Czech
PHRASE BOOK
& DICTIONARY

Easy to use features

- Handy thematic colour coding
- Quick Reference Section—opposite page
- Tipping Guide—inside back cover
- Quick reply panels throughout

How best to use this phrase book

• We suggest that you start with the **Guide to pronunciation** (pp. 6-9), then go on to **Some basic expressions** (pp. 10-15). This gives you not only a minimum vocabulary, but also helps you get used to pronouncing the language.

• Consult the **Contents** pages (3-5) for the section you need. In each chapter you'll find travel facts, hints and useful information. Simple phrases are followed by a list of words applicable to the situation.

• Separate, detailed contents lists are included at the beginning of the extensive **Eating out** and **Shopping guide** sections (Menus, p. 39, Shops and services, p. 97).

• If you want to find out how to say something in Czech, your fastest look-up is via the **Dictionary** section (pp. 164-189). This not only gives you the word, but is also cross-referenced to its use in a phrase on a specific page.

• If you wish to learn more about constructing sentences, check the **Basic grammar** (pp. 159-163).

• Note the **colour margins** are indexed in Czech and English to help both listener and speaker. And, in addition, there is also an **index in Czech** for the use of your listener.

• Throughout the book, this symbol ☛ suggests phrases your listener can use to answer you. If you still can't understand, hand this phrase book to the Czech-speaker to encourage pointing to an appropriate answer.

5th printing – January 1999

Printed in Spain

Contents

Travelling around 65

Sightseeing 80

Relaxing 86

Making friends 92

Shopping guide 97

Acknowledgements
We are particularly grateful to Anna Fraser and Jana Dankovikova for their help in the preparation of this book.

Guide to pronunciation

This chapter is intended to make you familiar with the phonetic transcription we have devised, and to help you get used to the sound system of Czech.

The imitated pronunciation should be read as if it were English (based on Standard British pronunciation), except for any special rules set out below.

Czech is one of the most phonetic of all European languages, and you should have little trouble pronouncing Czech once you've got accustomed to its diacritical marks: the *čárka* (´), the *kroužek* (˚), and the *háček* (ˇ).

Consonants

Letter	Approximate pronunciation	Symbol	Example	
b, d, f, g, k, m, n, p, t, v, z	are pronounced as in English			
c	like **ts** in ca**ts**	ts	**cesta**	tsesta
č	like **ch** in **ch**urch	ch	**klíč**	kleech
ď	like **d** in **d**uty; for American speakers close to **j** in **j**am	d^{y}	**Láďa**	lahd^{y}a
g	like **g** in **g**ood	g	**galerie**	galeriye
h	like **h** in **h**alf	h	**hlava**	hlava
ch	like **ch** in Scottish lo**ch**	kh	**chtít**	kht^{y}eet
j	like **y** in **y**es	y	**jídlo**	yeedlo
ň	like **nn** in a**nn**ual or **ny** in ca**ny**on	n^{y}	**píseň**	peesen^{y}
r	rolled (like a Scottish **r**)	r	**ruka**	rooka
ř	a sound unique to Czech; like a rolled **r** but flatten the tip of the tongue to make a short forceful buzz like **ž** (below)	rzh	**tři** **Dvořák**	trzhi dvorzhahk
s	like **s** in **s**et	s	**čas**	chas
š	like **sh** in **sh**ort	sh	**šest**	shest

t'	like **t** in **t**une; for American speakers close to **ch** in **ch**urch	t^y	**chut'**	$khoot^y$
w	like **v** in **v**an; found only in foreign words	v	**víno**	veeno
ž	like **s** in plea**s**ure	zh	**žena**	zhena

Notes

1) **ě** — the sign ˇ written over the letter **e** makes the preceding consonant soft. A similar effect is produced by pronouncing **y** as in **y**et.

When **t**, **d** and **n** precede **ě**, they become $\mathbf{t^y}$, $\mathbf{d^y}$ and $\mathbf{n^y}$. The same happens if they are followed by the letter **i** and **í**:

je**š**t**ě** ($yesht^ye$) **dě**kuji ($d^yekooyi$) **ni**c (n^yits)

When **b**, **p**, **v**, **f** and **m** precede **ě**, they become **by**, **py**, **vy**, **fy** and **mny** respectively:

pět (pyet) **vě**c (vyets) **mě**sto (mn^yesto)

2) Voiced consonants (**b**, **d**, $\mathbf{d^y}$, **h**, **z**, **zh**, **v**) become voiceless (**p**, **t**, $\mathbf{t^y}$, **kh**, **s**, **sh**, **f** respectively) at the beginning and end of a word, and before a voiceless consonant:

obě**d** (obyet) ztratit ($strat^yit$) tu**ž**ka (tooshka)

Voiceless consonants within a word become voiced if followed by a voiced consonant (this involves particularly k becoming g):

kde (gde) ni**k**do (n^yigdo)

Vowels

Vowels in Czech can be either short (**a**, **e**, **i**, **o**, **u**, **y**) or long (**á**, **é**, **í**, **ó**, **ú**, **ů**, **ý**). The length of the vowel is an essential feature since it can differentiate meanings of words which are otherwise written with the same spelling.

a	between the **a** in c**a**t and the **u** in c**u**t	a	**tam**	tam
á	like **a** in f**a**ther	ah	**máma**	mahma

e	like **e** in m**e**t; this is always pronounced, even at the end of a word	e	**den**	den
é	similar to the **e** in b**e**d but longer	eh	**mléko**	mlehko
i	like **i** in b**i**t	i	**pivo**	pivo
í	like **ee** in s**ee**	ee	**bílý**	beelee
o	like **o** in h**o**t	o	**slovo**	slovo
ó	like **o** in sh**o**rt; found only in foreign words	ō	**gól**	gōl
u	like **oo** in b**oo**k	oo	**ruka**	rooka
ú	like **oo** in m**oo**n	$\overline{oo}$	**úkol**	$\overline{oo}$kol
ů	like **ú** above	$\overline{oo}$	**vůz**	v$\overline{oo}$z
y	like **i** above	i	**byt**	bit
ý	like **ee** in s**ee**	ee	**bílý**	beelee

The letters **l** and **r** also operate as semi-vowels when they occur between two consonants or at the end of a word, following a consonant.

l	like **le** in cab**le**	^{u}l	**mohl**	moh^{u}l
r	like **ir** in b**ir**d	^{u}r	**krk**	k^{u}rk

Diphthongs

au	like **ow** in c**ow**	aoo	**auto**	aooto
ou	like **ow** in m**ow**, or the exclamation **oh**	oh	**mouka**	mohka

N.B. All vowels (long and short) should be pronounced the same way in all positions including at the end of a word, e.g.:

tam (tam) **Anna** (ana)

In places where confusion may arise over pronunciation, hyphens have been inserted in the phonetic transcription to help differentiate syllables:

mohl byste	(mo-h^{u}l bis-te)

Stress

Stress in Czech falls always on the first syllable of a word, though it is weaker than in English. Prepositions in Czech are generally pronounced together with their object as a single word, so the stress falls on the preposition.

Kolik to stojí **na den**?	(kolik to stoyee naden)

Note that stress and the length of vowels are two independent features: long vowels are not necessarily stressed vowels; on the other hand stressed vowels are not automatically long vowels.

Pronunciation of the Czech alphabet

A	krahtkeh a	Ň	eny
Á	dloh-heh a	O	krahtkeh o
B	beh	Ó	dloh-heh o
C	tseh	P	peh
Č	cheh	Q	kveh
D	deh	R	er
Ď	d^{y}eh	Ř	erzh
E	krahtkeh e	S	es
É	dloh-heh e	Š	esh
F	ef	T	teh
G	geh	Ť	t^{y}eh
H	hah	U	krahtkeh oo
CH	chah	Ú	oo schahrkoh
I	krahtkeh i	Ů	oo skroh-zhkem
Í	dloh-heh i	V	veh
J	yeh	W	dvo-yiteh veh
K	kah	X	iks
L	el	Y	ipsilon
M	em	Ý	dloh-heh ipsilon
N	en	Z	zet
		Ž	zhet

Some basic expressions

Yes.	**Ano.**	ano
No.	**Ne.**	ne
Please.	**Prosím.**	proseem
Thank you.	**Děkuji.**	d^{y}ekooyi
Thank you very much.	**Děkuji mnohokrát.**	d^{y}ekooyi mno-hokraht
That's all right/ You're welcome.	**To je v pořádku.**	to ye fporzhahtkoo

Greetings *Pozdravy*

Good morning.	**Dobré ráno.**	dobreh rahno
Good afternoon.	**Dobré odpoledne.**	dobreh otpoledne
Good evening.	**Dobrý večer.**	dobree vecher
Good night.	**Dobrou noc.**	dobroh nots
Goodbye.	**Nashledanou.**	nas-khledanoh
See you later.	**Uvidíme se později.**	oovid^{y}eeme se pozd^{y}eyi
Hello/Hi!	**Ahoj!**	a-hoy
This is Mr./Mrs./ Miss ...	**Tohle je pan/paní/ slečna ...**	to-hle ye pan/pan^{y}ee/ slechna
How do you do? (Pleased to meet you.)	**Těší mne.**	t^{y}eshee mn^{y}e
How are you?	**Jak se máte?**	yak se mahte
Very well, thanks. And you?	**Děkuji dobře. A Vy?**	d^{y}ekooyi dobrzhe. a vi
How's life?	**Jak se daři?**	yak se darzhi
Fine.	**Dobře.**	dobrzhe
I beg your pardon?	**Promiňte.**	promin^{y}te
Excuse me. (May I get past?)	**Dovolte/Promiňte prosím.**	dovolte/promin^{y}te proseem
Sorry!	**Pardon!**	pardon

Questions *Otázky*

Where?	**Kde?**	gde
How?	**Jak?**	yak
When?	**Kdy?**	gdi
What?	**Co?**	tso
Why?	**Proč?**	proch
Who?	**Kdo?**	gdo
Which?	**Který?**	kteree
Where is ...?	**Kde je ...?**	gde ye
Where are ...?	**Kde jsou ...?**	gde ysoh
Where can I find/ get ...?	**Kde bych našel(a)/ dostal(a) ...?***	gde bikh nashel(a)/dostal(a)
How far?	**Jak daleko?**	yak daleko
How long?	**Jak dlouho?**	yak dloh-ho
How much/ How many?	**Kolik?**	kolik
How much does this cost?	**Kolik to stojí?**	kolik to stoyee
When does ... open/ close?	**Kdy je ... otevřeno/ zavřeno?**	gdi ye ... otevrzheno/ zavrzheno
What do you call this/ that in Czech?	**Jak se to řekne česky?**	yak se to rzhekne cheskee
What does this/ that mean?	**Co to znamená?**	tso to znamenah

Do you speak ...? *Mluvíte ...?*

Do you speak English?	**Mluvíte anglicky?**	mlooveete anglitski
Does anyone here speak English?	**Mluví tady někdo anglicky?**	mloovee tadi n^{y}egdo anglitski
I don't speak (much) Czech.	**Já nemluvím (moc) česky.**	yah nemlooveem (mots) cheskee

* Alternatives for a female speaker are indicated in curved brackets.

Could you speak more slowly?	**Mohl[a] byste mluvit pomaleji?***	mo-h^{u}l [mo-hla] bis-te mloovit pomaleyi
Could you repeat that?	**Mohl[a] byste to opakovat?**	mo-h^{u}l [mo-hla] bis-te to opakovat
Could you spell it?	**Mohl[a] byste to hláskovat?**	mo-h^{u}l [mo-hla] bis-te to hlahskovat
How do you pronounce this?	**Jak se vyslovuje tohle?**	yak se vislovooye to-hle
Could you write it down, please?	**Mohl[a] byste to prosím napsat?**	mo-h^{u}l [mo-hla] bis-te to proseem napsat
Can you translate this for me?	**Mohl[a] byste to pro mne přeložit?**	mo-h^{u}l [mo-hla] bis-te to pro mne przhelozhit
Can you translate this for us?	**Mohl[a] byste to pro nás přeložit?**	mo-h^{u}l [mo-hla] bis-te to pronahs przhelozhit
Could you point to the ... in the book, please?	**Mohl[a] byste mi prosím v mé knihe ukázat ...?**	mo-h^{u}l [mo-hla] bis-te mi proseem vmeh kn^{y}ihe ookahzat
word	**to slovo**	to slovo
phrase	**ten výraz**	ten veeras
sentence	**tu větu**	too vyetoo
Just a moment.	**Malý moment.**	malee moment
I'll see if I can find it in my book.	**Já se podívám jestli to můžu najít v mé knihe.**	yah se pod^{y}eevahm yestli to m$\overline{oo}$zhoo na-yeet vmeh kn^{y}ihe
I understand.	**Rozumím.**	rozoomeem
I don't understand.	**Nerozumím.**	nerozoomeem
Do you understand?	**Rozumíte?**	rozoomeete

Can/May ...? *Žádosti ...?*

Can I have ...?	**Mohl(a) bych dostat ...?**	mo-h^{u}l (mo-hla) bikh dostat
Can we have ...?	**Mohli bychom dostat ...?**	mo-hli bikhom dostat

* Alternatives when addressing a female are indicated in square brackets.

Can you show me …?	**Mohl[a] byste mi ukázat …?**	mo-h^{u}l [mo-hla] bis-te mi ookahzat
I can't.	**Nemůžu.**	nemoozhoo
Can you tell me …?	**Mohl[a] byste mi říct …?**	mo-h^{u}l [mo-hla] bis-te mi rzheetst
Can you help me?	**Mohl[a] byste mi pomoci?**	mo-h^{u}l [mo-hla] bis-te mi pomotsi
Can I help you?	**Mohu vám pomoci?**	mo-hoo vahm pomotsi
Can you direct me to …?	**Mohl[a] byste mi říct jak najdu …?**	mo-h^{u}l [mo-hla] bis-te mi rzheets-t yak naydoo

Do you want …? *Chcete …?*

I'd like …	**Chtěl(a) bych …**	kht^{y}el(a) bikh
We'd like …	**Chtěli bychom …**	kht^{y}eli bikhom
What do you want?	**Co chcete?**	tso kh-tse-te
Could you give me …?	**Mohl[a] byste mi dát …?**	mo-h^{u}l [mo-hla] bis-te mi daht
Could you bring me …?	**Mohl[a] byste mi přinést …?**	mo-h^{u}l [mo-hla] bis-te mi przhi-nehst
Could you show me …?	**Mohl[a] byste mi ukázat …?**	mo-h^{u}l [mo-hla] bis-te mi ookahzat
I'm looking for …	**Hledám …**	hledahm
I'm hungry.	**Já mám hlad.**	yah mahm hlat
I'm thirsty.	**Já mám žízeň.**	yah mahm zheezen^{y}
I'm tired.	**Jsem unavený (unavená).**	ysem oonavenee (oonavenah)
I'm lost.	**Ztratil(a) jsem.**	strat^{y}il(a) ysem
It's important.	**To je důležité.**	to ye doolezhiteh
It's urgent.	**To je spěchá.**	to ye sp^{y}ekhah

It is/There is … *Je …?*

It is …	**To je …**	to ye
Is it …?	**Je to …?**	ye to
It isn't …	**Není …**	nen^{y}ee
Here it is.	**Tady to je.**	tadi to ye
Here they are.	**Tady jsou.**	tadi ysoh
There it is.	**Tam to je.**	tam to ye
There they are.	**Tam jsou.**	tam ysoh

There is/There are ...	**Tam je/Tam jsou ...**	tam ye/tam ysoh
Is there/Are there ...?	**Je tam/Jsou tam ...?**	ye tam/ysoh tam
There isn't/aren't ...	**Tam není/nejsou ...**	tam nen^{y}ee/neysoh
There isn't/aren't any.	**Tam není nic/Tam nejsou žádné.**	tam nen^{y}ee n^{y}its/tam neysoh zhahdneh

It's ... *To je ...*

beautiful/ugly	**krásné/ošklivé**	krahsneh/oshkliveh
better/worse	**lepší/horší**	lepshee/horshee
big/small	**velké/malé**	velkeh/maleh
cheap/expensive	**laciné/drahé**	latsineh/dra-heh
early/late	**brzo/pozdě**	b^{u}rzo/pozd^{y}e
easy/difficult	**jednoduché/složité**	yedno-dookheh/slozhiteh
free (vacant)/occupied	**volné/obsazené**	volneh/opsazeneh
full/empty	**plné/prázdné**	p^{u}lneh/prahzdneh
good/bad	**dobré/špatné**	dobreh/shpatneh
heavy/light	**těžké/lehké**	t^{y}ezhkeh/lekh-keh
here/there	**tady/tam**	tadi/tam
hot/cold	**horké/studené**	horkeh/studeneh
near/far	**blízko/daleko**	bleesko/daleko
next/last	**příští/poslední**	przheesht^{y}ee/posledn^{y}ee
old/new	**staré/nové**	stareh/noveh
old/young	**staré/mladé**	stareh/mladeh
open/shut	**otevřené/zavřené**	otevrzheneh/zavrzheneh
quick/slow	**rychlé/pomalé**	rikhleh/pomaleh
right/wrong	**správné/špatné**	sprahvneh/shpatneh

Quantities *Množství*

a little/a lot	**trochu/hodně**	trokhoo/hodn^{y}e
few/a few	**málo/několik**	mahlo/n^{y}ekolik
much	**moc**	mots
many	**hodně**	hodn^{y}e
more/less	**víc/míň**	veets/meen^{y}
more than/less than	**víc než/míň než**	veets nesh/meen^{y} nesh
enough/too much/some	**to stačí/to je moc/několik**	to stachee/to ye mots/n^{y}ekolik

A few more useful words *Další užitečná slova*

above	**nad**	nat
after	**po**	po
also	**také**	takeh
always	**vždycky**	vzh-ditski
and	**a**	a
at	**v**	f
before (time)	**před**	przhet
behind	**za**	za
below	**pod**	pot
between	**mezi**	mezi
but	**ale**	a-le
down	**dole**	dole
downstairs	**dolů**	doloo
during	**během**	byehem
for	**pro**	pro
from	**z**	s
in	**od,v**	ot,f
inside	**vevnitř**	vevn^{y}itrzh
near	**blízko**	bleesko
never	**nikdy**	n^{y}igdi
none	**žádný**	zhahdnee
not	**ne**	ne
nothing	**nic**	n^{y}its
now	**teď**	tet^{y}
on	**na**	na
only	**jenom**	yenom
or	**nebo**	nebo
outside	**venku**	venkoo
perhaps	**možná**	mozhnah
since	**od**	ot
soon	**brzo**	b^{u}rzo
then	**pak**	pak
through	**skrz**	sk^{u}rs
to	**do**	do
too (also)	**také**	takeh
towards	**směrem**	smn^{y}erem
under	**pod**	pot
until	**až do**	azh do
up	**nahoru**	na-horoo
upstairs	**nahoře**	na-horzhe
very	**velmi**	velmi
with	**s**	s
without	**bez**	bes

Arrival

Passport control *Pasová kontrola*

Although visa requirements are being reduced (British and U.S. citizens no longer need them) some nationals still have to have them. Visas can be obtained in advance from your embassy, or at the airport or major road crossings. Rail travellers cannot have a visa issued on the spot.

Here's my passport.	**Tady je můj pas.**	tadi ye m$\overline{oo}$y pas
I'll be staying ...	**Já se zdržím ...**	yah se zd^{u}rzheem
a few days	**několik dnů**	n^{y}ekolik dn$\overline{oo}$
a week	**týden**	teeden
2 weeks	**dva týdny**	dva teedni
a month	**měsíc**	mn^{y}eseets
I don't know yet.	**Já ještě nevím.**	yah yesht^{y}e neveem
I'm here on holiday.	**Já jsem tady na dovolené.**	yah ysem tadi nadovoleneh
I'm here on business.	**Já jsem tady na služební cestě.**	yah ysem tadi nasluzhebn^{y}ee tsest^{y}e
I'm just passing through.	**Já jenom projíždím.**	yah yenom proyeezhd^{y}eem
I'm sorry, I don't understand.	**Promiňte, ale já tomu nerozumím.**	promin^{y}te ale yah tomoo nerozoomeem
Does anyone here speak English?	**Mluví tady někdo anglicky?**	mloovee tadi n^{y}egdo anglitski

CELNICE
CUSTOMS

After collecting your baggage at the airport (*letiště*), you may have a choice: use the green exit if you have nothing to declare or leave via the red exit if you have items in excess of those allowed.

věci k proclení
goods to declare

nic k proclení
nothing to declare

The chart below shows what you can bring in duty-free.

Entering the Czech Republic	Cigarettes	Cigars	Tobacco	Spirits	Wine
	250	or	similar quantity	1 l. and 2 l.	
Into:					
Australia	200	or 250g.	or 250 g.	1 l. or	1 l.
Canada	200	and 50	and 900 g.	1.1 l. or	1 l.
Eire	200	or 50	or 250 g.	1 l. and	2 l.
N. Zealand	200	or 50	and 250 g.	1.1 l. and	4.5 l.
U.K.	200	or 50	or 250 g.	1 l. and	2 l.
U.S.A.	200	and 100	and *	1 l. or	1 l.

* A reasonable quantity.

I have nothing to declare.	**Nemám nic k proclení.**	nemahm n^{y}its kprotslen^{y}ee
I have ...	**Mám ...**	mahm
a carton of cigarettes	**krabici cigaret**	krabitsi tsigaret
a bottle of whisky	**láhev whisky**	lah-hef viski
It's for my personal use.	**To je pro osobní potřebu.**	to ye pro osobn^{y}ee potrzheboo
It's a gift.	**To je dárek.**	to ye dahrek

Váš pas, prosím.	Your passport, please.
Máte něco k proclení?	Do you have anything to declare?
Otevřete tu tašku.	Please open this bag.
Za tohle musíte zaplatit clo.	You'll have to pay duty on this.
Máte ještě další zavazadla?	Do you have any more luggage?

Baggage—Porter *Zavazadla—Vrátný*

Porters are only available at the airport, and occasionally at railway stations. Where no porters are available, you'll find luggage trolleys for the use of passengers. You can also ask the taxi driver to help you.

Porter!	**Vrátný!**	vrahtneeh
Please take (this/ my) ...	**Vezměte prosím (tohle/moje) ...**	vezmn^{y}ete proseem (to-hle/ mo-ye)
luggage suitcase (travelling) bag	**zavazadlo** **kufr** **(cestovní) tašku**	zavazadlo koofr (tsestovn^{y}ee) tashkoo
That one is mine.	**Tohle je moje.**	to-hle ye mo-ye
Take this luggage ...	**Vezměte tato zavazadla ...**	vezmn^{y}ete tato zavazadla
to the bus to the luggage lockers	**k autobusu** **k úschovně zavazadel**	kaooto-boosoo ko͞os-khovn^{y}e zavazadel
to the taxi	**k taxiku**	ktaksikoo
How much is that?	**Kolik to stojí?**	kolik to stoyee
There's one piece missing.	**Mně chybí jedno zavazadlo.**	mn^{y}e khibee yedno zavazadlo
Where are the luggage trolleys (carts)?	**Kde jsou vozíky pro zavazadla?**	gde ysoh vozeeki prozavazadla

Changing money *Výměna peněz*

Where's the currency exchange office?	**Kde je směnárna?**	gde ye smn^{y}enahrna
Can you change these traveller's cheques?	**Vyměňujete cestovní šeky?**	vimn^{y}en^{y}ooyete tsestovn^{y}ee sheki
I want to change some dollars/ pounds.	**Chci vyměnit dolary/libry.**	khtsi vimn^{y}en^{y}it dolari/ libri
Can you change this into koruna?	**Mohl[a] byste vyměnit tyto peníze za koruny?**	mo-h^{u}l [mo-hla] bis-te vimn^{y}en^{y}it tito pen^{y}eeze zakorooni
What's the exchange rate?	**Jaký je kurs?**	yakee ye kurs

BANK—CURRENCY, see page 129

Where is ...? *Kde je ...?*

Where is the ...?	**Kde je ...?**	gde ye
booking office	**pokladna**	pokladna
duty (tax)-free shop	**obchod bez cla**	op-khot bes-tsla
newsstand	**novinový stánek**	novinovee stahnek
restaurant	**restaurace**	restaoo-ratse
How do I get to ...?	**Jak se dostanu do ...?**	yak se dostanoo do
Is there a bus into town?	**Jede odsud autobus do města?**	yede otsut aoo-toboos domn^{y}esta
Where can I get a taxi?	**Kde seženu taxik?**	gde sezhenoo taksik
Where can I hire (rent) a car?	**Kde si mohu pronajmout auto?**	gde si mo-hoo prona-ymoht aoo-to

Hotel reservation *Hotelová rezervace*

Do you have a hotel guide (directory)?	**Máte seznam hotelů?**	mahte seznam hotel$\overline{oo}$
Could you reserve a room for me?	**Mohl[a] byste mi rezervovat pokoj?**	mo-h^{u}l [mo-hla] bis-te mi rezervovat pokoy
in the centre	**v centru**	vtsentroo
near the railway station	**poblíž nádraží**	pobleesh nahdrazhee
a single room	**jednolůžkový pokoj**	yednol$\overline{oo}$shkovee pokoy
a double room	**dvoulůžkový pokoj**	dvoh-l$\overline{oo}$shkovee pokoy
not too expensive	**ne moc drahý**	ne mots drahee
Where is the hotel?	**Kde je ten hotel?**	gde ye ten hotel
Do you have a street map?	**Máte mapu města?**	mahte mapoo mn^{y}esta

HOTEL/ACCOMMODATION, see page 22

Car hire (rental) *Půjčovna aut*

Car hire firms have offices at Prague international airport and major hotels and railway stations. You can also hire a vehicle through a tourist office or your hotel. You may require an international driving licence, and the most convenient method of payment is by credit card.

Note: It is illegal to drive with even a trace of alcohol under your belt.

I'd like to hire (rent) a ... car.	**Rád(a) bych si pronajmul ... auto.**	rahd(a) bikh si pronaymool ... aooto
small	**malé**	malee
medium-sized	**středně velké**	st^{u}rzhedn^{y}e velkeh
large	**velké**	velkeh
an automatic	**auto s automatickou rychlostí**	aooto saooto-matitskoh rikhlost^{y}ee
I'd like it for a day/ a week.	**Chci ho na jeden den/na týden.**	khtsi ho na yeden den/ nateeden
Are there any week-end arrangements?	**Jaké máte podmínky na víkend?**	yakeh mahte podmeenkii naveekent
Do you have any special rates?	**Máte speciální sazby?**	mahte spetsiahln^{y}ee sazbi
What's the charge per day/week?	**Kolik to stojí na den/na týden?**	kolik to stoyee naden/ nateeden
Is mileage included?	**Je to včetně poplatku za kilometr?**	ye to fchetn^{y}e poplatku zakilomet^{u}r
What's the charge per kilometre?	**Kolik je sazba za kilometr?**	kolik je sazba zakilomet^{u}r
I'd like to leave the car in ...	**Chtěl(a) bych to auto nechat v ...**	kht^{y}el(a) bikh to aooto nekhat f
I'd like full insurance.	**Chci plné pojištění.**	kh-tsi p^{u}lneh poyisht^{y}en^{y}ee
How much is the deposit?	**Kolik musím dát zálohy?**	kolik mooseem daht zahlo-hi
I have a credit card.	**Mám úvěrovou kartu.**	mahm oovyerovoh kartoo
Here's my driving licence.	**Tady je můj řidičský průkaz.**	tadi ye m$\overline{oo}$y rzhid^{y}ichskee pr$\overline{oo}$kas

CAR, see page 75

Taxi *Taxi*

The best place to find a taxi is at a taxi rank (*stanoviště taxi*), generally located outside hotels, railway stations and department stores. The meter indicates the fare, but there may be extra charges for leaving the city limits, so it's advisable to state your destination before entering the cab.

It's customary to leave a tip in addition to the amount shown on the meter.

Where can I get a taxi?	**Kde najdu taxi?**	gde naydoo taxi
Where is the taxi rank (stand)?	**Kde je stanoviště taxi?**	gde ye stanovisht^{y}e taxi
Could you get me a taxi?	**Mohl[a] byste mi zavolat taxi?**	mo-h^{u}l [mo-hla] bis-te mi zavolat taxi
What's the fare to . . .?	**Kolik to stojí do . . .?**	kolik to stoyee do
How far is it to . . .?	**Jak daleko je to do . . .?**	yak daleko ye to do
Take me to . . .	**Zavezte mne . . .**	zaveste mne
this address	**na tuto adresu**	natooto adresoo
the airport	**na letiště**	nalet^{y}isht^{y}e
the town centre	**do středu města**	dost^{u}rzhedoo mn^{y}esta
the . . . Hotel	**do Hotelu . . .**	do-hoteloo
the railway station	**na nádraží**	nanahdrazhee
Turn . . . at the next corner.	**Zahněte . . . na příštím rohu.**	zahn^{y}ete . . . na przheesht^{y}eem rohoo
left/right	**vlevo/vpravo**	vlevo/fpravo
Go straight ahead.	**Jeď'te rovně.**	yed^{y}te rovn^{y}e
Please stop here.	**Zastavte tady prosím.**	zastafte tadi proseem
I'm in a hurry.	**Spěchám.**	spyekhahm
Could you drive more slowly?	**Mohl byste jet pomaleji?**	mo-h^{u}l bis-te yet pomaleyi
Could you help me carry my luggage?	**Můžete mi pomoci nést mà zavazadla?**	mo͞ozhete mi pomotsi nehst mah zavazadla
Could you wait for me?	**Mohl byste na mne počkat?**	mo-h^{u}l bis-te namne pochkat
I'll be back in 10 minutes.	**Já se vrátím za deset minut.**	yah se vraht^{y}eem zadeset minoot

TIPPING, see inside back-cover

Hotel—Other accommodation

You should book accommodation well in advance, as the principal hotels are often filled to capacity. The busiest periods are the summer season and when trade fairs, exhibitions or major international conferences are being held, particularly in Prague.

Hotel
(hotel)

Hotels are officially classified according to the scope and standard of their services, from A* de luxe at the top, through A*, B*, B and, for the basic requirements, C.

Interhotel
(inter hotel)

These highest rating hotels have the superior rooms and elaborate facilities (translation, secretarial and fax services) expected by businessmen, as well as shops on the premises, multiple bars and restaurants.

Botel
(botel)

For an alternative to the conventional hotel you can stay in a converted river-boat. Prague has several, moored on the Vltava and ranking as three star hotels.

Motel
(motel)

For the motorist there are a few motels, with prices similar to B* hotels.

Chatové osady
(khatoveh osadi)

These cabins are mainly found in Slovakia, graded A*, A and B. As you must often pay for all the beds in the cabin (typically 2 or 4), they can be less practical for those travelling alone.

Mládežnická ubytovna
(mlahdezhnitskah oobitovna)

Although there is no extensive network of youth hostels, some accommodation caters exclusively for young people (under 30), such as the *Juniorhotel* chain.

Pensión
(pensioon)

A list of registered guesthouses can be obtained from the local tourist information office. Signs in the street (usually in German) also indicate where private rooms are available. You may find that your host prefers you to pay in foreign currency.

Sanatorium
(sanatorioom)

Karlovy Vary (Carlsbad) has long been famous for its mineral springs, but there are over 35 spa towns in the Czech and Slovak Republics. Bookings for treatment are arranged through the state Spa bureau, Balnea.

Turistická ubytovna (tooristitska oobitovna) — A hostel with dormitories, but rarely with anywhere to cook. There are two grades, depending on how many beds per room.

Can you recommend a hotel/guesthouse?	**Mohl[a] byste mi doporučit hotel/ pensión?**	mo-h^{u}l [mo-hla] bis-te mi doporoochit hotel/ pensio͞on
Are there any flats (apartments) vacant?	**Jsou tady nějaké volné byty?**	ysoh tadi n^{y}eyakeh volneh biti

Checking in—Reception *Registrace*

My name is ...	**Jmenuji se ...**	ymenooyi se
I have a reservation.	**Mám rezervaci.**	mahm rezervatsi
We've reserved two rooms.	**Máme zamluvené dva pokoje.**	mahme zamluveneh dva pokoye
Here's the confirmation.	**Tady je to potvrzení.**	tadi ye to potvrzen^{y}ee
Do you have any vacancies?	**Máte volný pokoj?**	mahte volnee pokoy
I'd like a ...	**Chtěl(a) bych ...**	kht^{y}el(a) bikh
single room	**jednolůžkový pokoj**	yednolo͞oshkovee pokoy
double room	**dvoulůžkový pokoj**	dvoh-lo͞oshkovee pokoy
We'd like a room ...	**Rádi bychom pokoj ...**	rahd^{y}i bikhom pokoy
with twin beds	**se dvěma postelemi**	sedvyema postelemi
with a double bed	**se dvojitou postelí**	sedvoyitoh postelee
with a bath	**s koupelnou**	skohpelnoh
with a shower	**se sprchou**	sesp^{u}rkhoh
with a balcony	**s balkónem**	sbalko͞onem
with a view	**s vyhlídkou**	svihleetkoh
at the front	**na přední straně**	nap^{u}rzhedn^{y}ee stran^{y}e
at the back	**na zadní straně**	nazadn^{y}ee stran^{y}e
It must be quiet.	**Musí být tichý.**	moosee beet t^{y}ikhee
Is there ...?	**Má to ...?**	mah to
air conditioning	**klimatizaci**	klimatizatsi
a conference room	**konferenční sál**	konferenchn^{y}ee sahl
a laundry service	**prádelní službu**	prahdeln^{y}ee sluzhboo
a private toilet	**soukromou toaletu**	sohkromoh toaletoo
a radio/television in the room	**rádio/televizi v pokoji**	rahdiyo/televizi fpokoyi
hot water	**horkou vodu**	horkoh vodoo
room service	**pokojovou službu**	pokoyovoh sluzhboo

CHECKING OUT, see page 31

Could you put an extra bed in the room?	**Mohli byste nám dát jednu postel navíc?**	mo-hli bis-te nahm daht yednoo postel naveets

How much? *Kolik?*

What's the price ...?	**Kolik to stojí ...?**	kolik to stoyee
per day	**na den**	naden
per week	**na týden**	nateeden
for bed and breakfast	**na nocleh se snídaní**	nanotsle-h sesn^{y}eedan^{y}ee
excluding meals	**bez jídla**	bez yeedla
for full board (A.P.)	**se všemi jídly**	se-fshemi yeedli
for half board (M.A.P.)	**s večeří a snídaní**	svecherzhee a sn^{y}eedan^{y}ee
Does that include ...?	**Zahrnuje to ...?**	zahrnooye to
breakfast	**snídani**	sn^{y}eedan^{y}i
service	**službu**	sloozhboo
value-added tax (V.A.T.)	**daň z-přidané hodnoty**	dan^{y} sprzhidaneh hodnoti
Is there any reduction for children?	**Máte slevu pro děti?**	mahte slevoo prod^{y}et^{y}i
Do you charge for the baby?	**Musíme platit za to miminko?**	mooseeme plat^{y}it zato miminko
That's too expensive.	**To je moc drahé.**	to ye mots dra-heh
Do you have anything cheaper?	**Nemáte něco lacinějšího?**	memahte n^{y}etso latsin^{y}eyshee-ho

How long? *Jak dlouho?*

We'll be staying ...	**Zůstaneme ...**	zo͞ostaneme
overnight only	**na jednu noc**	nayednoo nots
a few days	**několik dnů**	n^{y}ekolik dno͞o
a week (at least)	**týden (nejméně)**	teeden (neymehn^{y}e)
I don't know yet.	**Ještě nevím.**	jesht^{y}e neveem

Decision *Rozhodnutí*

May I see the room?	**Mohl(a) bych se podívat na ten pokoj?**	mo-h^{u}l (mo-hla) bikh se pod^{y}eevat na ten pokoy

NUMBERS, see page 147

That's fine. I'll take it.	**To je v pořádku. Já si ho vezmu.**	to ye fporzhahtkoo. yah si ho vezmoo
No. I don't like it.	**Mně se nelíbí.**	mn^{y}e se neleebee
It's too . . .	**Je moc . . .**	ye mots
cold/hot	**studený/horký**	stoodenee/horkee
dark/small	**tmavý/malý**	tmavee/malee
noisy	**hlučný**	hluchnee
I asked for a room with a bath.	**Já jsem chtěl(a) pokoj s koupelnou.**	jah ysem kht^{y}el(a) pokoy skohpelnoh
Do you have anything . . .?	**Máte něco . . .?**	mahte n^{y}etso
better	**lepšího**	lepshee-ho
bigger	**většího**	vjetshee-ho
cheaper	**lacinějšího**	latsin^{y}ejshee-ho
quieter	**tiššího**	t^{y}ishshee-ho
Do you have a room with a better view?	**Máte pokoj s lepší vyhlídkou?**	mahte pokoy slepshee vihleetkoh

Registration *Registrace*

Upon arrival at a hotel or guesthouse you'll be asked to fill in a registration form (*registrační formulář*—registrachn^{y}ee formoolahrzh).

Jméno/Křestní jméno	Name/First name
Trvalé bydliště/Ulice/Číslo	Home town/Street/Number
Národnost/Zaměstnání	Nationality/Occupation
Datum/Místo narození	Date/Place of birth
Ubytováni od/do	Staying from/to
Příjezd z/Odjezd do	Coming from/Going to
Číslo pasu	Passport number
Místo/Datum	Place/Date
Cena	Price
Podpis	Signature

What does this mean?	**Co to znamená?**	tso to znamenah

Ukažte mi, prosím, pas.	May I see your passport, please?
Mohl[a] byste vyplnit tento registrační formulář?	Would you mind filling in this registration form?
Tady se, prosím, podepište.	Please sign here.
Jak dlouho tady zůstanete?	How long will you be staying?

What's my room number?	**Jaké mám číslo pokoje?**	yakeh mahm cheeslo pokoye
Will you have our luggage sent up?	**Přinesete nám zavazadla?**	przhinesete nahm zavazadla
Where can I park my car?	**Kde můžu zaparkovat?**	gde mo͞ozhoo zaparkovat
Does the hotel have a garage/parking?	**Má tento hotel garáž/parkoviště?**	mah tento hotel garahzh/ parkovisht^{y}e
I'd like to leave this in the hotel safe.	**Chci nechat tyto věci v hotelovém sejfu.**	khtsi nekhat tito vyetsi vhotelovehm seyfoo

Hotel staff *Hoteloví zaměstnanci*

hall porter	**nosič**	nosich
maid	**pokojská**	pokoyskah
manager	**ředitel**	rzhed^{y}itel
porter	**vrátný**	vrahtnee
receptionist	**recepční**	retsepchn^{y}ee
switchboard operator	**centrála**	tsentrahla
waiter	**číšník**	cheeshn^{y}eek
waitress	**číšnice**	cheeshn^{y}itse

If you want to address members of the staff, you don't use the actual names shown above, but a general introductory phrase: *promiňte* (promin^{y}teh).

TELLING THE TIME, see page 153

General requirements *Základní potřeby*

The key to room ..., please.	**Klíč na pokoj ..., prosím.**	kleech napokoy ... proseem
Could you wake me at ... please?	**Mohl[a] byste mě vzbudit ve ... prosím?**	mo-h^{u}l [mo-hla] bis-te mn^{y}e vzbood^{y}it ve ... proseem
When is breakfast/ lunch/dinner served?	**Kdy se podává snídaně/ oběd/ večeře?**	gdi se podahvah sn^{y}eedan^{y}e/obyet/ vecherzhe
May we have breakfast in our room, please?	**Mohu snídat v pokoji?**	mo-hoo sn^{y}eedat fpokoyi
Is there a bath on this floor?	**Je na tomto patře koupelna?**	ye natomto patrzhe kohpelna
What's the voltage?	**Jaké je napětí?**	yakeh ye nap^{y}et^{y}ee
Where's the shaver socket (outlet)?	**Kde je zástrčka na holicí strojek?**	gde ye zahst^{u}rchka na-holitsee stroyek
Can you find me a ...?	**Mohl[a] byste mi sehnat ...?**	mo-h^{u}l [mo-hla] bis-te mi sehnat
babysitter	**hlídání dětí**	hleedahn^{y}ee d^{y}et^{y}ee
secretary	**sekretářku**	sekretahrzhkoo
typewriter	**psací stroj**	psatsee stroy
May I have a/an/ some ...?	**Můžete mi dát ...?**	m$\overline{oo}$zhete mi daht
ashtray	**popelník**	popeln^{y}eek
bath towel	**velký ručník**	velkee roochn^{y}eek
(extra) blanket	**(víc) dek**	(veets) dek
envelopes	**obálky**	obahlki
(more) hangers	**(víc) ramínek**	(veets) rameenek
hot-water bottle	**ohřívací láhev**	o-h^{u}rzheevatsee lah-hef
ice cubes	**ledové kostky**	ledoveh kostki
needle and thread	**jehlu a nit**	ye-hloo a n^{y}it
(extra) pillow	**(víc) polštářů**	(veets) polshtahrzh$\overline{oo}$
reading lamp	**noční lampu**	nochn^{y}ee lampoo
soap	**mýdlo**	meedlo
writing paper	**dopisní papír**	dopisn^{y}ee papeer
Where's the ...?	**Kde je ...?**	gde ye
bathroom	**koupelna**	kohpelna
dining-room	**jídelna**	yeedelna
emergency exit	**nouzový východ**	nohzovee veekhot
lift (elevator)	**výtah**	veetakh
Where are the toilets?	**Kde jsou toalety?**	gde ysoh toaleti

BREAKFAST, see page 40

Telephone—Post (mail) *Telefon—Pošta*

Can you get me Prague 123-45-67?	**Můžete mne spojit s Prahou? 123-45-67?**	mo͞ozhete mne spoyit sprahoh jedna dvye trzhi pyet shest sedm
Do you have any stamps?	**Máte známky?**	mahte znahmki
Would you post (mail) this for me, please?	**Mohl[a] byste tohle pro mě poslat?**	mo-h^{u}l [mo-hla] bis-te to-hle promn^{y}e poslat
Are there any letters for me?	**Máte pro mě nějaké dopisy?**	mahte promn^{y}e n^{y}eyakeh dopisi
Are there any messages for me?	**Jsou tady pro mě nějaké zprávy?**	ysoh tadi promn^{y}e n^{y}eyakeh sprahvi
How much is my telephone bill?	**Kolik je můj telefonní účet?**	kolik ye mo͞oy telefon^{y}ee o͞ochet

Difficulties *Problémy*

The ... doesn't work.	**nefunguje ...**	nefoongooye
air conditioning	**klimatizace**	klimatizatse
bidet	**bidet**	bidet
fan	**větrák**	vyetrahk
heating	**topení**	topen^{y}ee
light	**světlo**	svyetlo
radio	**rádio**	rahdiyo
television	**televize**	televize
The tap (faucet) is dripping.	**Kohoutek kape.**	kohohtek kape
There's no hot water.	**Neteče teplá voda.**	neteche teplah voda
The washbasin is blocked.	**Umyvadlo je ucpané.**	oomivadlo ye ootspaneh
The window is jammed.	**Okno je zablokované.**	okno ye zablokovaneh
The curtains are stuck.	**Záclony nejsou pohyblivé.**	zahtsloni neysoh po-hibliveh
The bulb is burned out.	**Žárovka je prasklá.**	zhahrofka ye prasklah
My bed hasn't been made up.	**Mně nikdo neustlal.**	mn^{y}e n^{y}igdo ne-oostlal

POST OFFICE AND TELEPHONE, see page 132

The ... is broken.	**Je pokažená ...**	ye pokazhenah
blind	**roleta**	roleta
lamp	**lampa**	lampa
plug	**zástrčka**	zahst^{u}rchka
shutter	**okenice**	okenitse
switch	**vypínač**	vipeenach
Can you get it repaired?	**Můžete to spravit?**	mo͞ozhete to spravit

Laundry—Dry cleaner's *Prádelna—Čistírna*

I'd like these clothes ...	**Tyhle šaty bych chtěl(a) ...**	tihle shati bikh kht^{y}el(a)
cleaned	**vyčistit**	vichist^{y}it
ironed	**vyžehlit**	vizhehlit
pressed	**vyžehlit**	vizhehlit
washed	**vyprat**	viprat
When will they be ready?	**Kdy to bude hotové?**	gdi to bude hotovee
I need them ...	**Já to potřebuji ...**	Yah to potrzhebooyi
today	**dnes**	dnes
tonight	**dnes večer**	dnes vecher
tomorrow	**zítra**	zeetra
before Friday	**do pátku**	dopahtkoo
Can you ... this?	**Můžete tohle ...?**	mo͞ozhte to-hle
mend	**spravit**	spravit
patch	**záplatovat**	zahplatovat
stitch	**sešít**	sesheet
Can you sew on this button?	**Můžte mi přišít knoflík?**	mo͞ozhete mi przhisheet knofleek
Can you get this stain out?	**Můžete vyčistit tuhle skvrnu?**	mo͞ozhete vichist^{y}it too-hle skv^{u}rnoo
Is my laundry ready?	**Je moje prádlo hotové?**	ye mo-ye prahdlo hotoveh
This isn't mine.	**Tohle není moje.**	to-hle nen^{y}ee moye
There's something missing.	**Něco tady chybí.**	n^{y}etso tadi khibee
There's a hole in this.	**V tomhle je díra.**	vtomhle ye d^{y}eera

Hairdresser—Barber *Kadeřnictví—Holič*

Is there a hairdresser in the hotel?	**Máte v hotelu kadeřnictví?**	mahte v-hoteloo kaderzhn^{y}itstvee
Can I make an appointment for Thursday?	**Můžu se zamluvit na čtvrtek?**	m$\overline{oo}$zhoo se zamloovit na-ch^{u}tv^{u}rtek
I'd like a cut and blow dry.	**Chtěla bych ostříhat a vyfoukat.**	kht^{y}ela bikh ostrzhee-hat a vifohkat
I'd like a haircut, please.	**Chci se nechat ostříhat.**	khtsi se nekhat ost^{u}rzhee-hat
bleach	**odbarvit**	odbarvit
blow-dry	**foukaná**	fohkanah
colour rinse	**přeliv**	p^{u}rzhelif
dye	**obarvení**	obarven^{y}ee
hair gel	**pomáda na vlasy**	pomahda navlasi
manicure	**manikůra**	manik$\overline{oo}$ra
permanent wave	**trvalá**	t^{u}rvalah
setting lotion	**tužidlo**	toozhidlo
shampoo and set	**umýt a natočit**	oomeet a natochit
with a fringe (bangs)	**s ofinou**	s ofinoh
I'd like a shampoo for ... hair.	**Chtěl(a) bych šampón na ... vlasy.**	khtel(a) bikh shamp$\overline{oo}$n na ... vlasi
normal/dry/greasy (oily)	**normální/suché/ mastné**	normahln^{y}ee/sookheh/ mastsneh
Do you have a colour chart?	**Máte ukázky barvy?**	mahte ookahski barvi
Don't cut it too short.	**Ne moc na krátko.**	ne mots nakrahtko
A little more off the ...?	**Trochu víc ubrat ...?**	trokhoo veets oobrat
back	**vzadu**	vzadoo
neck	**na krku**	nak^{u}rkoo
sides	**na stranách**	nastranahkh
top	**nahoře**	na-horzhe
I don't want any hairspray.	**Nechci žádný lak.**	nekh-tsi zhahdnee lak
I'd like a shave.	**Chtěl bych oholit.**	kht^{y}el bikh o-holit

DAYS OF THE WEEK, see page 151

Would you trim my ..., please?	**Můžete přistřihnout moje ...**	moozhete przhi-strzhih-noht mo-ye
beard	**vousy**	vohsi
moustache	**knír**	kn^{y}eer
sideboards (sideburns)	**licousy**	litsohsi

Checking out *Odchod*

May I have my bill, please?	**Prosím účet.**	proseem oochet
I'm leaving early in the morning.	**Odjíždím zítra brzo ráno.**	odyeezhd^{y}eem zeetra b^{u}rzo rahno
Please have my bill ready.	**Připravte mi prosím účet.**	przhiprafte mi proseem oochet
We'll be checking out around noon.	**My budeme odjíždět kolem poledne.**	mi boodeme odyeezhd^{y}et kolem poledne
I must leave at once.	**Musím odjet okamžitě.**	mooseem odyet okamzhit^{y}e
Is everything included?	**Započítal jste všechno?**	zapocheetal yste fshekhno
Can I pay by credit card?	**Můžu platit úvěrovou kartou?**	moozhoo plat^{y}it oovyerovoh kartoh
I think there's a mistake in the bill.	**Myslím, že v tom účtu je chyba.**	misleem zhe ftom oochtoo ye khiba
Can you get us a taxi?	**Můžete nám objednat taxi?**	moozhete nahm obyednat taksi
Could you have our luggage brought down?	**Mohli byste nám snést zavazadla?**	mo-hli bis-te nahm snehst zavazadla
Here's the forwarding address.	**Tady je naše adresa.**	tadi ye nashe adresa
You have my home address.	**Vy máte naši domácí adresu.**	vi mahte nashi domahtsee adresoo
It's been a very enjoyable stay.	**Moc se nám tady líbilo.**	mots se nahm tadi leebilo

TIPPING, see inside back-cover

Camping *Stanování*

Camping sites (*stanový tábor*—stanovi tahbor) and motor camps (*autokemping*) are aimed at the economy-minded vacationer. These are grouped into four categories according to their facilities, but even the lowest class (a single star *) are equipped with toilets and water supply. To conserve the environment, camping outside a designated site is not allowed.

Is there a camp site near here?	**Je tu blízko kemping?**	ye too bleesko kemping
Can we camp here?	**Můžeme tady stanovat?**	m$\overline{oo}$zheme tadi stanovat
Do you have room for a tent/caravan (trailer)?	**Máte místo pro stan/pro obytný přívěs?**	mahte meesto prostan/pro obitnee przheev^{y}es
What's the charge ...?	**Kolik to stojí? ...**	kolik to stoyee
per day	**za den**	zaden
per person	**za osobu**	za osoboo
for a car	**za auto**	za aooto
for a tent	**za stan**	zastan
for a caravan (trailer)	**za obytný přivěs**	za obitnee przhiv^{y}es
Is tourist tax included?	**Je to včetně turistického poplatku?**	ye to fchetn^{y}e turistitskeh-ho poplatkoo
Is there/Are there (a) ...?	**Je tady/jsou tady ...?**	ye tadi/ysoh tadi
drinking water	**pitná voda**	pitnah voda
electricity	**elektřina**	elektrzhina
playground	**dětské hřiště**	d^{y}etskeh hrzhisht^{y}e
restaurant	**restaurant**	restaoorant
shopping facilities	**obchod**	opkhot
swimming pool	**koupaliště**	kohpalisht^{y}e
Where are the showers/toilets?	**Kde jsou sprchy/záchody?**	gde ysoh sp^{u}rkhi/zah-khodi
Where can I get butane gas?	**Kde můžu sehnat plynovou bombu?**	gde m$\overline{oo}$zhoo sehnat plinovoh bomboo
Is there a youth hostel near here?	**Je tady poblíž mládežnická ubytovna?**	ye tadi pobleezh mlahdezhnitskah oobitovna

CAMPING EQUIPMENT, see page 106

Eating out

There are many different types of places in which to enjoy a meal or a drink. They vary from traditional inns and snack bars to luxury restaurants serving international cuisine.

Buffet
(boofet)

A fast food buffet, found mainly at bus or railway stations. These often sell cigarettes and biscuits, as well as open sandwiches.

Cukrárna
(tsookrahrna)

Proper sweet or pastry shop. Specialities include excellent gateaux, choux pastries and cream cakes of many varieties. Good coffee is served, often accompanied by a glass of water in true Viennese style. These places also sell ice-cream. Some shops are take-away only, while others function as cafés as well.

Hospoda
(hospoda)

The traditional eating and drinking establishment, serving good cheap food and draft beer. On the whole very good value. These local taverns are known as *hostinec* (hostinets) or *krčma* (k^{u}rtsma) in Slovakia.

Kavárna
(kavahrna)

This coffee shop is the equivalent of the continental *café*, serving coffee, soft-drinks, mineral water and pastries. Some old traditional establishments provide newspapers hung in wooden long-handled frames.

Pivnice
(pivnitse)

The famed Czech beer hall is the place to drink good beer; most also serve full meals. Its furnishings are generally spartan, but the atmosphere more than makes up for the décor.

Restaurace
(restaoo-ratse)

The generic name for all restaurants; classified according to location, facilities and type of food into 4 categories *I-IV cenová*, I being the best. The categories are always stated at the top of the menu below the restaurant name. There are an increasing number of restaurants serving foreign food — Chinese, Italian, French, Hungarian and others — with menus generally providing German and English translations of dishes.

Rychlé občerstvení
(rikhleh obcherstvenee)

A stand-up fast food establishment selling a variety of tasty snacks, savouries, cakes, hot and cold drinks, draft beer and spirits.

Samoobsluha (samo-obsloo-ha) — The self-service restaurant, also known as an *automat*, is the cheapest place to eat. There is generally something tasty on offer.

Vinárna (vinahrna) — A wine bar. These may be open all day (*denní vinárna*) or at night (*noční vinárna*). Some are owned by wine cooperatives and sell exclusively their own wine.

Meal times *Kdy jíst*

Most eating places serve food and drink all day and, except for expensive tourist restaurants, there are no set menus. It is possible to have just soup or a cold meal almost at any time of day after 1 o'clock.

Breakfast—*snídaně*—from about 5.30 a.m. in snack bars
from 7.30 a.m. in most other places
Lunch—*oběd*—from 11 a.m. to 3 p.m.
Dinner—*večeře*—from 6 p.m. to 10 or 11 p.m.

As work starts very early in the Czech and Slovak republics, people tend to eat early.

Czech and Slovak cuisine *Česká i slovenská kuchyně*

Czech people like their food and their beer and good cooking is very much appreciated. The traditional diet is related to southern German food but there are many Czech specialities. The best known of these are Czech dumplings (*knedlíky*) which accompany meals served with various sauces. Dumplings here are a substitute for rice, pasta or potatoes. However, they have also crept into the dessert category, where they are made from sweet-based dough, filled with fruit, boiled and served with sugar and soured cream. Forget your waistline if you see "*Meruňkové* (or *švestkové*) *knedlíky*"—apricot (or plum) dumplings on the menu. They are definitely worth it!

Vegetarian food (*zeleninová jídla*) is becoming increasingly available in restaurants. The choice is often limited, but lentils cooked in delicious sweet and sour sauce shouldn't be missed.

There is a vast choice of salami and sausages, as these are very popular and good. Hot wurst sausages (with mustard) are sold from small kiosks on the streets. In contrast to these Germanic specialities, Slovakian cooking is more influenced by Hungarian cuisine, with the appearance of goulash and flavouring with pepper and paprika.

Co si přejete?	What would you like?
Můžu vám doporučit toto.	I recommend this.
Co chcete k pití?	What would you like to drink?
Nemáme...	We don't have ...
Chtěli byste...?	Would you like ...?

Hungry? *Máte hlad?*

I'm hungry/ I'm thirsty.	**Mám hlad/ Mám žízeň.**	mahm hlat/mahm zheezen^{y}
Can you recommend a good restaurant?	**Můžete nám doporučit dobrou restauraci?**	m$\overline{oo}$zhete nahm doporoochit dobroh restaooratsi
Are there any inexpensive restaurants around here?	**Jsou tu blízko nějaké lacinější restaurace?**	ysoh too bleesko n^{y}ey-akeh latsin^{y}eyshee restaooratse

If you want to be sure of getting a table in a well-known restaurant, it may be better to book in advance.

I'd like to reserve a table for 4.	**Chci si zamluvit stůl pro 4.**	kh-tsi si zamloovit st$\overline{oo}$l pro chtirzhi
We'll come at 8.	**Přijdeme v 8 hodin.**	przhiydeme f osm hod^{y}in
Could we have a table ...?	**Máte volný stůl...?**	mahte volnee st$\overline{oo}$l
in the corner	**v rohu**	vrohoo
by the window	**u okna**	oo okna
outside	**venku**	venkoo
on the terrace	**na terase**	naterase
in a non-smoking area	**v nekuřácké části**	vnekoorzhah-ts-keh chahst^{y}i

Asking and ordering *Žádosti a objednávky*

Waiter/Waitress!	**Pane vrchní/slečno!**	pane vr-khn^{y}ee/slechno
I'd like something to eat/drink.	**Chtěl(a) bych něco k jídlu/k pití.**	kht^{y}el(a) bikh n^{y}etso k yeedloo/k pit^{y}ee
May I have the menu, please?	**Prosím jídelní lístek?**	proseem yeedeln^{y}ee leestek
Do you have a set menu*/local dishes?	**Máte standardní menu/místní speciality?**	mahte standardn^{y}ee menoo/meestn^{y}ee spetsiy-aliti
What do you recommend?	**Co nám doporučujete?**	tso nahm doporoochooyete
Do you have anything ready quickly?	**Máte něco rychlého?**	mahte n^{y}etso rikhleh-ho
I'm in a hurry.	**Mám naspěch.**	mahm naspyekh
I'd like ...	**Chtěl(a) bych ...**	kht^{y}el(a) bikh
Could we have a/an ..., please?	**Mohl[a] byste mi dát ...?**	mo-h^{u}l [mo-hla] biste mi daht
ashtray	**popelník**	popeln^{y}eek
cup	**šálek**	shahlek
fork	**vidličku**	vidlich-koo
glass	**sklenici**	sklen^{y}itsi
knife	**nůž**	noosh
napkin (serviette)	**ubrousek**	oobrohsek
plate	**talíř**	taleerzh
spoon	**lžíci**	lzheetsi
May I have some ...?	**Přineste mi prosím...**	przhineste mi proseem
bread	**chleba**	khleba
butter	**máslo**	mahslo
lemon	**citrón**	tsitroon
oil	**olej**	oley
pepper	**pepř**	pep^{u}rzh
salt	**sůl**	sool
seasoning	**koření**	korzhen^{y}ee
sugar	**cukr**	tsookr
vinegar	**ocet**	otset

* A set menu is a number of pre-chosen courses, usually cheaper than à la carte.

Special diet *Speciální Strava*

The following expressions will be particularly useful for those who are on a diet or who have other special dietary requirements.

I'm on a diet.	**Mám dietu.**	mahm dietoo
I'm vegetarian.	**Jsem vegetarián.**	ysem vegetariahn
I don't drink alcohol.	**Nepiju alkohol.**	nepiyoo alko-hol
I don't eat meat.	**Nejím maso.**	neyeem maso
I mustn't eat food containing ...	**Nesmím jíst nic v čem je ...**	nesmeem yeest n^{y}its fchem ye
flour	**mouka**	mohka
fat	**tuk**	took
salt	**sůl**	s$\overline{oo}$l
sugar	**cukr**	tsookr
Do you have ... for diabetics?	**Máte ... pro diabetiky?**	mahte...pro diy-abetiki
cakes	**zákusky**	zahkooski
fruit juice	**ovocnou šťávu**	ovotsnoh sht^{y}ahvoo
a special menu	**speciální jídla**	spetsiy-ahln^{y}ee yeedla
Do you have any vegetarian dishes?	**Máte bezmasá jídla?**	mahte bezmasah yeedla
Could I have ... instead of dessert?	**Mohl[a] bych si dát ... místo dezertu?**	mo-h^{u}l [mo-hla] bich si daht ... meesto dezertoo
Can I have an artificial sweetener?	**Máte umělé sladidlo?**	mahte oomn^{y}eleh slad^{y}idlo

And ...

I'd like some more.	**Já bych si rád přidal.**	yah bikh si raht przhidal
Can I have more ..., please?	**Mohl bych si přidat ...?**	mo-hl bikh si przhidat
Just a small portion.	**Jen malou porci.**	yen maloh portsi
Nothing more, thanks.	**Už nic, děkuji.**	oozh n^{y}its d^{y}ekooyi
Where are the toilets?	**Kde jsou toalety?**	gde ysoh toaleti

What's on the menu? *Co máte k jídlu?*

Most restaurants display a menu outside, but many do not serve set menus but à la carte meals. Certain dishes (most often chops or steaks) can be ordered only after 6 p.m. (*jídla podávaná po 18. hodině*). There are dishes suitable for certain diets (*dietní jídla*), for vegetarians (*zeleninová jídla*) and for children (*dětská jídla*).

Under the headings below you'll find alphabetical lists of dishes that might be offered on a Czech menu with their English equivalents. You can simply show the book to the waiter. If you want some fruit, for instance, let *him* point to what's available on the appropriate list. Use pages 36 and 37 for ordering in general.

Reading the menu *Jídelní lístek*

On most Czech menus you'll find the size of the portions in grammes indicated to the left of the item. If the restaurant has run out of the dish, it is simply crossed out on the menu.

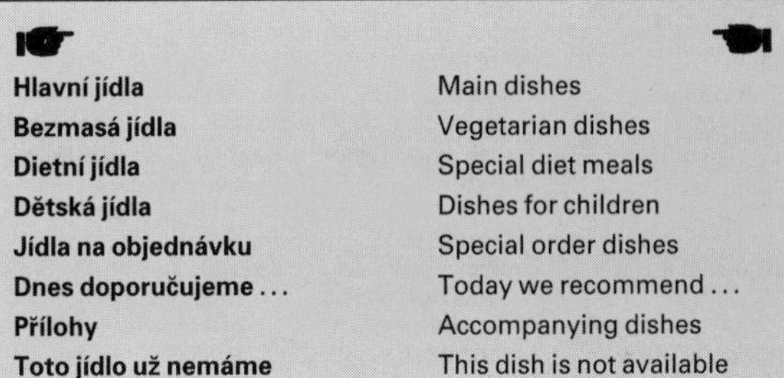

Hlavní jídla	Main dishes
Bezmasá jídla	Vegetarian dishes
Dietní jídla	Special diet meals
Dětská jídla	Dishes for children
Jídla na objednávku	Special order dishes
Dnes doporučujeme ...	Today we recommend ...
Přílohy	Accompanying dishes
Toto jídlo už nemáme	This dish is not available

deserty/zákusky	dezerti/zahkooski	desserts
drůbež	droobesh	poultry
kuře	koorzhe	chicken
mořské ryby	morzhskeh ribi	seafood
moučníky	mohchneeki	sweets
nápoje	nahpoye	beverages
ovoce	ovotse	fruit
pivo	pivo	beer
polévky	polehfki	soups
předkrmy	przhetk^{u}rmi	entrees
předkrmy	przhetkrmi	appetizers
studené	stoodenee	cold
teplé	tepleh	warm
ryby	ribi	fish
rychlé občerstvení	rikhleh obcherstvenee	snacks
saláty	salahti	salads
sýr	seer	cheese
těstoviny	t^{y}estovini	pasta
uzeniny	oozenini	cold cuts
vaječná jídla	va-yechnah yeedla	egg dishes
víno	veeno	wine
zelenina	zelen^{y}ina	vegetables
zmrzlina	zm^{u}rzlina	ice cream
zvěřina	zvyerzhina	game

Breakfast *Snídaně*

The Czech breakfast can vary from a simple meal, perhaps just a coffee and *loupáček*, a croissant-like roll, to an altogether more substantial affair, with cold meats, bacon and eggs. Cereals are not common, and if available at all, the choice is limited. Use the list below to specify what you would like.

I'd like breakfast, please.	**Prosil(a) bych snídani.**	prosil(a) bikh sn^{y}eedan^{y}i
I'll have a/an/ some …	**Dám si…**	dahm si
bacon and eggs	**slaninu s vajíčkem**	slan^{y}inoo sva-yeechkem
boiled egg	**vařené vajíčko**	varzheneh va-yeechko
soft/hard	**na měkko/na tvrdo**	namn^{y}eko/natv^{y}rdo
eggs	**vejce**	veytse
fried eggs	**smažená vejce**	smazhenah veytse
scrambled eggs	**míchaná vejce**	meekhanah veytse
poached eggs	**ztracená vejce**	stratsenah veytse
fruit juice	**ovocnou štávu**	ovotsnoh sht^{y}ahvoo
grapefruit	**grapefruitový džus**	greypfrootovee dzhoos
orange	**pomerančovy džus**	pomeranchovee dzhoos
ham and eggs	**šunku s vajíčky**	shoonkoo sva-yeechki
jam	**džem**	dzhem
marmalade	**pomerančový džem**	pomeranchovee dzhem
toast	**topinku**	topinkoo
yoghurt	**jogurt**	yogoort
May I have some …?	**Chtěl(a) bych …**	kht^{y}el(a) bikh
bread	**chleba**	khleba
butter	**máslo**	mahslo
(hot) chocolate	**(horkou) čokoládu**	(horkoh) chokolahdoo
coffee	**kávu**	kahvoo
decaffeinated	**bez kofeinu**	beskofeyeenoo
black/with milk	**černou/s mlékem**	chernoh/smlehkem
honey	**med**	met
milk	**mléko**	mlehko
cold/hot	**studené/teplé**	stoodeneh/tepleh
pepper	**pepř**	pep^{u}rzh
rolls	**rohlíky**	ro-hleeki
salt	**sůl**	sool
tea	**čaj**	cha-y
with milk	**s mlékem**	smlehkem
with lemon	**s citrónem**	s-tsitrōnem
(hot) water	**(horkou) vodu**	(horkoh) vodoo

Starters (Appetizers) *Předkrmy*

Although the Czechs do not have a great tradition of eating hors d'oeuvres, why not try the succulent speciality of Prague ham (*pražská šunka* — prazhskah shoonkah), served with cucumber or cheese.

I'd like an appetizer.	**Chtěl(a) bych předkrm.**	kh-t^{y}el(a) bikh przhetk^{u}rm
What would you recommend?	**Co doporučujete?**	tso doporoochooyete

chuť'ovky	choot^{y}ovki	savouries
játrová paštika	yahtrovah pashtika	liver paté
kyselé okurky	kiseleh okoorki	sour pickles
langoše	langoshe	fried pastry coated in garlic
moravský salám	moravski salahm	Moravian salami
nakládané houby	naklahdaneh hohbi	pickled mushrooms
obložené chlebíčky	oblozheneh khlebveekh-ki	open sandwich
palačinky s masitou náplní	palachinki	pancakes with meat fillings
párky	pahrki	frankfurters
ředkvičky	rzhedkvichki	radishes
ruské vejce	rooskeh ve-ytse	egg mayonnaise
sardinky	sardinki	sardines
špekáčky	spekahchki	wieners
sýrový nářez	seerovee nahrzhes	
šunka	shoonka	ham
tlačenka	tlachenka	collared pork
tvaroh	tvarokh	farmer cheese
uherský salám	ooherski salahm	Hungarian salami
uzený jazyk	oozenee yazik	smoked tongue
zavináče	zavinah-che	rollmops

Soups and stews *Polévky a dušená jídla*

Soups have long been the basis for midday meals in Bohemia and are still excellent value in restaurants, some being a meal in their own right. Soups are often flavoured with herbs, in particular chives, marjoram, parsley and caraway seeds. Clear soups (*vývar*) will often contain noodles (*s nudlemi*) or small liver-based dumplings (*s knedlíčky*).

bramborová polévka	bramborovah polehfka	potato soup
česneková polévka	chesnekovah pohlefka	garlic soup
čočková polévka	chochkovah polehfka	lentil soup
dršťková polévka	d^{u}rsht^{y}kovah polehfka	tripe soup with herbs
fazolová polévka	fazolovah polehfka	bean soup
hovězí vývar (s nudlemi)	hovyez^{y}ee veevar (snoodlemi)	beef broth (with noodles)
hrachová polévka s uzeným masem	hrakhovah polehvka soozeneem masem	pea soup with smoked meat
kapustová polévka	kapoostovah polehfka	cabbage soup
kmínová polévka	kmeenovah polehfka	caraway seed soup
pórková polévka	pōrkovah polehfka	leek soup
rajská polévka	ra-yskah polehfka	tomato soup
rybí polévka	rib^{y}ee polehfka	fish soup
slepičí vývar s nudlemi	slepich^{y}ee veevar snoodlemi	chicken broth with vermicelli
slepičí polévka	slepich^{y}ee polehfka	chicken consomme
zeleninová polévka	zeleninovah polehfka	vegetable soup
zelná polévka s klobásou	zalnah polehfka sklobahsoh	cabbage soup with smoked sausage

boršč/ruská polévka (borshch/rooskah polehfka)	Russian-style borsch, made from beef, vegetables (mainly beetroot) and sour cream
gulášová polévka (goolashovah polehfka)	Hungarian goulash soup made with beef chunks, potatoes, onions, tomatoes and peppers, richly spiced with paprika, caraway seeds and garlic
ovarová polévka ze zabijačky (ovarovah polehfka zezabi-yachki)	a rich pork soup flavoured with garlic and marjoram and served with boiled barley or rice; has a special place in carnival week
Staročeská (plzeňská) pivní polévka (starocheskah (plzen^{y}skah) pivn^{y}ee polehfka)	Old Czech or Pilsen-style beer soup, based on a light beer, thickened with bread cubes and egg yolks

Fish and seafood *Ryby*

The traditional Czech fish is carp, but several other fresh-water fish are available, such as trout or pike. Carp is normally served baked (*kapr pečený*) or fried in breadcrumbs (*kapr smažený*). A speciality is "Blue carp" (*kapr na modro*) in which the fish is boiled in stock containing vinegar, root vegetables and various spices including thyme, allspice, bay leaf and lemon peel.

I'd like some fish.	**Já bych si dal rybu.**	yah bikh si dal riboo
What kind of seafood do you have?	**Jaké máte mořské ryby?**	yakeh mahte morzhskeh ribi

candát	candaht	pike perch
caviár	caviahr	caviar
humr	hoom^{u}r	lobster
kapr	kap^{u}r	carp
krab	krap	crab
losos	losos	salmon
mořský krab	morzhskee krap	shrimp
mořský okoun	morzhskee okohn	bass
okoun říční	okohn rzheechnee	perch
platýs	platees	halibut
pstruh	pstroo-h	trout
rybí filé	ribee fileh	fish fillet
sardinka	sardinka	sardine
sled'	sled	herring
štika	shtika	pike
treska	treska	cod
tuňák	toon^{Y}ahk	tuna
úhoř	ō-horzh	eel
ústřice	ōstrzhitse	oysters

kapr dušený na černo (kap^{u}r dooshenee nacherno) — carp in a black sauce of peppercorns, prunes, and dark beer

kapr na kmině (kap^{u}r nakmeen^{Y}e) — carp baked with caraway seeds

kapr na modro (kap^{u}r namodro) — carp cooked in stock with wine and spices served with butter

pstruh na másle (pstroo-h namahsl-e) — grilled trout with herb butter

pstruh na smetaně (pstroo-h nasmetan^{Y}e) — poached trout in cream

baked	**pečené**	pecheneh
fried	**smažené**	smazheneh
grilled	**grilované**	grilovaneh
marinated	**marinované**	marinovaneh
poached	**do ztracena**	dostratsena
sautéed	**na másle**	namahsle
smoked	**uzené**	oozeneh
steamed	**uvařené v páře**	oovarzheneh fpahrzhe

Meat *Maso*

The national dish encountered everywhere is pork, served with sauerkraut and dumplings. However, Czech cuisine offers a considerable variety of meat, served in many ways with various types of sauces.

What kind of meat do you have?	**Jaké máte druhy masa?**	yakeh mahte droo-hi masa
beef	**hovězí**	hovyezee
lamb	**jehněčí**	ye-hn^{y}echee
pork	**vepřové**	veprzhoveh
veal	**telecí**	teletsee

biftek	biftek	steak
brzlík	b^{u}rzleek	sweetbreads
bůček	b$\overline{oo}$chek	belly pork
čevapčiči	chevapchichi	meatballs
dušené hovězí	doosheneh hovyezee	pot roast
hovězí oháňka	hovyezee o-hahn^{y}ka	oxtail
hřbet	h^{u}rzhbet	saddle
jazyk	yazik	tongue
jehněčí kýta	ye-hn^{y}echee keehta	leg of lamb
jelítko	yeleetko	blood sausage
jitrnice	yit^{u}rni-tse	white sausage
kotleta	kotleta	chop/cutlet
králík	krahleek	rabbit
kýta	keeta	leg of pork
ledvinky	ledvinki	kidneys
masová směs na roštu	masovah smn^{y}es naroshtoo	mixed grill
masové kuličky	masoveh koolichki	meatballs
mleté maso	mleteh maso	mince
párky	parki	frankfurters
roštená	roshtenah	entrecote
salám	salahm	salami
selátko	selahtko	suckling pig
skopové	skopoveh	mutton
slanina	slan^{y}ina	bacon
špek	shpek	speck
svíčková	sveechkovah	tenderloin
uzená šunka	oozenah shoonka	(smoked) ham
uzené	oozeneh	gammon
vepřová hlava	veprzhovah hlava	pig's head
vepřové droby	veprzhoveh drobi	black pudding
vepřové kotlety	veprzhoveh kotleti	pork chops
vuřt	voorzht	sausage

baked	**pečený**	pechenee
boiled	**vařené**	varzheneh
braised	**dušené**	doosheneh
fried	**smažené**	smazheneh
grilled	**grilované**	grilovaneh
roast	**pečeně**	pecheneh
sautéed	**na másle**	namahsle
smoked	**uzené**	oozeneh
stewed	**dušené**	doosheneh
very rare	**na krvavo**	nak^{u}rvavo
underdone (rare)	**lehce udělané**	lekh-tse ood^{y}elaneh
medium	**středně udělané**	strzhedn^{y}e ood^{y}elaneh
well-done	**dobře udělané**	dobrzhe ood^{y}elaneh

Meat dishes *Masitá jídla*

guláš z hovězího masa na smetaně	goolash zhovyezee-ho masa nasmetan^{y}e	beef goulash with cream sauce
hovězí dušené na hříbkách	hovyezee doosheneh na-hrzheebkah-kh	beef ragout with mushrooms
hovězí tokáň	hovyezee tokah^{y}n	beef in a wine and tomato purée
pečeně se slaninou	pecheneh se slan^{y}inoh	larded roast
přírodní řízek	przheerodnee rzheezek	unbreaded cutlet
roštěnky na pivě	rosht^{y}enki napiv^{y}e	carbonade, a stew of beef and onions cooked in beer
segedínský guláš	segedeenskee goolash	goulash of three meats with sauerkraut
smažene karbanátky	smazhen-e karbanahtki	fried burgers
smažený řízek	smazheni rzheezek	breaded veal cutlet
tatarský biftek	tatarski biftek	steak tartare
vepřové kotlety na pivě	veprzhoveh kotleti napiv^{y}e	pork chops in beer
vepřové žebírko	veprzhoveh zhebeerko	stewed rib of pork
vepřový guláš se zelím	veprzhovee goolash sezeleem	pork goulash with sauerkraut
dušené telecí maso na víně	doosheneh teletsee maso na veen^{y}e	veal braised with wine
vídeňský řízek	veeden^{y}skee rzheezek	Weinerschnitzel cutlet
zadělávané dršt'ky	zadyelahvaneh d^{u}rsht^{y}ki	tripe in white sauce
živáňská	zhivahn^{y}skah	a Slovak grilled skewer
znojemská pečeně	zno-yemskah pechen^{y}e	slices of roast beef in a gherkin sauce

guláš (goolash)	goulash; a Hungarian soup made from beef, onions, potatoes, paprika, caraway, garlic, vegetables and tiny dumplings
moravští vrabci (moravshtee vraptsi)	"Moravian sparrows", roasted pieces of pork sprinkled with caraway seeds
pražská hovězí pečeně (prazhskah hovyezhee pechen^{y}e)	Prague-style roast beef, a joint stuffed with fried diced ham, peas, egg, onion and spices
pražské telecí hrudí (prazhskeh teletsi hroodee)	Prague-style breast of veal, stuffed with a mixture of eggs, ham, peas and whipped cream, and roasted with butter
svíčková pečeně na smetaně (sveetskovah pechen^{y}e nasmetan^{y}e)	a tasty cut of beef in a special sour cream and spice sauce
šunka po staročesku (shoonka postarocheskoo)	old-Bohemian style boiled ham, with a sauce of plums, prunes, walnuts and wine
vepřová krkovička po selsku (veprzhovah k^{u}rkovitska poselskoo)	neck of pork, rubbed with garlic and roasted with onions
znojemská roštěná (zno-yemskah rosht^{y}enah)	sirloin à la Znojmo, fried then stewed with onions

Game and poultry *Zvěřina a Drůbež*

Roast duck is a very common Czech dish, as is braised rabbit and goose breast smeared in garlic and roasted in its own juices. Many recipes for poultry and game include cranberries, while caraway is also often used to ease the digestion of fat.

bažant	bazhant	pheasant
divoký kanec	d^{y}ivokee kanets	wild boar
holub	holoop	pigeon
husa	hoosa	goose
kachna	kakhna	duck
kachňátko	kakhn^{y}ahtko	duckling
kapoun	kapohn	capon
koroptev	koroptef	partridge
křepelka	krzhepelka	quail

krůta	kro͞ota	turkey
kuře	koorzhe	chicken
kuře na roštu prsa/stehno/křídlo	koorzhe na rhoshtoo p^{u}rsa/ste-hno/ krzheedlo	roast chicken breast/leg/wing
perlička	perlichka	guinea fowl
sluka	slooka	woodcock
srnčí	s^{u}rnchee	venison
tetřívek	tetrzheevek	grouse
zajíc	za-yeets	hare

Special dishes *Speciality*

bažant dušený na žampiónech	bazhant dooshenee nazhampiōnekh	pheasant casserole with mushroom
bažant na slanině	bazhant naslanin^{y}e	roast pheasant with bacon
divoký králík na česneku	divokee krahleek nachesnekoo	wild rabbit with garlic
dušena kachna s brusinkami	dooshena kakhna sbroosinkami	braised duck with cranberries
guláš z daňčího masa	goolahsh zdan^{y}chee-ho masa	venison goulash
husí játra smažená	hoosee yahtra smazhenah	fried goose liver in breadcrumbs
husí krky plněné	hoosee k^{u}rki p^{u}ln^{y}eneh	stuffed goose neck
husí žaludky zadělávané	hoosee zhaloodki zad^{y}elahvaneh	goose stomach in white sauce
koroptev pečená na červeném zelí	koroptef pechenah nachervenehm zelee	roast partridge with red cabbage
krocan s kaštanovou nádivkou	krotsan skashtanovoh nahdivkoh	roast turkey stuffed with chestnuts
kuře pečené s nádivkou	koorzhe pecheneh snahdivkoh	roast chicken with chicken liver stuffing
pečená husí játra s mandlemi	pechenah hoosee yahtra smandlemi	goose liver with almonds
perlička pečená	perlitska pechenah	roast guinea fowl
srnčí hřbet dušený na víně	s^{u}rnchee h^{u}rzhbet dooshenee naveen^{y}e	saddle of venison braised with wine
zajíc na černo	za-yeets nacherno	stewed hare in thick, dark, sweet sauce
zajíc na divoko	za-yeets nad^{y}ivoko	larded hare cooked with onion and vegetables in red wine
zajíc na smetaně	za-yeets nasmetan^{y}e	hare in cream sauce

Potatoes *Brambory*

Potatoes are the most common staple and are used in an amazing variety of ways. You might be lucky and find a place selling *bramborák* or a spicy potato pancake which is made of grated potatoes with marjoram and garlic. There are also, of course, potato dumplings as well as excellent potato soup.

bramborák	bramborahk	potato cakes made from raw potatoes
bramborová kaše	bramborovah kash-e	mashed potatoes
bramborové hranolky	bramboroveh hranolki	chips (French fries)
bramborové knedlíky	bramboroveh knedleeki	potato dumplings
plněné uzeným	p[u]ln[y]eneh oozeneem	with smoked meat
s cibulkou	stsiboolkoh	with onions
bramborové omelety se špenátem	bramboroveh omeletoo seshpenahtem	potato omelettes with spinach
bramborové placky	bramboroveh platski	potato pancake
bramborové šišky	bramboroveh shishki	small flour and potato dumplings
bramborové škubánky	bramboroveh shkoobahnki	potato pudding
bramborové taštičky s masitou nádivkou	bramboroveh tashtitski smasitoh nahdivkoh	potato ravioli with meat stuffing

In addition, you'll also want to try these specialities:

chlupaté knedlíky se zelím (khloopateh knedleeki sezeleem) Bohemian potato dumplings with cabbage, made from raw grated potato, flour and egg

škubánky s mákem (shkoobahnki smahkem) potato dumplings with poppy seeds and sugar

Rice, noodles and dumplings *Rýže, nudle a knedlíky*

Dumplings will always be found on a Czech menu in some form, whether floating in your soup, as an accompaniment to a main course or filled with fruit and served as a dessert.

fleky zapečené se zelím	fleki zapecheneh sezeleem	pasta baked with cabbage
houskový knedlík	hoh-skovee knedleek	bread dumpling

knedlíky s vejci	knedleeki sveytsi	dumpling with egg
kynuté knedlíky	kinooteh knedleeki	jam-filled dumplings
makarony	makaroni	macaroni
noky	noki	gnocchi
nudle	nood-le	noodles
s mákem	smahkem	with poppy seeds
rýžová kaše	reezhovah kash-e	rice purée
špagety	shpageti	spaghetti
těstoviny	t^{y}estovini	noodles
zapékané nudle	zapehkaneh nood-le	noodles baked with egg and cheese

buchty (bookhti) baked yeast dumpling filled with cottage cheese, jam, apples or plums

švestkové knedlíky (shvestkoveh knedleeki) plum dumplings topped with melted butter, crushed poppy seeds and sugar

Sauces *Omáčky*

A sauce in Czech cooking means really one thing — a thick, cream-based sauce flavoured with various vegetables, herbs and spices. These sauces form the perfect accompaniment to Czech dumplings.

The most common sauces which are served with beef are tomato (*rajská omáčka*), dill (*koprová omáčka*) or mushrooms (*houbová omáčka*). The tastiest is the so-called "candle roast sauce" (*svíčková omáčka*), derived from marinaded roast fillet of beef, and served sieved and flavoured with thyme and cream.

These are some of the terms appearing on menus, describing how meat and poultry may be cooked or served.

na česneku	nachesnekoo	with garlic
na pivě	napivye	with a beer sauce, flavoured with spices
na smetaně	nasmetan^{y}e	in a cream sauce
na víně	navinye	in wine
se žloutkovou omáčkou	sezhlohtkovoh omahchkoh	with an egg yolk sauce

na černo (nacherno) in a "black" sauce made with peppercorns, allspice, gingerbread, cheese, tomato purée and red wine

Vegetables *Zelenina*

artyčoky	artichoki	artichokes
brambory	brambori	potatoes
celer	tseler	celery
červená řepa	chervenah repa	beetroot
chřest	khrzhest	asparagus
cibule	tsiboo-le	onions
cikorka	tsikorka	endive (chicory)
čočka	chochka	lentils
dýně	deen^{y}e	squash
dýně	deen^{y}e	vegetable marrow
fazole	fazole	beans
fazole na kyselo	fazo-le nakeeselo	sour beans
červené fazole	cherveneh fazole	kidney beans
zelené fazolky	zeleneh fazolki	green beans
fenykl	fenik^{u}l	fennel
houby	hohbi	mushrooms
hrášek	hrahshek	peas
jedlé kaštany	yedleh kashtani	chestnuts
kukuřice	kookoorzhitse	sweetcorn
květák	kvyetahk	cauliflower
lilek	lilek	aubergine (eggplant)
mrkev	m^{u}rkef	carrots
obilí	obilee	corn
okurka	okoorka	cucumber
pálivá paprika	pahlivah paprika	chili
papriky	papriki	peppers
sladké	slatkeh	sweet
zelené/červené	zeleneh/cherveneh	green/red
pórek	po͞orek	leeks
rajská jablíčka	ra-yskah yableechka	tomatoes
ředkvičky	rzhetkvichki	radishes
růžičková kapusta	ro͞ozhichkovah kapoosta	Brussels sprouts
salát	salaht	lettuce
sladké brambory	slatkeh brambori	sweet potatoes
špenát	shpenaht	spinach
tuřín	toorzheen	turnips
tykev	tikef	pumpkin
žampióny	zhampiōni	wild mushrooms
zelí	zelee	cabbage
kyselé zelí	kiseleh zhelee	sauerkraut

Some vegetarian dishes:

plněné papriky v rajčatové omáčce	plneneh papriki vraychatoveh omahch-tse	stuffed peppers in tomato sauce

čočka na kyselo	chochka nakiselo	savoury lentils
houby s krupkami	hoh-bi skroopkami	mushrooms with pearl barley
smažené květákové nočky	smazheneh kv^{y}etahkoveh nochki	fried cauliflower dumplings
špenátové smaženky s houbami	shpenahtoveh smazhenki s-hohbami	spinach rissoles with mushrooms
zadělávaný květák se sýrem	zad^{y}elahvanee kvyetahk seseerem	cauliflower with cream sauce and cheese
zeleninové karbanátky	zeleninové karbanahtki	fried vegetable rissoles in breadcrumbs

Salads *Saláty*

A salad may be served as a starter, an accompaniment to a meal, or as a main dish in itself.

Here are just a few to whet your appetite:

bramborový salát	bramborovee salaht	potato salad
celerový salát	tselerovee salaht	celeriac salad
čočkový salát	chochkovee salaht	lentil salad
fazolkový salát	fazolkovee salaht	French bean salad
hlávkový salát	hlahvkovee salaht	green salad
jarní míchaný salát	jarnee meekhanee salaht	mixed fresh vegetable salad
okurkový salát	okoorkovee salaht	cucumber salad
paprikový salát	paprikovee salaht	green pepper salad
rajčatový salát	raychatovee salaht	tomato salad
salát z červené řepy	salaht scherveneh rzhepi	beet salad
salát z červeného zelí	salaht scherveneh-ho zelee	red cabbage salad
salát z kyselého zelí	salaht zkooseleh-ho zelee	sauerkraut salad

Herbs and spices *Bylinky a koření*

anýz	anees	aniseed
bazalka	bazalka	basil
bobkový list	bopkovee list	bay leaf
česnek	chesnek	garlic
drobná cibulka	drobnah tsiboolka	shallot
estragon	estragon	tarragon

hořčice	horzhchitse	mustard
hřebíček	hrzhebeechek	cloves
kapary	kapari	capers
kmín	kmeen	caraway
kopr	kop^{u}r	dill
křen	krzhen	horseradish
majoránka	ma-yorahnka	marjoram
máta	mahta	mint
muškátový oříšek	mooshkahtovee orzheeshek	nutmeg
nakládane okurky	naklahdaneh okoorki	gherkins
oregano	oregahno	oregano
paprika	paprika	paprika
pažitka	pazhitka	chives
pepř	pep^{u}rzh	pepper
petržel	pet^{u}rzhel	parsley
potočnice	potochn^{y}itse	watercress
rozmarýnka	rozmareenka	rosemary
šafrán	shafrahn	saffron
šalvěj	shalvyey	sage
skořice	skorzhitse	cinnamon
sůl	so͞ol	salt
tymián	timiy-ahn	thyme
vanilka	vanilka	vanilla
zázvor	zahzvor	ginger

To follow ... *A potom...*

If you're still hungry, you may have room for some cheese, some fruit or perhaps a dessert.

Cheese *Sýr*

Although cheese spreads, made from curd cheese and cream and flavoured with onions and paprika or fruits, are used frequently in Czech cuisine, the country itself does not produce a great variety of different cheeses. However, here are some cheeses you will come across:

brynza	brinza	sheep cheese
ementál	ementahl	Swiss cheese
plísňový sýr	pleesn^{y}ovee seer	blue cheese
smetanový sýr	smetanovee seer	cream cheese
syrečky	seerechki	beer cheese

And here are some cheese-based dishes to look out for:

smažené sýrové knedlíčky se smetanou	smazheneh seeroveh knedleetski sesemetanoh	fried cheese dumplings with cream
smažený sýr v těstíčku	smazhenee seer ft^y^esteechkoo	cheese fried in batter
smažený sýr	smazheni seer	fried cheese in breadcrumbs
sýrové pavézky	seeroveh pavehzki	cheese cutlets
tvarohové palačinky	tvaro-hoveh palachinki	cottage cheese pancakes

Fruit and nuts *Ovoce a ořechy*

Do you have any fresh fruit?	**Máte nějaké čerstvé ovoce?**	mahte n^y^eyakeh cherstveh ovotse
I'd like a (fresh) fruit cocktail.	**Dám si ovocný pohár.**	dahm si ovotsnee po-hahr

ananas	ananas	pineapple
angrešt	angresht	gooseberries
banán	banahn	banana
borůvky	boroofki	bilberries
borůvky	boroofki	blueberries
broskev	broskef	peach
burské oříšky	boorskeh orzheeshki	peanuts
černý rybíz	chernee ribees	blackcurrants
citrón	tsitrōn	lemon
limetka	limetka	lime
datle	datle	dates
fíky	feeki	figs
grapefruit	greypfroot	grapefruit
hrozinky	hrozinki	raisins
hrozny	hrozni	grapes
hruška	hrooshka	pear
jablko	yablko	apple
jahody	ya-hodi	strawberries
kaštany	kashtani	chestnuts
kdoule	kdohle	quince
kokos	kokos	coconut
lískové ořechy	leeskoveh orzhekhi	hazelnuts
maliny	malini	raspberries
mandle	mandle	almonds
meloun	melohn	melon

meruňky	meroon^{y}ki	apricots
nektarinka	nektarinka	nectarine
mandarinka	mandarinka	tangerine
pomeranč	pomeranch	orange
rebarbora	rebarbora	rhubarb
sultánky	sooltahnki	sultanas
sušené ovoce	soosheneh ovotse	dried fruit
sušené švestky	soosheneh shvestki	prunes
švestky	shvestki	plums
třešně	trzheshn^{y}e	cherries
vlašské ořechy	vlashskeh orzhekhi	walnuts

Desserts—Pastries *Moučníky—Zákusky*

The Czechs have long prided themselves on their pastry cooking—and with good reason. You'll find many rich and heavyweight items to tempt you on the restaurant menu or in the window of a bakery or pastry shop (*cukrárna* — tsookrahrna).

Here are some phrases to help you arrive at your decision. But be warned—it won't be easy!

I'd like a dessert, please.	**Dal bych si moučník.**	dal bikh si mohchn^{y}eek
What do you recommend?	**Co mi doporučíte?**	tso mi doporoocheete
Something light, please.	**Něco lehčího.**	n^{y}etso lekh-cheeho
Just a small portion.	**Jen malou porci.**	yen maloh portsi

bublanina	booblanina	sponge with fruit
třešňová bublanina	trzheshnovah booblanina	sponge biscuits with cherries
buchta	bukhta	buns
cukroví	tsookrovee	cookies
dort	dort	rich cream cake, topped with chocolate icing and almonds

dukátové buchtičky	dookahtoveh bookhtichki	tiny doughnuts
jemný drobenkový koláč	yemnee drobenkovee kolahch	cheese crumble pie
koblihy	koblihi	doughnuts
koláčky	kolahchki	sweet buns
kompot	kompot	stewed fruit
krém	krem	custard
makový koláč	makovee kolahch	poppy-seed cake
marokánky	marokahnki	macaroons
nepečené kuličky	nepecheneh koolitski	chocolate truffles
omeleta se zavařeninou	omeleta sezavarzheninoh	jam omelette
ovocné koláče	ovotsneh kolahche	fruit cake slices
palačinky	palachinki	crêpes
rakvičky	rakvitski	meringue with whipped cream
šlehačka	shle-hatska	whipped cream
štrůdl	shtrood[u]l	apple strudel
švestkový koláč na plech	shvestkovee kolahch naplekh	plum pie with crumble
svítek	zveetek	baked pancake often served with stewed fruit
trubičky se šlehačkou	troobitski seshle-hatskoh	puff pastry cream cornets
tvarohové palačinky	tvaro-hovee palachinki	cottage cheese pancakes

If ice cream is your weakness, try one (or all!) of the following flavours:

zmrzlina	zm[u]rzlina	ice cream
čokoládová	chokolahdovah	chocolate
oříšková	orzhishkovah	nut
vanilková	vanilkovah	vanilla
zmrzlinový pohár	zm[u]rzlinovee po-hahr	sundae
zázvorky	zahzvorki	ginger snaps

Specialities *Speciality*

domažlický velký koláč (domazhlitskee velkee kolahch) a large pie à la Domažlice, patterned with strips of cottage cheese, plum cheese and poppy seed filling

dort z karlovarských oplatek (dort skarlovarskeekh oplatek)	"Carlsbad layer cake", made from thin wafers sandwiching a walnut and cocoa butter filling, and topped with icing
jablkový závin (yab[u]lkovee zahvin)	apple baked in flaky pastry, using entire apples stuffed with sugar, cinnamon and raisins
lívance (leevant-se)	small pancakes, spread with plum cheese and a layer of cottage or curd cheese, and topped with yoghurt or thick sour cream
moravské koláče (moravskeh kolahch)	Moravian buns, filled twice during cooking with first curd cheese and then plum cheese, and sprinkled with crumble
perník (perneek)	gingerbread cookie made with honey, almonds and spices
piškotová balenka (pishkotovah balenka)	Swiss roll served with redcurrant jam and whipped cream
švestkové knedlíky (shvestkoveh knedleeki)	plum dumplings sprinkled with sieved curd cheese and sugar and covered with melted butter
žemlovka (zhemlofka)	baked apples in a soft pudding with white bread, milk, raisins, cinnamon and eggs

Drinks *Nápoje*

Beer *Pivo*

Czech beer is justifiably world famous, based on a brewing tradition going back over one thousand years. It is in this region that the world's most prized hops are grown, renowned for their delicacy of fragrance and exported worldwide. The country also boasts two great brewing towns: *Plzeň* (p[u]lzen[y]), home of the world's most widely produced style of beer (Pilsner or Pils), and *České Budějovice*, (cheskeh bood[y]e-yovitse) and formerly named Budweis.

Not surprisingly, with such an excellent array to choose from, beer consumption among the Czech is amongst the highest in the world, and the best place to enjoy the local brew is in one of the many beer halls (*pivnice* — pivnitse).

Lager (*světlé pivo*) comes in two strengths — 10% (*desítka*) and 12% (*dvanáctka*). Black beer (*černé* or *tmavé pivo*) is also very popular and there are beer halls and pubs around Prague like *U Fleků* which specialize in this type of beer.

Here are just a few of the most well-known beers to look out for:

Plzeňský Prazdroj (p[u]lzenskee prazdro-y) — exported as *Pilsner Urquell*, the original pilsner lager is dry and golden, with an aromatic, hoppy flavour and soft drinkability

Budvar (boodvar) — this well-rounded lager has a depth of spicy-sweet maltiness and goes particularly well with food

Speciální pivo (spetsiahlnee pivo) — "special beer" is a stronger beer of 13-20 degrees; beers of this type include *Bránické, Flekovské, Tomášské* and *Senátor.*

Staropramen svetlé (staropramen svetleh) — a soft, sweetish, light beer from the largest brewery in Prague

Zlatý Bažant (slatee bazhant) — the fresh, dry "Golden Pheasant" is the most famous Slovak beer

I'd like a beer.	**Chtěl(a) bych pivo.**	kht[y]el(a) bikh pivo
a dark beer	**černé pivo**	cherneh pivo
a light beer	**světlé pivo**	sv[y]etleh pivo
a bottle of beer	**láhev piva**	lah-hef piva
a draught beer	**sudové pivo**	soodoveh pivo
half a litre	**malé pivo**	maleh pivo
What's yours?	**Co si dáte?**	tso si dahte
I'll have another.	**Dejme se ještě jednu.**	de-yme si yeshtee yednoo

NA ZDRAVÍ
(nasdravee)
CHEERS

Wine *Víno*

There are many home-grown wines in the Czech and Slovak republics, though the amount that is exported is very small.

Southern Moravia and Southern Slovakia produce excellent white wines and there are many cellars you can visit, particularly in Bratislava.

Wines to look out for are the popular whites: *Vlašský ryzlink*, *Rulandské bílé*, *Müller-Thurgau*, *Veltlínské zelené* and *Ryzlink rýnský*; the reds *Klaštorné červené* and *Rulandské červené*, as well as *Sekt Cremant Rose*, a red champagne.

May I please have the wine list?	**Přineste mi, prosím, nápojový lístek?**	przhineste mi proseem nahpo-yovee leestek
I would like a bottle of white /red wine.	**Chtěl(a) bych láhev bílého/červeného vína.**	kht^{y}el(a) bikh lah-hef beeleh-ho/cherveneh-ho veena
I'd like a glass of ...	**Rád(a) bych sklenici ...**	rahd(a) bikh sklenitsi
Waiter/waitress, bring me another ..., please.	**Pane/paní vrchní, ještě ..., prosím.**	paneh/pan^{y}ee v^{u}rkh^{y}nee yeshte ... proseem

red	**červené**	chervenee
white	**bilé**	beelee
rosé	**růžové**	roozhoveh
sparkling	**šumivé**	shoomivee
dry	**suché**	sookhee
sweet	**sladký**	sladkee

Other alcoholic drinks *Jiné alkoholické nápoje*

I'd like a/ an ...	**Chtěl(a) bych ...**	khtěl(a) bikh
aperitif	**aperitiv**	aperitif
cognac	**koňak**	kon^{y}ak
gin	**gin**	dzhin
liqueur	**likér**	likehr
rum	**rum**	room

vermouth	**vermut**	vermoot
vodka	**vodku**	votkoo
whisky	**whisky**	viski
neat (straight)	**čistou**	chistoh
on the rocks	**s ledem**	sledem
with a little water	**s trochou vody**	strokhoh vodi
Give me a gin and tonic, please.	**Dejte mi, prosím, gin a tonik.**	deyte mi proseem dzhin a tonik
Just a dash of soda, please.	**Jen trochu sodovky.**	yen trokhoo sodofki

It is said that Bohemia has the best beer, Moravia the best wine and Slovakia the best spirits. Why not put this to the test by trying the very popular Slovakian drink *borovička* (borovitska)? It has a very distinctive taste, but perhaps the closest comparison is with gin.

If you want to try something else with a local flavour, we would recommend the following:

Karlovarská Becherovka (karlovarskah bekherovka)	a herbaceous drink originating from Karlovy Vary, served chilled as an aperitif and often drunk with tonic, lemon and ice
meruňkovice (meroon[y]kovitse)	an apricot brandy
slivovice (slivovit-se)	plum brandy, often served with snack meals or as a pick-me-up during the day
stará myslivecká (starah mislivetskah)	a powerful, sweet aperitif
Zubrovka (zoobrofka)	vodka flavoured with a herb extract

Nonalcoholic drinks *Nealkoholické nápoje*

At some stage you're bound to be in need of a refreshing mineral water (*minerálka*), bottled at one of the many well-known Czech spas. Lemonade (*limonáda*) is the traditional generic soft drink, but fruit juices and international brands of colas are now also widely available.

Tea tends to be weak, more of the Chinese rather than Indian variety, and is served with lemon and sugar on the side.

Here are a few phrases to help you order just what you want:

apple juice	**jablečná šťáva**	yablechnah sht^{y}ahva
(hot) chocolate	**kakao**	kakao
fruit juice	**ovocná šťáva**	ovotsnah sht^{y}ahva
grapefruit juice	**grapefruitový džus**	greypfro͞otovee dzhoos
herb tea	**bylinkový čaj**	bilinkovee cha-y
lemon juice	**citronová šťáva**	tsitrōnovah sht^{y}ahva
lemonade	**limonáda**	limonahda
milk	**mléko**	mlehko
milkshake	**koktejl**	kokteyl
mineral water	**minerálka**	minerahlka
fizzy (carbonated)	**šumivá**	shoomivah
still	**nešumivá**	neshoomivah
orange juice	**pomerančový džus**	pomeranchovee dzhoos
orangeade	**oranžáda**	oranzhahda
tea	**čaj**	cha-y
cup of tea	**šálek čaje**	shahlek cha-ye
with milk/lemon	**s mlékem/s citrónem**	smlehkem/stsitrōnem
iced tea	**ledový čaj**	ledovee cha-y
tomato juice	**rajská šťáva**	ra-yskah sht^{y}ahva
tonic water	**tonik**	tonik

Coffee *Káva*

The most common coffee you can get is excellent Turkish coffee (*turecká káva*). It is also the cheapest coffee around.

In a good café your coffee should come with a glass of water. It should be thick and strong with finely ground coffee forming a layer on top of the liquid. Other types of coffee are also available, including espresso, cappuccino and instant coffee.

I'd like a/an ...	**Chtěl(a) bych ...**	kht^{y}el(a) bikh
coffee	**kávu**	kahvoo
black coffee	**černou kávu**	chernoh kahvoo
coffee with cream	**kávu se šlehačkou**	kahvoo seshle-hachkoh
white coffee	**s mlékem**	smlehkem
caffeine-free coffee	**kávu bez kofeinu**	kahvoo beskofeynoo
espresso coffee	**espresso**	espreso
Turkish coffee	**tureckou kávu**	tooretskoh kahvoo
Vienna coffee	**vídeňskou kávu**	veeden^{y}tskoh kahvoo

Complaints *Stížnosti*

If you do have a complaint that is not satisfactorily redressed, try asking for the complaints book (*kniha přání a stížností*—kniha przhahn^{y}ee a steezhnostee). Although newly privatized restaurants are no longer required to keep them, your request alone should rectify the problem.

There's a plate/glass missing.	**Tady chybí talíř/ sklenička.**	tadi khibee taleerzh/ sklen^{y}ichka
I don't have a knife/ fork/spoon.	**Já nemám nůž/ vidličku/žíci.**	yah nemahm n$\overline{oo}$sh/ vidlichkoo/zheetsi
That's not what I ordered.	**To jsem si neobjednal(a).**	to ysem si neobyednal(a)
I asked for ...	**Já jsem chtěl(a)...**	yah ysem kht^{y}el(a)
There must be some mistake.	**Tady se někdo spletl.**	tadi se n^{y}egdo splet^{u}l
May I change this?	**Můžu si to vyměnit?**	m$\overline{oo}$zhoo si to vimn^{y}en^{y}it
I asked for a small portion (for the child).	**Já jsem chtěl(a) malou porci (pro dítě).**	yah ysem kht^{y}el(a) maloh portsi (prod^{y}eet^{y}e)
The meat is ...	**To maso je...**	to maso ye
overdone	**příliš udělané**	przheelish ood^{y}elaneh
underdone	**nedodělané**	nedod^{y}elaneh
too rare	**moc syrové**	mots siroveh
too tough	**tvrdé**	tv^{u}rdeh
This is too ...	**Tohle je moc...**	to-hle ye mots
bitter/salty/sweet	**hořké/slané/sladké**	horzhkeh/slaneh/slatkeh
I don't like this.	**To mi nechutná.**	to mi nekhootnah
The food is cold.	**To jídlo je studené.**	to yeedlo ye stoodeneh
This isn't fresh.	**Tohle není čerstvé.**	to-hle nen^{y}ee cherstveh
What's taking you so long?	**Proč vám to tak dlouho trvá?**	proch vahm to tak dloh-ho t^{u}rvah
Have you forgotten our drinks?	**Nezapomněl(a) jste na naše pití?**	nezapomn^{y}el(a) yste nanashe pit^{y}ee
The wine doesn't taste right.	**To víno má divnou chůt'.**	to veeno mah d^{y}ivnoh khoot^{y}
This isn't clean.	**Tohle není čisté.**	to-hle nen^{y}ee chisteh
Would you ask the head waiter to come over?	**Zavolal[a] byste pana vrchního?**	zavolal[a] biste pana vr-khn^{y}ee-ho

The bill (check) *Účet*

A tip of about 10% for the waiter is expected. Credit cards are generally accepted in all establishments frequented by tourists. Signs are posted indicating which cards are accepted.

I'd like to pay.	**Prosím účet.**	proseem o͞ochet
We'd like to pay separately.	**My budeme platit zvlášť.**	mi boodeme plat^{y}it zv^{u}lahsht^{y}
I think there's a mistake in this bill.	**V tom účtu je asi chyba.**	ftom o͞ochtoo ye asi khiba
What's this amount for?	**Za co je tohle?**	zatso ye to-hle
Is service included?	**Zahrnuje to služby?**	za-hrnooye to sloozhbi
Is the cover charge included?	**Je tady poplatek za stůl?**	ye tadi poplatek zasto͞ol
Is everything included?	**Je v tom všechno?**	ye ftom fshekhno
Do you accept traveller's cheques?	**Přijímáte cestovní šeky?**	przhiyeemahte tsestovn^{y}ee sheki
Can I pay with this credit card?	**Mohu platit touto úvěrovou kartou?**	mo-hoo plat^{y}it o͞ovyerovoh kartoh
Please round it up to …	**Můžete to zaokrouhlit na …**	mo͞ozhete to zaokroh-hlit na
Keep the change.	**Nechte si drobné.**	nekhte si drobneh
That was delicious.	**To bylo vynikající.**	to bilo vin^{y}ika-yeetsee
We enjoyed it, thank you.	**Moc nám to chutnalo, děkujeme.**	mots nahm to khootnalo d^{y}ekooyeme

SLUŽBA JE ZAPOČÍTANÁ
SERVICE INCLUDED

TIPPING, see inside back-cover

Snacks—Picnic *Rychlé občerstvení—Piknik*

The following words and phrases will come in handy if you want a quick snack. You should be able to find what you want at a *buffet* or *cukrárna* (pastry shop). If not, the local grocer's (*obchod s potravinami*) will have the provisions you need.

Give me two of these and one of those.	**Dejte mi dva takové a jeden takový.**	deyte mi dva takoveh a yeden takovee
to the left/right	**nalevo/napravo**	nalevo/napravo
above/below	**nad tím/pod tím**	natt^{y}eem/pott^{y}eem
It's to take away.	**Zabalit.**	zabalit
I'd like a piece of cake.	**Chtěl(a) bych jeden kousek dortu.**	kht^{y}el(a) bikh yeden kohsek dortoo
burger	**karbanátek**	karbanahtek
fried sausage	**opečený vuřt**	opechenee voorzht
hot dog	**párek v rohlíku**	pahrek fro-hleekoo
omelette	**omeletu**	omeletoo
open sandwich	**chlebíček**	khlebeechek
with ham	**se šunkou**	seshoonkoh
with cheese	**se sýrem**	seseerem
potato salad	**bramborový salát**	bramborovee salaht
sandwich	**sendvič**	sendvich

Bread *Chleb*

Czech bread was traditionally based on rye (*žitný chleb*), but its modern equivalent is made from a mixture of rye and wheat.

Brown bread (*hnědý chléb*) is rich, soft and malty and can be eaten on its own.

White bread is mostly available in the form of rolls (*rohlíky*) which are like straight, salty croissants, or tiny plaited rolls with coarse salt and caraway seeds (*housky* — hohski). This type of bread is very similar to its French equivalent in that it is good only when fresh.

Here's a basic list of other food and drink items that might come in useful when shopping for a picnic.

I'd like a/an/ some ...	**Chtěl(a) bych ...**	kht^{y}el(a) bikh
apples	**jablka**	yab^{u}lka
bananas	**banány**	banahni
biscuits (Br.)	**sušenky**	sooshenki
beer	**pivo**	pivo
(loaf of) bread	**(bochník) chleba**	(bokhneek) khleba
butter	**máslo**	mahslo
cake	**dort**	dort
cheese	**sýr**	seer
chips (Am.)	**brambůrky**	bramb$\overline{oo}$rki
chocolate bar	**čokoládu**	chokolahdoo
coffee	**kávu**	kahvoo
cold cuts	**studené maso**	stoodeneh maso
cookies	**cukroví**	tsookrovee
crisps	**brambůrky**	bramb$\overline{oo}$rki
dates	**datle**	datle
eggs	**vajíčka**	va-yeechka
gherkins (pickles)	**nakládané okurky**	naklahdaneh okoorki
grapes	**hrozny**	hrozni
ham	**šunka**	shoonka
ice cream	**zmrzlinu**	zm^{u}rzlinoo
lemonade	**limonáda**	limonahda
milk	**mléko**	mlehko
mineral water	**minerálka**	minerahlka
mustard	**hořčici**	horzhchitsi
oranges	**pomeranče**	pomeranche
pepper	**pepř**	pep^{u}rzh
rolls	**housky**	hohski
salt	**sůl**	s$\overline{oo}$l
sausage	**klobásu**	klobahsoo
soft drink	**nealkoholický nápoj**	nealko-holitskee nahpoy
sugar	**cukr**	tsook^{u}r
tea	**čaj**	cha-y
wine	**vinó**	veen$\bar{o}$
yoghurt	**jogurt**	yogoort

Travelling around

Plane *Letadlo*

Domestic air services are run by ČSA, operating between Prague, Bratislava, Pieštany Poprad and Košice. For flights in summer it is best to book a week in advance.

Is there a flight to Prague?	**Je možné letět do Prahy?**	ye mozhneh let^{y}et dopra-hi
Is it a direct flight?	**Je to přímý let?**	ye to przheemee let
When's the next flight to Brno?	**Kdy letí příští letadlo do Brna?**	gdi let^{y}ee przheesht^{y}ee letadlo dob^{u}rna
Is there a connection to Poprad?	**Má to spojení do Popradu?**	mah to spoyen^{y}ee dopopradoo
I'd like a ticket to Karlovy Vary.	**Chtěl(a) bych letenku do Karlových Varů.**	kht^{y}el(a) bikh letenkoo dokarloveekh var$\overline{oo}$
single (one-way)	**jedním směrem**	yedn^{y}eem smn^{y}erem
return (round trip)	**zpáteční**	spahtechn^{y}ee
business class	**business třídu**	biznis trzheedoo
aisle seat	**sedadlo u uličky**	sedadlo oo oolichki
window seat	**sedadlo u okna**	sedadlo oo okna
What time do we take off?	**V kolik hodin to letí?**	fkolik hod^{y}in to let^{y}ee
What time should I check in?	**Kdy se musíme odbavit?**	gdi se mooseeme odbavit
Is there a bus to the airport?	**Jede na letiště autobus?**	yede na let^{y}isht^{y}e aooto-boos
What's the flight number?	**Jaké je číslo letu?**	yakeh ye cheeslo letoo
What time do we arrive?	**V kolik je přílet?**	fkolik ye przheelet
I'd like to ... my reservation.	**chtěl(a) bych ... mou rezervaci.**	kht^{y}el(a) bikh ... moh rezervatsi
cancel	**zrušit**	zrooshit
change	**změnit**	zmn^{y}en^{y}it
confirm	**potvrdit**	potv^{u}rd^{y}it

PŘÍLETY ARRIVAL

ODLETY DEPARTURE

Train *Vlak*

The Czech State Railway *České státní dráhy* (ČSD) runs an extensive network with first- and second-class service covering the entire country and allowing access to most places. Trains are generally comfortable and frequent, but are not always punctual or very clean, so go for the fastest possible service. Since trains tend to get crowded, it's advisable to avoid travel on Friday afternoons and Saturday mornings, if possible.

For certain trains you need to buy not only a train ticket, but also book a seat reservation (*místenku*). This can be done at the reservation office (*rezervace*) at the station or the advance sales office (*předprodejní kancelář*). On the timetable, trips requiring reservation are marked with an R in a box where this is essential, in a circle where advisable. International reservations can be made at the ARES or ČEDOK offices.

First class compartments seat six people only, second class seat eight. There are also special compartments for smokers. Tickets can be purchased from railway stations and travel agencies. There is a variety of reduced fares, such as student tickets or tourist passes. Inter-Rail cards are valid in the Czech and Slovak Republics.

Expresní (espresnee) — The express train runs between major towns and is the quickest service

Rychlík (rikhleek) — The through train is a relatively fast service, stopping only at major towns; surcharges often payable on these trips

Spěšný (sp^{y}eshnee) — This train is not as fast a service as the through train, and makes more frequent stops

Osobní vlak (osobnee vlak) — Also known colloquially as *lokálka*, this train stops at every station on its route, and should be avoided on longer trips

Spací vagón (spatsee vagohn) — While sleepers (*lůžko*) tend to be expensive, these cheap couchettes are operated by the state railway on overnight trains and run on all long journeys across the country. These should be booked as far in advance as possible

To the railway station *Na nádraží*

Where's the railway station?	**Kde je nádraží?**	gde ye nahdrazhee
Taxi!	**Taxi!**	taxi
Take me to the ... main railway station	**Zavezte mne na ... hlavní nádraží**	zaveste mne na hlavn[y]ee nahdrazhee
What's the fare?	**Kolik to stojí?**	kolik to stoyee

NÁSTUP	ENTRANCE
VÝSTUP	EXIT
K NÁSTUPIŠTÍM	TO THE PLATFORMS
INFORMACE	INFORMATION

Where's the ...? *Kde je ...?*

Where is/are (the) ...?	**Kde je/jsou ...?**	gde ye/ysoh
bar	**výčep**	veechep
booking office	**pokladna**	pokladna
currency exchange office	**směnárna**	smn[y]enahrna
left-luggage office (baggage check)	**úschovna zavazadel**	$\overline{oo}$s-khovna zavazadel
lost property (lost and found) office	**ztráty a nálezy**	strahti a nahlezi
luggage lockers	**skříňka na zavazadla**	skrzheen[y]ka nazavazadla
newsstand	**novinový stánek**	novinovee stahnek
platform 7	**sedmé nástupiště**	sedmeh nahstoopisht[y]e
reservations office	**pokladna pro rezervaci**	pokladna prorezervatse
restaurant	**restaurace**	restaoo-ratse
snack bar	**občerstvení**	opcherstven[y]ee
ticket office	**pokladna**	pokladna
waiting room	**čekárna**	chekahrna
Where are the toilets?	**Kde jsou toalety?**	gde ysoh toaleti

TAXI, see page 21

Inquiries *Dotazy*

When is the ... train to Pilsen?	**Kdy jede ... vlak do Plzňe?**	gdi yede ... vlak dop^{u}lzn^{y}e
first/last/next	**první/poslední/ příští**	prvn^{y}ee/posledn^{y}ee/ przheesht^{y}ee
What time does the train to Karlovy Vary leave?	**V kolik odjíždí vlak do Karlových Varů?**	fkolik odyeezhd^{y}ee vlak dokarloveekh var$\overline{oo}$
What's the fare to Olomouc?	**Kolik stojí lístek do Olomouce?**	kolik stoyee leestek do olomohtse
Is it a through train?	**Je to rychlík?**	ye to rikhleek
Is there a connection to ...?	**Má to spojení do ...?**	mah to spoyen^{y}ee do
Do I have to change trains?	**Musím přestupovat?**	mooseem przhestoopovat
Is there enough time to change?	**Mám čas na přestup?**	mahm chas naprzhestoop
Is the train running on time?	**Jede ten vlak na čas?**	yede ten vlak nachas
What time does the train arrive in Vienna?	**V kolik přijedeme do Vídně?**	fkolik przhiyedeme doveedn^{y}e
Is there a dining car/ sleeping car on the train?	**Je v tom vlaku jídelní vůz/spací vůz?**	ye ftom vlakoo yeedeln^{y}ee v$\overline{oo}$s/spatsee v$\overline{oo}$s
Does the train stop in Konopiště?	**Staví ten vlak v Konopišti?**	stavee ten vlak fkonopisht^{y}i
Which platform does the train to Košice leave from?	**Ze kterého nástupiště jede vlak do Košic?**	ze-ktereh-ho nahstoopisht^{y}e yede vlak dokoshits
Which platform does the train from Prague arrive at?	**Na které nástupiště přijede vlak z Prahy?**	naktereh nahstoopisht^{y}e przhiyede vlak spra-hi
I'd like a timetable.	**Máte jízdní řád?**	mahte yeezdn^{y}ee rzhaht

PŘÍJEZD
ARRIVAL

ODJEZD
DEPARTURE

Musíte přestoupit ve ...	You have to change at ...
Přestoupíte ve ... na lokálku.	Change at ... and get a local train.
Sedmé nástupiště je ...	Platform 7 is ...
tamhle/nahoře **nalevo/napravo**	over there/upstairs on the left/on the right
Vlak do ...	There's a train to ...
Váš vlak jede z osmého nástupiště.	Your train will leave from platform 8.
Vlak má ... minut zpoždění.	It's running ... minutes late.
První třída je vepředu/uprostřed/vzadu.	First class at the front/in the middle/at the rear.

Tickets *Jízdenky*

I'd like a ticket to Česke Budějovice.	**Chtěl(a) bych jízdenku do Českých Budějovic.**	kht^{y}el(a) bikh yeezdenkoo docheskeekh bood^{y}eyovits
single (one-way)	**jedním směrem**	yedn^{y}eem smn^{y}erem
return (round trip)	**zpáteční**	spahtechn^{y}ee
first/second class	**první/druhou třídu**	p^{u}rvn^{y}ee/droohoh trzheedoo
half price	**za poloviční cenu**	zapolovichn^{y}ee tsenoo

Reservation *Rezervace*

Do I need a reservation?	**Potřebuji místenku?**	potrzhebuyi mistenkoo
I'd like to reserve a ...	**Chci si rezervovat ...**	kh-tsi si rezervovat
seat (by the window)	**jedno místo (u okna)**	yedno meesto (oo okna)
berth	**lůžko**	l͞ooshko
upper	**horní**	horn^{y}ee
middle	**střední**	strzhedn^{y}ee
lower	**spodní**	spodn^{y}ee
berth in the sleeping car	**lůžko ve spacím voze**	l͞ooshko vespatseem voze

All aboard *Nastupovat*

Is this the right platform for the train to Hradec Králove?	**Jede vlak do Hradce Králové z tohoto nástupiště?**	yede vlak do-hrattse krahloveh sto-hoto nahstoopisht^{y}e
Is this the right train to Břeclav?	**Je tohle vlak do Břeclavi?**	ye to-hle vlak dobrzhetslavi
Excuse me. Could I get past?	**Promiňte, prosím. Mohl(a) bych projít?**	promin^{y}te proseem. mo-h^{u}l(a) bikh proyeet
Is this seat taken?	**Je tohle sedadlo obsazené?**	ye to-hle sedadlo opsazeneh

KUŘÁCI
SMOKER

NEKUŘÁCI
NONSMOKER

I think that's my seat.	**Tohle je asi moje místo.**	to-hle ye asi moye meesto
Would you let me know before we get to Cheb?	**Mohl[a] byste mi říct než přijedeme do Chebu?**	mo-h^{u}l[a] bis-te mi rzheets-t nesh przhiyedeme dokheboo
What station is this?	**Co je to za stanici?**	tso ye to zastan^{y}itsi
How long does the train stop here?	**Jak dlouhá je tato zastávka?**	yak dloh-hah ye tato zastahfka
When do we arrive in Ostrava?	**Kdy přijedeme do Ostravy?**	gdi przhiyedeme do ostravi

Sleeping *Lůžkový vůz*

Are there any free compartments in the sleeping car?	**Máte volná lůžka ve spacím voze?**	mahte volnah l$\overline{oo}$shka ve spatseem voze
Where's the sleeping car?	**Kde je lůžkový vůz?**	gde ye l$\overline{oo}$shkovee v$\overline{oo}$s
Where's my berth?	**Kde je moje lůžko?**	gde ye moye l$\overline{oo}$shko

I'd like a lower berth.	**Chtěl(a) bych spodní lůžko**	kht^{y}el(a) bikh spodn^{y}ee $\overline{loo}$shko
Would you make up our berths?	**Mohl[a] byste nám ustlat?**	mo-h^{u}l [mo-hla] bis-te nahm oostlat
Would you wake me at 7 o'clock?	**Vzbuďte nás, prosím, v sedm hodin.**	vzboot^{y}te nahs proseem fsed^{u}m hod^{y}in

Eating *Jídelní vůz*

There is usually a dining car or buffet on the faster express trains.

Where's the dining car?	**Kde je jídelní vůz?**	gde ye yeedeln^{y}ee v$\overline{oo}$s

Baggage—Porters *Zavazadla—Nosiči*

Porter!	**Nosič!**	nosich
Can you help me with my luggage?	**Můžete nám vzít zavazadla?**	m$\overline{oo}$zhete nahm vzeet zavazadla
Where are the luggage trolleys (carts)?	**Kde jsou vozíky na zavazadla?**	gde ysoh vozeeki nazavazadla
Where are the luggage lockers?	**Kde jsou skříňky na zavazadla?**	gde ysoh skrzheen^{y}ki nazavazadla
Where's the left-luggage office (baggage check)?	**Kde je úschovna zavazadel?**	gde ye $\overline{oo}$skhovna zavazadel
I'd like to leave my luggage, please.	**Já si tady chci nechat zavazadla.**	yah si tadi kh-tsi nekhat zavazadla
I'd like to register (check) my luggage.	**Chci si nechat odbavit zavazadla.**	kh-tsi si nekhat odbavit zavazadla

ODBAVENÍ ZAVAZADEL

REGISTERING (CHECKING) BAGGAGE

PORTERS, see also page 18

Underground (subway) *Metro*

Prague is the only city large enough to have an underground. It is the fastest and most convenient way of getting around the city. Each station is made of a different type of stone and all the stations are kept scrupulously clean. The system runs from 5 a.m. to 12.30 p.m. with great frequency.

Metro stations are clearly marked by an "M" symbol as part of a downward-pointing arrow. Buy a ticket from one of the machines in the entrance hall, entitling you to unlimited travel within an hour and a half. Passes are also available, valid for 24 hours on all forms of public transport.

Maps of the Metro system are posted in the stations and inside trains, while recorded announcements en route identify the stops.

Where's the nearest underground station?	**Kde je nejbližší stanice metra?**	gde ye neyblishee stan^{y}itse metra
Does this train go to …?	**Tahle linka jede do …?**	ta-hle linka yede do
Where do I change for …?	**Kde musím přestoupit na …?**	gde mooseem przhestohpit na
Is the next station …?	**Příští stanice je …?**	przheesht^{y}ee stan^{y}itse ye
Which line should I take to …?	**Která linka jede do …?**	kterah linka yede do

Coach (long-distance bus) *Dálkový autobus*

Inter-city bus routes link all cities but are generally more expensive, though faster than the trains. On some routes, it is advisable to book your seat beforehand. You may be charged extra for your baggage.

When's the next coach to …?	**Kdy jede příští autobus do …?**	gdi yede przheesht^{y}ee aooto-boos do
Does this coach stop at …?	**Staví tento autobus ve …?**	stavee tento aooto-boos ve
How long does the journey (trip) take?	**Jak dlouho ta cesta trvá?**	yak dloh-ho ta tsesta t^{u}rvah

Note: Most of the phrases on the previous pages can be used or adapted for travelling on local transport.

Bus—Tram (streetcar) *Autobus—Tramvaj*

There are no conductors on most city transport. You are expected to have bought a ticket in advance. Tickets can be bought from the tobacconist's (*tabák*), newspaper shops or hotel receptions.

Tickets must be validated in a stamping machine upon boarding and should be retained. Otherwise you may be surprised with a hefty fine from an undercover inspector!

The tram (*tramvay* or *eletrika*) operates in some city centres and there are trolley-buses in a few towns.

I'd like a booklet of tickets.	**Chtěl(a) bych blok jízdenek.**	kht^{y}el(a) bikh blok yeezdenek
Which tram (streetcar) goes to the town centre?	**Která tramvaj jede do centra?**	kterah tramva-y yede dotsentra
Where can I get a bus to the opera?	**Odkud jede autobus k opeře?**	otkoot yede aooto-boos k operzhe
Which bus do I take to Wencelas Square?	**Který autobus jede na Václavské náměstí?**	kteree aooto-boos yede navahtslafskeh nahmn^{y}est^{y}ee
Where's the bus stop?	**Kde je stanice autobusů?**	gde ye stan^{y}etse aooto-bos$\overline{oo}$
When is the ... bus to the Lesser Quarter?	**Kdy jede ... autobus na Malou Stranu?**	gdi yede ... aooto-boos namaloh stranoo
first/last/next	**první/poslední/ příští**	p^{u}rvn^{y}ee/posledn^{y}ee/ przheesht^{y}ee
How much is the fare to ...?	**Kolik to stojí do ...?**	kolik to stoyee do
Do I have to change buses?	**Musím přestoupit?**	mooseem przhestohpit
How many bus stops are there to ...?	**Kolik je to stanic do ...?**	kolik ye to stan^{y}its do
Will you tell me when to get off?	**Řekněte mi kdy mám vystoupit?**	rzheknete mi gdy mahm vistohpit
I want to get off at the National Gallery.	**Chci vystoupit u Národní galerie.**	kh-tsi vistohpit oo nahrodn^{y}ee galeriye

ZASTÁVKA AUTOBUSU	BUS STOP
ZASTÁVKA NA POŽÁDÁNÍ	REQUEST STOP

Boat service *Lodní doprava*

In addition to excursions down the Vltava from Prague, the only major boat service runs from Bratislava to Vienna along the Danube (*Dunaj* —doonay).

When does the next boat for … leave?	**Kdy jede příští loď do …?**	gdi yede przheesht^{y}ee lod^{y} do
Where's the embarkation point?	**Kde se nalodíme?**	gde se nalod^{y}eeme
How long does the crossing take?	**Jak dlouho trvá přeplava?**	yak dloh-ho t^{u}rvah przheplava
Which port(s) do we stop at?	**Ve kterých přístavištích zastavíme?**	vektereekh przheestavisht^{y}eekh zastaveeme
boat	**jet lodí**	yet lod^{y}ee
cabin	**kabinu**	kabinoo
single/double	**jednolůžkovou/ dvoulůžkovou**	yednol$\overline{oo}$shkovoh/dvoh-l$\overline{oo}$shkovoh
deck	**paluba**	palooba
ferry	**převoz**	przhevos
hydrofoil	**křídlový člun**	krzheedlovee chloon
life belt/boat	**záchranný pas/ člun**	zah-khranee pahs/ chloon
port	**přístav**	przheestaf
river cruise	**cesta říční lodí**	tsesta rzheechn^{y}ee lod^{y}ee
ship	**loď**	lot^{y}
steamer	**parník**	parn^{y}eek

Other means of transport *Jiné dopravní prostředky*

Hitchhiking is a relatively safe means of getting around, though cheap public transportation may reduce its attraction for some. *Note:* The hitchhiking sign is a downward wave of the arm with your open hand facing the traffic.

cable car	**lanovka**	lanofka
helicopter	**helikoptéra**	helikoptehra
moped	**moped**	mopeht
motorbike/scooter	**motocykl/skúter**	mototsik^{u}l/sk$\overline{oo}$tr
to hitchhike	**stopování**	stopovahn^{y}ee
to walk	**jít pěšky**	yeet pyeshki
bicycle hire	**půjčovna kol**	p$\overline{oo}$ychovna kol
I'd like to hire a bicycle.	**Chci si pronajmout kolo.**	kh-tsi si prona-ymoht kolo

Car *Auto*

The road system is of a reasonable standard, with express highways (E roads) linking the larger towns. To bring your own car into the country, you'll require a valid international driving licence, car registration papers and a green card extending your regular car insurance policy.

The speed limit is 68 m.p.h. (110 k.p.h.) on main highways, 56 m.p.h. (90 k.p.h.) on other roads and 37 m.p.h. (60 k.p.h.) in towns. Speeding fines are levied on the spot by police. Seatbelts are obligatory and alcohol is totally forbidden to drivers.

You may need to obtain petrol coupons (*poukázka na benzin* — poh-kahzka nabenzin) at the border, as petrol may not be sold at pumps for cash.

Where's the nearest filling station?	**Kde je nejbližší benzinová pumpa?**	gde ye neyblishee benzeenovah poompa
Fill it up, please.	**Prosím, plnou nádrž.**	proseem p^{u}lnoh nahd^{u}rsh
Give me ... litres of petrol (gasoline).	**Dejte mi ... litrů benzinu.**	deyte mi ... litroo benzeenoo
super (premium)/ regular/unleaded/ diesel	**super/normálu/ bezolovnatého benzinu/nafty**	sooper/normahloo/ besolovnateh-ho benzeenoo/nafti
Please check the ...	**Zkontrolujte prosím ...**	skontrolooyte proseem
battery	**baterii**	bateriyi
brake fluid	**brzdovou kapalinu**	b^{u}rzdovoh kapalinoo
oil/water	**olej/vodu**	oley/vodoo
Would you check the tyre pressure?	**Mohl[a] byste zkontrolovat tlak pneumatik?**	mo-h^{u}l [mo-hla] bis-te skontrolovat tlak pneoo-matik
1.6 front, 1.8 rear.	**Jedna celá šest vpředu, jedna celá osm vzádu.**	yedna tselah shest veprzhedoo yedna tselah osoom vzadoo
Please check the spare tyre, too.	**Zkontrolujte i náhradní pneumatiku.**	skontrolooyte i nahradn^{y}ee pneoo-matikoo
Can you mend this puncture (fix this flat)?	**Můžete spravit tuhle píchlou duši?**	moozhete spravit too-hle peekhloh dooshi

CAR HIRE, see page 20

Would you change the ..., please?	**Mohl[a] byste vyměnit ...?**	mo-h^{u}l [mo-hla] bis-te vimn^{y}en^{y}it
bulb	**žárovku**	zhahrofkoo
fan belt	**náhonný řemen větráku**	nah-honee rzhemen vyetrahkoo
spark(ing) plugs	**svíčky**	sveechki
tyre	**pneumatiku**	pneoo-matikoo
wipers	**stěrače**	st^{y}era-che
Would you clean the windscreen (windshield)?	**Mohl[a] byste umýt přední sklo?**	mo-h^{u}l [mo-hla] bis-te oomeet przhedn^{y}ee sklo

Asking the way—Street directions *Ptát se na cestu—Směr*

Can you tell me the way to ...?	**Mohl[a] byste mi říct jak se dostanu do ...?**	mo-h^{u}l [mo-hla] bis-te mi rzheets-t yak se dostanoo do
In which direction is ...?	**Kterým směrem je ...?**	ktereem smn^{y}erem ye
How do I get to ...?	**Jak se dostanu do ...?**	yak se dostanoo do
Are we on the right road for ...?	**Jdeme správným směrem na ...?**	ydeme sprahvneem smn^{y}erem na
How far is the next village?	**Jak daleko je to do příští vesnice?**	yak daleko ye to doprzheesht^{y}ee vesn^{y}itse
How far is it to ... from here?	**Jak daleko je to odsud do ...?**	yak daleko ye to otsood do
Is there a motorway (expressway)?	**Je tam dálnice?**	ye tam dahln^{y}itse
How long does it take by car/on foot?	**Jak dlouho to trvá autem/pěšky?**	yak dloh-ho to t^{u}rvah aootem/pyeshki
Can I drive to the centre of town?	**Můžu dojet do centra města?**	m$\overline{oo}$zhoo doyet dotsentra mn^{y}esta
Is traffic allowed in the town centre?	**Je centrum otevřené pro auta?**	ye tsentroom otevrzheneh pro aoota
Can you tell me where ... is?	**Mohl[a] byst mi říct kde je ...?**	mo-h^{u}l [mo-hla] bis-te mi rzheets-t gde ye
How can I find this place/address?	**Jak se dostanu na toto místo/na tuto adresu?**	yak se dostanoo natoto meesto/natooto adresoo
Where's this?	**Kde je tohle?**	gde ye to-hle
Can you show me on the map where I am?	**Mohl[a] byste mi ukázat na mapě kde jsem?**	mo-h^{u}l [mo-hla] bis-te mi ookahzat na mapye gde ysem

Vy jste na špatné silnici.	You're on the wrong road.
Jědte/běžte rovně.	Go straight ahead.
To je tam dole po levé/pravé straně.	It's down there on the left/ right.
naproti/za ... **vedle/po ...** **na sever/na jih** **na východ/na západ**	opposite/behind ... next to/after ... north/south east/west
Jědte/běžte na první/druhou křižovatku.	Go to the first/second crossroads (intersection).
Zahněte vlevo u semaforu.	Turn left at the traffic lights.
Zahněte vpravo na příštím rohu.	Turn right at the next corner.
Jědte/běžte ... ulicí.	Take the ... road.
To je jednosměrná ulice.	It's a one-way street.
Musíte se vrátit do ...	You have to go back to ...
Sledujte směrovky do Plzně.	Follow signs for Pilsen.

Parking *Parkování*

Visitors to Prague are advised to avoid the congestion by parking their cars outside the centre and taking public transport from there. Cars parked in a restricted zone without a parking permit (*parkovací lístek*) may be towed away.

Where can I park?	**Kde můžu zaparkovat?**	gde moozhoo zaparkovat
Is there a car park nearby?	**Je tu blízko parkoviště?**	ye too bleesko parkovisht^{y}e
May I park here?	**Můžu tady parkovat?**	moozhoo tadi parkovat
How long can I park here?	**Jak dlouho tu můžu parkovat?**	yak dloh-ho too moozhoo parkovat
What's the charge per hour?	**Kolik se platí za hodinu?**	kolik se plat^{y}ee zahod^{y}inoo
Do you have some change for the parking meter?	**Máte drobné na parkovací hodiny?**	mahte drobneh naparkovatsee hod^{y}ini

Breakdown—Road assistance *Porucha—Pomoc na silnici*

The "yellow angels", mobile mechanics of the Autoturist Road Service, come to the aid of motorists in distress. There are several garages for repairs around the country. Look for emergency telephones on the highway, or dial 158 for the police. An increasing number of private garages offer a more flexible service to the state-run ones; they tend to stay open later and offer a quicker service.

Where's the nearest garage?	**Kde je nejbližší garáž?**	gde ye neyblishee garahsh
My car has broken down.	**Mně se pokazilo auto.**	mn^{y}e se pokazilo aooto
May I use your phone?	**Mohl[a] bych si zatelefonovat?**	mo-h^{u}l [mo-hla] bikh si zatelefonovat
I've had a breakdown at ...	**Mně se porouchalo auto ve ...**	mn^{y}e se poroh-khalo aooto ve
Can you send a mechanic?	**Můžete mi poslat mechanika?**	m$\overline{oo}$zhete mi poslat mekhanika
My car won't start.	**Moje auto nechce startovat.**	moye aooto nekh-tse startovat
The battery is dead.	**Baterie je vybitá.**	bateriye ye vibitah
I've run out of petrol (gasoline).	**Došel(a) mi benzin.**	doshel(a) mi benzeen
I have a flat tyre.	**Píchl(a) jsem.**	peekh^{u}l (peekhla) ysem
The engine is overheating.	**Motor se přehřívá.**	motor se przhehrzheevah
There's something wrong with the ...	**Nefunguje dobře ...**	nefoongooye dobrzhe
brakes	**brzdy**	b^{u}rzdi
carburettor	**karburátor**	karboorahtor
exhaust pipe	**výfuk**	veefook
radiator	**chladič**	khlad^{y}ich
wheel	**kolo**	kolo
Can you send a breakdown van (tow truck)?	**Mohli byste poslat havarijní službu?**	mo-huli bis-te poslat prohavariyn^{y}ee sloozhboo
How long will you be?	**Jak vám to bude dlouho trvat?**	yak vahm to boode dloh-ho t^{u}rvat
Can you give me an estimate?	**Jaká je odhadní cena?**	yakah ye odhadn^{y}ee tsena

Accident—Police *Nehoda—Policie*

Please call the police.	**Zavolejte, prosím, policii.**	zavoleyte proseem politsiyi
There's been an accident. It's about 2 km. from ...	**Tady se stala nehoda. Je to asi dva kilometry od ...**	tadi se stala ne-hoda. ye to asi dva kilometri ot
Where's there a telephone?	**Kde najdu telefon?**	gde na-ydoo telefon
Call a doctor/an ambulance quickly.	**Zavolejte rychle lékaře/ambulanci.**	zavoleyte rikhle lehkarzhe/ amboolantsi
There are people injured.	**Jsou tady zranění lidé.**	ysoh tadi zran[y]en[y]ee lideh
What's your name and address?	**Jak se jmenujete a kde bydlíte?**	yak se ymenooyete a gde bidleete
What's your insurance company?	**Kterou pojišťovnu používáte?**	kteroh poyisht[y]ovnoo po-oozheevahte

Road signs *Dopravní značky*

DEJ PŘEDNOST	Give way
KONEC DÁLNICE	End of expressway
JEDNOSMĚRNÝ PROVOZ	One way
NA SILNICI SE PRACUJE	Roadworks (Men working)
NEBEZPEČÍ	Danger
NEBEZPEČI SMYKU	Danger of skidding
NEVSTUPUJTE	No entry
OBJÍŽDKA	Diversion (Detour)
OPATRNĚ	Caution
PĚŠÍ ZÓNA	Pedestrian zone
PODCHOD	Subway
POZOR	Attention
STŮJ	Stop
SNÍŽIT RYCHLOST (ZPOMALIT)	Slow down
ŠKOLA	School
VCHOD	Entrance
VJEZD ZAKÁZÁN	No admittance
VÝCHOD	Exit
ZÁKAZ PŘEDJÍŽDĚNÍ	No overtaking (passing)
ZÁKAZ VJEZDU	No entry
ZÁKAZ PARKOVÁNÍ	No parking
ZÁKAZ ZASTAVENÍ	No stopping

Sightseeing

Where's the tourist office?	**Kde jsou turistické informace?**	gde ysoh tooristitskeh informatse
What are the main points of interest?	**Která jsou nejzajímavější místa?**	kterah ysoh neyza-yeemavyeyshee meesta
We're here for ...	**My jsme tady ...**	mi ysme tadi
only a few hours	**jen několik hodin**	yen n^{y}ekolik hod^{y}in
a day	**jeden den**	yeden den
a week	**jeden týden**	yeden teeden
Can you recommend a sightseeing tour?	**Můžete nám doporučit vyhlídkovou cestu?**	moozhete nahm doporoochit vihleetkovoh tsestoo
Where do we leave from?	**Odkud to odjíždí?**	otkoot to odyeezhd^{y}ee
Will the bus pick us up at the hotel?	**Zastaví se pro nás ten autobus v hotelu?**	zastavee se pronahs ten aooto-boos v-hoteloo
How much does the tour cost?	**Kolik ta exkurse stojí?**	kolik ta exkoor-ze stoyee
What time does the tour start?	**V kolik hodin začíná ta exkurse?**	fkolik hod^{y}in zacheenah ta exkoor-ze
Is lunch included?	**Je v tom započítaný oběd?**	ye ftom zapocheetanee obyet
What time do we get back?	**V kolik hodin budeme zpátky?**	fkolik hod^{y}in boodeme spahtki
Do we have free time in ...?	**Máme volný čas v ...?**	mahme volnee chas f
Is there an English-speaking guide?	**Je tam anglicky mluvící průvodce?**	ye tam anglitski mlooveetsee proovot-tse
I'd like to hire a private guide for ...	**Mohu si najmout soukromého průvodce na ...**	mo-hoo si na-ymoht sohkromeh-ho proovot-tse na
half a day	**půl dne**	pool dne
a day	**den**	den

Where is/Where are the . . .?	**Kde je/Kde jsou . . .?**	gde ye/gde ysoh
abbey	**opatství**	opat-stvee
art gallery	**galerie**	galehri-ye
artists' quarter	**čtvrť umělců**	ch^{u}tv^{u}rt^{y} oomn^{y}eltsoo
botanical gardens	**botanická zahrada**	botanitskah za-hrada
building	**budova**	boodova
business district	**obchodní čtvrť**	opkhodn^{y}ee ch^{u}tv^{u}rt^{y}
castle	**zámek**	zahmek
catacombs	**katakomby**	katakombi
cathedral	**katedrála**	katedrahla
cave	**jeskyně**	yeskin^{y}e
cemetery	**hřbitov**	h^{u}rzhbitof
city centre	**městské centrum**	mn^{y}estskeh tsentroom
chapel	**kaple**	kaple
church	**kostel**	kostel
concert hall	**koncertní hala**	kontsertn^{y}ee hala
convent	**klášter**	klahshter
court house	**soud**	sout
downtown area	**centrum města**	tsentroom mn^{y}esta
embankment	**nábřeží**	nahbrzhezhee
exhibition	**výstava**	veestava
factory	**továrna**	tovahrna
fair	**pouť**	poht^{y}
flea market	**trh**	t^{u}rkh
fortress	**pevnost**	pevnost
fountain	**fontána**	fontahna
gardens	**zahrady**	za-hradi
harbour	**přístav**	przheestaf
lake	**jezero**	yezero
library	**knihovna**	kn^{y}ihovna
market	**trh**	t^{u}rkh
memorial	**pomník**	pomn^{y}eek
monastery	**klášter**	klahshter
monument	**památník**	pamahtneek
museum	**muzeum**	moozeoom
old town	**staré město**	stareh mn^{y}esto
opera house	**operní divadlo**	opern^{y}ee d^{y}ivadlo
palace	**palác**	palahts
park	**park**	park
parliament building	**budova parlamentu**	boodova parlamentoo
planetarium	**planetárium**	planetahriyoom
river	**řeka**	rzheka
royal palace	**královský palác**	krahlofskee palahts
ruins	**zřícenina**	zrzheetsen^{y}ina
shopping area	**obchodní čtvrť**	opkhodn^{y}ee ch^{u}tv^{u}rt^{y}
square	**náměstí**	nahmn^{y}est^{y}ee

stadium	**stadión**	stadiyon
statue	**socha**	sokha
stock exchange	**bursa**	boorza
theatre	**divadlo**	d^{y}ivadlo
tomb	**hrobka**	hropka
tower	**věž**	vyesh
town hall	**radnice**	radn^{y}itse
university	**universita**	ooniverzita
zoo	**zoologická zahrada**	zo-ologitskah za-hrada

Admission *Vstupné*

Is ... open on Sundays?	**Je ... otevřeno v neděli?**	ye ... otevrzheno vned^{y}eli
What are the opening hours?	**Jaká je otevírací doba?**	yakah ye oteveeratsee doba
When does it close?	**V kolik se zavírá?**	fkolik se zaveerah
How much is the entrance fee?	**Kolik stojí vstup?**	kolik stoyee fstoop
Is there any reduction for (the) ...?	**Je tu sleva pro ...?**	ye too sleva pro
children	**děti**	d^{y}et^{y}i
disabled	**tělesně postižené**	t^{y}elesn^{y}e post^{y}izheneh
groups	**skupiny**	skoopini
pensioners	**důchodce**	dookhot-tse
students	**studenty**	stoodenti
Do you have a guidebook (in English)?	**Máte průvodce v angličtině?**	mahte proovot-tse f anglicht^{y}in^{y}e
Can I buy a catalogue?	**Mohu si koupit katalog?**	mo-hoo si kohpit katalog
Is it all right to take pictures?	**Může se tu fotografovat?**	moozhe se too fotografovat

VSTUP ZDARMA	ADMISSION FREE
ZÁKAZ FOTOGRAFOVÁNÍ	NO CAMERAS ALLOWED

Who—What—When? *Kdo—Co—Kdy?*

What's that building?	**Co je to za budovu?**	tso ye to zaboodovoo
Who was the ...?	**Kdo byl ten ...?**	gdo bil ten
architect	**architekt**	arkhitekt
artist	**umělec**	oomn^{y}elets
painter	**malíř**	maleerzh
sculptor	**sochař**	sokharzh
Who built it?	**Kdo to postavil?**	gdo to postavil
Who painted that picture?	**Kdo namaloval tento obraz?**	gdo namaloval tento obras
When did (s)he live?	**Kdy žil(a)?**	gdi zhil(a)
When was it built?	**Kdy to bylo postavené?**	gdi to bilo postaveneh
Where's the house where ... lived?	**Kde je ten dům kde bydlel(a) ...?**	gde ye ten d$\overline{oo}$m gde bidlel(a)
We're interested in ...	**My máme zájem o ...**	mi mahme zahyem o
antiques	**starožitnosti**	starozhitnost^{y}i
archaeology	**archeologii**	arkheologiyi
art	**umění**	oomn^{y}en^{y}ee
botany	**botaniku**	botanikoo
ceramics	**keramiku**	keramikoo
coins	**mince**	mintse
fine arts	**krásné umění**	krahsneh oomn^{y}en^{y}ee
furniture	**nábytek**	nahbitek
geology	**geologii**	geologiyi
handicrafts	**řemesla**	rzhemesla
history	**historii**	historiyi
medicine	**medicínu**	meditseenoo
music	**hudbu**	hoodboo
natural history	**přírodovědu**	przheerodovyedoo
ornithology	**ornitologii**	ornitologiyi
painting	**malířství**	maleerzhstvee
pottery	**hrnčířství**	h^{u}rncheerzhstvee
religion	**náboženství**	nahbozhenstvee
sculpture	**sochařství**	sokharzhstvee
zoology	**zoologii**	zo-ologiyi
Where's the ... department?	**Kde je ... oddělení?**	gde ye ... odd^{y}elen^{y}ee

It's . . .	**To je . . .**	to ye
amazing	**neuvěřitelné**	ne-oovyerzhitelneh
awful	**hrozné**	hrozneh
beautiful	**krásné**	krahsneh
boring	**nudné**	noodneh
gloomy	**chmurné**	khmoorneh
impressive	**impozantní**	impozantn^{y}ee
interesting	**zajímavé**	za-yeemaveh
magnificent	**překrásné**	przhekrahsneh
pretty	**hezké**	heskeh
strange	**zvláštní**	zv^{u}lah-sh-tn^{y}ee
superb	**ohromné**	o-hromneh
terrifying	**úděsné**	$\overline{oo}$d^{y}esneh
tremendous	**obrovské**	obrofskeh
ugly	**ošklivé**	oshkliveh

Churches—Religious services *Kostely—Bohoslužby*

The Czech and Slovak republics are primarily Catholic, but synagogues and Protestant churches are also found in larger towns. Most churches are open to the public all day, but part of a church may be closed during a religious service.

Is there a . . . near here?	**Je tady blízko . . .?**	ye tadi bleesko
Catholic church	**katolický kostel**	katolitskee kostel
Protestant church	**českobratrský kostel**	cheskobrat^{u}rskee kostel
mosque	**mešita**	meshita
synagogue	**synagoga**	sinagoga
What time is . . .?	**V kolik hodin je . . .?**	fkolik hod^{y}in ye
mass/the service	**bohoslužba**	bo-hosloozhba
Where can I find a . . . who speaks English?	**Kde najdu . . . který mluví anglicky?**	gde na-ydoo . . . kteree mloovee anglitski
priest/minister/ rabbi	**kněze/ českobratrského kněze/rabína**	kn^{y}eze/cheskobrat^{u}rskeh-ho kn^{y}eze/rabeena
I'd like to visit the church.	**Rád(a) bych se podíval do kostela.**	rahd(a) bikh se pod^{y}eeval do kostela

In the countryside *Na venkově*

Is there a scenic route to ...?	**Je tady vyhlidková trasa do ...?**	ye tadi vi-hleetkovah trasa do
How far is it to ...?	**Jak je to daleko do ...?**	yak ye to daleko do
Can we walk there?	**Můžeme tam jít pěšky?**	moozheme tam yeet pyeshki
How high is that mountain?	**Jak je vysoká ta hora?**	yak ye visokah ta hora
What kind of ... is that?	**Co je to za ...?**	tso ye to za
animal	**zvíře**	zveerzhe
bird	**ptáka**	ptahka
flower	**květinu**	kvyet^{y}inoo
tree	**strom**	strom

Landmarks *Orientační body*

bridge	**most**	most
cliff	**útes**	ootes
farm	**statek**	statek
field	**pole**	po-le
footpath	**pěšina**	pyeshina
forest	**les**	les
garden	**zahrada**	za-hrada
hill	**kopec**	kopets
house	**dům**	doom
lake	**jezero**	yezero
meadow	**louka**	lohka
mountain	**hora**	hora
(mountain) pass	**průsmyk**	proosmik
peak	**vrchol**	v^{u}rkhol
pond	**rybník**	ribn^{y}eek
river	**řeka**	rzheka
road	**cesta**	tsesta
sea	**moře**	morzhe
spring	**pramen**	pramen
valley	**údolí**	oodolee
village	**vesnice**	vesn^{y}itse
vineyard	**vinice**	vin^{y}itse
wall	**zeď**	zet^{y}
waterfall	**vodopád**	vodopaht
wood	**les**	les

ASKING THE WAY, see page 76

Relaxing

Cinema (movies)—Theatre *Kino—Divadlo*

Many foreign language films are dubbed into Czech (marked in listings by a square symbol against the title), but others appear in the original with subtitles. Seats are generally reserved, so it is best to book early.

Visitors to Prague should try to visit the Laterna Magika, or one of the other pantomime theatres offering an exciting mixture of music, mime, ballet and film; a puppet show (*loutkové divadlo*); or look out for a street theatre (*pouliční divadlo*).

What's on at the cinema tonight?	**Co dávají dnes v kině?**	tso dahva-yee dnes fkin^{y}e
What's playing at the ... theatre?	**Co dávají dnes v ... divadle?**	tso dahva-yee dnes f ... d^{y}ivadle
What sort of play is it?	**Jaká je to hra?**	yakah ye to hra
Who's it by?	**Kdo to napsal?**	gdo to napsal
Can you recommend a ...?	**Můžete nám doporučit ...?**	m$\overline{oo}$zhete nahm doporoochit
good film	**dobrý film**	dobree film
comedy	**komedii**	komediyi
musical	**muzikál**	moozikahl
folk dance show	**lidové tance**	lidoveh tantse
Where's that new film directed by ... being shown?	**Kde dávají ten nový film režírovaný ...?**	gde dahva-yee ten novee film rezheerovanee
Who's in it?	**Kdo v tom hraje?**	gdo ftom hra-ye
Who's playing the lead?	**Kdo hraje hlavní roli?**	gdo hra-ye hlavn^{y}ee roli
Who's the director?	**Kdo to režíruje?**	gdo to rezheerooye
At which theatre is that new play by ... being performed?	**Kde se hraje ta nová hra kterou napsal(a) ...?**	gde se hra-ye ta novah hra kteroh napsal(a)
Where's a pantomime on today?	**Kde dávají dnes pantomimu?**	gde dahva-yee dnes pantomimoo

What time does it begin?	**V kolik to začíná?**	fkolik to zacheenah
Are there any seats for tonight?	**Máte nějaké lístky na dnes večer?**	mahte n^{y}eyakeh leestki nadnes vecher
How much are the seats?	**Kolik stojí ty lístky?**	kolik stoyee ti leestki
I'd like to reserve 2 seats for the show on Friday evening.	**Chci zamluvit dvě místa na páteční představení.**	kh-tsi zamloovit dvye meesta napahtechn^{y}ee przhet-staven^{y}ee
Can I have a ticket for the matinée on Tuesday?	**Máte lístek na odpolední představení v úterý?**	mahte leestek na-otpoledn^{y}ee przhet-staven^{y}ee f $\overline{oo}$teree
I'd like a seat in the stalls (orchestra).	**Chtěl(a) bych lístek v přízemí.**	kht^{y}el(a) bikh leestek fprzheezemee
Not too far back.	**Ne moc daleko vzadu.**	ne mots daleko vzadoo
Somewhere in the middle.	**Někde uprostřed.**	n^{y}egde ooprostrzhet
How much are the seats in the circle (mezzanine)?	**Kolik stojí lístky na prvním balkóně?**	kolik stoyee leestki nap^{u}rvn^{y}eem balkōn^{y}e
May I have a programme, please?	**Program, prosím.**	program proseem
Where's the cloakroom?	**Kde je šatna?**	gde ye shatna

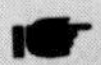

Bohužel, máme vyprodáno.	I'm sorry, we're sold out.
Je tu jen pár lístků na první balkón.	There are only a few seats left in the circle (mezzanine).
Ukažte mi lístek.	May I see your ticket?
Tohle je vaše sedadlo.	This is your seat.

DAYS OF THE WEEK, see page 151

Opera—Ballet—Concert *Opera—Balet—Koncert*

Prague offers an excellent choice of glamorous musical events, particularly during the Spring International Music Festival. Whether it's the Czech Philharmonic Orchestra or a small ensemble playing on the Charles Bridge (*Karlův most*), you'll find something here to suit your tastes.

Can you recommend a(n) ...?	**Můžete nám doporučit ...?**	m$\overline{\text{oo}}$zhete nahm doporoochit
ballet	**balet**	balet
concert	**koncert**	kontsert
opera	**operu**	operoo
operetta	**operetu**	operetoo
Where's the opera house/the concert hall?	**Kde je to operní divadlo/koncertní hala?**	gde ye to opern^{y}ee d^{y}ivadlo/kontsertn^{y}ee hala
What's on at the opera tonight?	**Co dávají dnes večer v opeře?**	tso dahva-yee dnes vecher f operzhe
Who's singing/dancing?	**Kdo zpívá/tančí?**	gdo speevah/tanchee
Which orchestra is playing?	**Který orchestr hraje?**	kteree orkhestr hra-ye
What are they playing?	**Co je na programu?**	tso ye naprogramoo
Who's the conductor/soloist?	**Kdo je dirigentem/solistou?**	gdo ye dirigentem/sōlistoh

Nightclubs—Discos *Noční kluby—Diskotéky*

Can you recommend a good nightclub?	**Můžete nám doporučit dobrý noční klub?**	m$\overline{\text{oo}}$zhete nahm doporoochit dobree nochn^{y}ee kloop
Is there a floor show?	**Je tam varieté?**	ye tam variyeteh
What time does the show start?	**V kolik hodin začíná představení?**	fkolik hod^{y}in zacheenah przhet-staven^{y}ee
Is evening dress required?	**Musíme jít ve večerních šatech?**	mooseeme yeet ve vechen^{y}eekh shatekh
Where can we go dancing?	**Kde si můžeme zatančit?**	gde si m$\overline{\text{oo}}$zheme zatanchit
Is there a discotheque in town?	**Je někde ve městě diskotéka?**	ye n^{y}egde vemn^{y}est^{y}e diskotehka
Would you like to dance?	**Chtěl[a] byste si zatančit?**	kht^{y}el[a] bis-te si zatanchit

Sports *Sporty*

The Czechs and Slovaks are sport-loving people, and you'll probably find sport a good topic of conversation. Popular summer sports include tennis, football, volleyball and swimming. Most parks and open-air swimming pools have a volleyball court, and tennis courts are plentiful. These are often flooded in winter and used for skating.

Hunting (*lov*), is a popular tradition, with a planned breeding and protection of game, organized by Čedok and Tatratour in Slovakia. All-inclusive package tours are available. For anglers, there are many lakes and rivers. Permits can be obtained through travel agencies.

Hiking (*jít na tramp*) is a popular activity, particularly in the High Tatras (*Vysoké Tatry*), and other mountain areas in Slovakia. There are over 40,000 km. of marked paths, tracks and routes. Good hiking maps (*turistické mapy*) are available in some areas.

Is there a football (soccer) match anywhere this Saturday?	**Hraje se někde v sobotu fotbal?**	hra-ye se n^{y}egde vsobotoo fotbal
Which teams are playing?	**Kdo hraje?**	gdo hra-ye
Can you get me a ticket?	**Můžete mi sehnat lístek?**	m$\overline{oo}$zhete mi se-hnat leestek

basketball	**košíková**	kosheekovah
boxing	**rohování**	rohovahn^{y}ee
car racing	**automobilové závody**	aootomobiloveh zahvodi
cycling	**cyklistika**	tsiklistika
football (soccer)	**fotbal**	fotbal
horse racing	**dostihy**	dost^{y}ihi
(horse-back) riding	**jezdectví**	yezdets-tvee
mountaineering	**horolezectví**	horolezets-tvee
skiing	**lyžování**	lizhovahn^{y}ee
swimming	**plavání**	plavahn^{y}ee
tennis	**tenis**	tenis
volleyball	**volejbal**	voleybal

I'd like to see a boxing match.	**Chci jít na zápas v boxu.**	kh-tsi yeet nazahpas vboksoo
What's the admission charge?	**Kolik je vstupné?**	kolik ye fstoopneh
Where's the nearest golf course?	**Kde je nejbližší golfové hřiště?**	gde ye neyblishshee golfoveh hrzhisht^{y}e
Where are the tennis courts?	**Kde jsou tenisové kurty?**	gde ysoh tenisoveh koorti
What's the charge per ...?	**Kolik to stojí za ...?**	kolik to stoyee za
day/round/hour	**den/kolo/hodinu**	den/kolo/hod^{y}inoo
Can I hire (rent) rackets?	**Můžu si pronajmout rakety?**	mo͞ozhoo si prona-ymoht raketi
Where's the race course (track)?	**Kde je dostihová dráha?**	gde ye dost^{y}ihovah drah-ha
Is there any good fishing/hunting around here?	**Dá se tady někde dobře lovit ryby/střílet?**	dah se tadi n^{y}egde dobrzhe lovit ribi/strzheelet
Do I need a permit?	**Potřebuji povolení?**	potrzhebooye povolen^{y}ee
Where can I get one?	**Kde ho dostanu?**	gde ho dostanoo
Can one swim in the lake/river?	**Smí se plavat v tom jezeře/v té řece?**	smee se plavat ftom yezerzhe/f teh rzhetse
Is there a swimming pool here?	**Je tady někde koupaliště?**	ye tadi n^{y}egde kohpalisht^{y}e
Is it open-air or indoor?	**Je to koupaliště nebo krytý bazén?**	ye to kohpalisht^{y}e nebo kritee bazehn
Is it heated?	**Je to vytápěné?**	ye to vitahpyeneh
Is there a sandy beach?	**Je tam písčitá pláž?**	ye tam peeschitah plahsh

On the beach *Na pláži*

Is it safe to swim here?	**Může se tu plavat?**	mo͞ozhe se too plavat
Is there a lifeguard?	**Je tam plavčík?**	ye tam plafcheek
Is it safe for children?	**Je to bezpečné pro děti?**	ye to bespechneh prod^{y}et^{y}i
The lake is very calm.	**To jezero je velmi klidné.**	to yezero ye velmi klidneh
Are there any dangerous currents?	**Je tady nebezpečný proud?**	ye tadi nebespechnee proht

I want to hire (rent) a/an/ some ...	**Chci si pronajmout ...**	kh-tsi si prona-ymoht
bathing hut (cabana)	**plaveckou kabinu**	plavetskoh kabinoo
deck chair	**lehátko**	le-hahtko
motorboat	**motorový člun**	motorovee chloon
rowing boat	**lod'ku**	lot^{y}koo
sailing boat	**plachetnici**	plakhetn^{y}itsi
skin-diving equipment	**potápěčské vybavení**	potahpyechskeh vibaven^{y}ee
sunshade (umbrella)	**slunečník**	sloonechn^{y}eek
water-skis	**vodní lyže**	vodn^{y}ee lizhe
windsurfer	**windsurfer**	vintserf^{u}r

SOUKROMÁ PLÁŽ	PRIVATE BEACH
ZÁKAZ KOUPÁNÍ	NO SWIMMING

Winter sports *Zimní sporty*

Cross-country skiing is more common than downhill. In the winter ice-hockey and skating are also popular.

Is there a skating rink near here?	**Je tady blízko kluziště?**	ye tadi bleesko kloozisht^{y}e
I'd like to ski.	**Chtěl(a) bych si zalyžovat.**	kht^{y}el(a) bikh si zalizhovat
downhill/cross-country skiing	**sjezd/běh na lyžích**	syest/bye-h nalizheekh
Are there any ski runs for ...?	**Jsou tady sjezdovky pro ...?**	ysoh tadi syezdofki pro
beginners	**začátečníky**	zachahtechn^{y}eeki
average skiers	**průměrné lyžaře**	pro͞om^{y}erneh lizharzhe
good skiers	**dobré lyžaře**	dobreh lizharzhe
Can I take skiing lessons?	**Můžu si vzít hodiny lyžování**	mo͞ozhoo si vzeet hod^{y}ini lizhovahn^{y}ee
Are there any ski lifts?	**Jsou tady lyžařské vleky?**	ysoh tadi lizharzhskeh vleki
I want to hire ...	**Chci si pronajmout ...**	kh-tsi si prona-ymoht
poles	**lyžhařské hole**	lizharzhskeh hol-e
skates	**brusle**	broosle
ski boots	**lyžařské boty**	lizharzhskeh boti
skiing equipment	**lyžařské vybavení**	lizharzhskeh vibaven^{y}ee
skis	**lyže**	lizhe

Making friends

Introductions *Představování*

Czech society is quite formal. People address each other as Mr. (*pan*), Mrs. (*paní*) or Miss (*slečna*—slechna), and use the polite form of you (*vy*) for quite a long time after their first meeting. The familiar form (*ty*) and first names are used when both parties feel comfortable with the change.

May I introduce . . ?	**Dovolte mi představit . . ?**	dovolte mi przhet-stavit
Mr Novotny and Mrs Novotna, this is . .	**Pan Novotný a paní Novotná, tohle je . .**	pan novotnee a pan^{y}ee novotnah to-hle ye
My name is . .	**Jmenuji se . .**	ymenooyi se
Pleased to meet you!	**Těší mě!**	t^{y}eshee mn^{y}e
What's your name?	**Jak se jmenujete?**	yak se ymenooyete
How are you?	**Jak se máte?**	yak se mahte
Fine, thanks. And you?	**Děkuji, dobře. A vy?**	d^{y}ekooyi dobrzhe. a vi

Follow up *A dále*

How long have you been here?	**Jak jste tady dlouho?**	yak yste tadi dloh-ho
We've been here a week.	**My jsme tady už týden.**	mi ysme tadi ush teeden
Is this your first visit?	**Je to vaše první návštěva?**	ye to vashe p^{u}rvn^{y}ee nahfsht^{y}eva
No, we came here last year.	**Ne, my jsme tady byli už vloni.**	ne mi ysme tadi bili oosh vlon^{y}i
Are you enjoying your stay?	**Líbí se vám tady?**	leebee se vahm tadi
Yes, I like it very much.	**Ano, nám se tady moc líbí.**	ano nahm se tadi mots leebee
What do you think of the country/people?	**Co si myslíte o naší zemi/o našich lidech?**	tso si misleete onashee zemi/onashikh lidekh
Where do you come from?	**Odkud jste?**	oktoot yste
I'm from . .	**Já jsem ze . .**	yah ysem ze
What nationality are you?	**Jaké jste národnosti?**	yakeh yste nahrodnost^{y}i

COUNTRIES, see page 146

I'm ...	**Jsem ...**	ysem
American	**Američan(ka)**	americhan(ka)
British	**Brit**	brit
Canadian	**Kanaď'an(ka)**	kanad^{y}an(ka)
English	**Angličan(ka)**	Anglichan(ka)
Irish	**Irčan(ka)**	irchan(ka)
Where are you staying?	**Kde jste ubytovaní?**	gde yste oobitovan^{y}ee
Are you on your own?	**Jste tady sam?**	yste tadi sahm
I'm with my ...	**Já jsem s ...**	yah ysem s
wife	**svou ženou**	svoh zhenoh
husband	**svým manželem**	sveem manzhelem
family	**svou rodinou**	svoh rod^{y}inoh
children	**svými dětmi**	sveemi đetmi
parents	**svými rodiči**	sveemi rod^{y}ichi
boyfriend/girlfriend	**svým mládencem/ svou dívkou**	sveem mlahdentsem/svoh d^{y}eefkoh

father/mother	**otec/matka**	otets/matka
son/daughter	**syn/dcera**	sin/tsera
brother/sister	**bratr/sestra**	brat^{u}r/sestra
uncle/aunt	**strýc/teta**	streets/teta
nephew/niece	**synovec/neteř**	sinovets/neterzh
cousin	**bratranec/sestřenice**	bratranets/ sestrzhenitse

Are you married/ single?	**Jste ženatý (vdaná)/svobodný?**	yste zhenatee (vdanah)/ svobodnee
Do you have children?	**Máte děti?**	mahte d^{y}et^{y}i
What do you do?	**V jakém oboru pracujete?**	fyakehm oboroo pratsooyete
I'm a student.	**Já jsem student(ka).**	yah ysem stoodent(ka)
What are you studying?	**Co studujete?**	tso stoodooyete
I'm here on a business trip.	**Já jsem tady služebně.**	yah ysem tadi sloozhebn^{y}e
Do you travel a lot?	**Cestujete hodně?**	tsestooyete hodn^{y}e
We're here on holiday.	**My jsme tady na dovolené.**	me ysme tadi nadovoleneh
Do you play cards/ chess?	**Hrajete karty/ šachy?**	hra-yete karti/shakhi

The weather *Počasí*

What a lovely day!	**To je krásný den!**	to ye krahsnee den
What awful weather!	**To je hrozné počasí!**	to ye hrozneh pochasee
Isn't it cold/hot today?	**Že je dnes zima/ horko?**	ze ye dnes zima/horko
Is it usually as warm as this?	**Je normálně takové teplo?**	ye normahln^{y}e takoveh teplo
Do you think it's going to ... tomorrow?	**Myslíte, že zítra bude ...?**	misleete zhe zeetra boode
be a nice day	**hezky**	heski
rain	**pršet**	p^{u}rshet
snow	**sněžit**	sn^{y}ezhit
What's the weather forecast?	**Jaká je předpověd?**	yakah ye przhetpovyet^{y}

cloud	**zamračeno**	zamracheno
fog	**mlha**	m^{u}lha
frost	**mráz**	mrahs
ice	**náledí**	nahled^{y}ee
lightning	**blesk**	blesk
moon	**měsíc**	mn^{y}eseets
rain	**déšť**	dehsht^{y}
sky	**obloha**	oblo-ha
snow	**sníh**	sn^{y}eekh
star	**hvězda**	hvyezda
sun	**slunce**	sloontse
thunder	**hrom**	hrom
thunderstorm	**bouřka**	bohrzhka
wind	**vítr**	veet^{u}r

Invitations *Pozvání*

Would you like to have dinner with us on ...?	**Mohli byste přijít na večeři v ...?**	mo-hli bis-te przhiyeet navecherzhi v
May I invite you to lunch?	**Rádi bychom vás pozvali na oběd.**	rahd^{y}i bikhom vahs pozvali na obyet

DAYS OF THE WEEK, see page 151

Can you come round for a drink this evening?	**Mohli byste přijít dnes večer na skleničku?**	mo-hli bis-te przhiyeet dnes vecher nasklen^{y}ichkoo
There's a party. Are you coming?	**Máme společhost. Přijdete?**	mahme spolechnost. przhiydete
That's very kind of you.	**To je od vás moc milé.**	to ye odvahs mots mileh
Great. I'd love to come.	**Děkuji. Přijdu rád.**	d^{y}ekooye. przhiydoo raht
What time shall we come?	**V kolik hodin máme přijít?**	fkolik hod^{y}in mahme przhiyeet
May I bring a friend?	**Můžu přivést kamaráda?**	m$\overline{oo}$zhoo przhivehst kamarahda
I'm afraid we have to leave now.	**My už musíme opravdu jít.**	mi oosh mooseeme opravdoo yeet
Next time you must come to visit us.	**Příště musíte přijít k nám.**	przheesht^{y}e mooseete przhiyeet knahm
Thanks for the evening. It was great.	**Děkujeme za moc milý večer. Bylo to vynikající.**	d^{y}ekooyeme zamots milee vecher. bilo to vin^{y}ikayeetsee

Dating *Schůzka*

Do you mind if I smoke?	**Bude vám vadit když si zapálím?**	boode vahm vad^{y}it gdish si zapahleem
Would you like a cigarette?	**Chcete cigaretu?**	kh-tsete tsigaretoo
Do you have a light, please?	**Máte zapalovač?**	mahte zapalovach
Why are you laughing?	**Proč se smějete?**	proch se smn^{y}eyete
Is my Czech that bad?	**Mluvím česky tak špatně?**	mlooveem cheski tak shpatn^{y}e
Do you mind if I sit here?	**Můžu se sem posadit?**	m$\overline{oo}$zhoo se sem posad^{y}it
Can I get you a drink?	**Chtěl[a] byste něco k pití?**	kht^{y}el[a] bis-te n^{y}etso k pit^{y}ee
Are you waiting for someone?	**Čekáte na někoho?**	chekahte nan^{y}eko-ho

Are you free this evening?	**Máte dnes večer volno?**	mahte dnes vecher volno
Would you like to go out with me tonight?	**Mohli bychom se večer sejít?**	mo-hli bikhom se vecher seyeet
Would you like to go dancing?	**Chtěl[a] byste si jít zatančit?**	kht^{y}el[a] bis-te si yeet zatanchit
I know a good discotheque.	**Vím o dobré diskotéce.**	veem odobreh diskotehtse
Shall we go to the cinema (movies)?	**Chcete do kina?**	kh-tsete dokina
Would you like to go for a drive?	**Půjdeme se projet?**	p$\overline{oo}$ydeme se proyet
Where shall we meet?	**Kde se sejdeme?**	gde se seydeme
I'll pick you up at your hotel.	**Vyzvednu vás před hotelem.**	vizvednoo vahs przhethotelem
I'll call for you at 8.	**Stavím se pro vás v osm hodin.**	staveem se provahs f osoom hod^{y}in
May I take you home?	**Můžu vás doprovodit domů?**	m$\overline{oo}$zhoo vahs doprovod^{y}it dom$\overline{oo}$
Can I see you again tomorrow?	**Uvidíme se znovu zítra?**	oovid^{y}eeme se znovoo zeetra
I hope we'll meet again.	**Doufám, že se ještě uvidíme.**	dohfahm zhe se yesht^{y}e oovid^{y}eeme

... and you might answer:

I'd love to, thank you.	**Moc rád(a), děkuji.**	mots rahd(a) d^{y}ekooyi
Thank you, but I'm busy.	**Děkuji, ale já mám moc práce.**	d^{y}ekooye ale yah mahm mots prahtse
No, I'm not interested, thank you.	**Ne, já opravdu nemám zájem.**	ne yah opravdoo nemahm zahyem
Leave me alone, please!	**Nechte mne, prosím!**	nekhte mne proseem
Thank you, it's been a wonderful evening.	**Děkuji za krásný večer.**	d^{y}ekooye za krahsnee vecher
I've enjoyed myself.	**Moc jsem se pobavil(a).**	mots ysem se pobavil(a)

Shopping Guide

This shopping guide is designed to help you find what you want with ease, accuracy and speed. It features:

1. A list of all major shops, stores and services (p. 98).
2. Some general expressions required when shopping to allow you to be specific and selective (p. 100).
3. Full details of the shops and services most likely to concern you. Here you'll find advice, alphabetical lists of items and conversion charts listed under the headings below.

LAUNDRY, see page 29/HAIRDRESSER'S, see page 30

Shops, stores and services *Obchody, obchodní domy a služby*

Most shops are open from 8 a.m. to 6 p.m., though food shops start opening from 6 a.m. and some shops close for lunch between 12 and 2 o'clock. Big department stores tend to work non-stop from 8 a.m. to 7 p.m. Many shops are closed all or part of Monday.

The shopper will be presented in town centres with a fascinating combination of state-run shops and an ever increasing number of private enterprises. In the former, you may come across rather antiquated procedures. For example, you cannot enter some shops without a basket, so pick one up at the door or stand in line and wait for someone to leave.

Where's the nearest ...?	**Kde je nejbližší ...**	gde ye neyblishee
antique shop	**starožitnictví**	starozhitnʸits-tvee
art gallery	**umělecká galerie**	umnʸeletskah galeri-ye
baker's	**pekařství**	pekarzhstvee
bank	**banka**	banka
barber's	**holičství**	holichstvee
beauty salon	**salón krásy**	salōn krahsi
bookshop	**knihkupectví**	knikh-koopets-tvee
butcher's	**řeznicví**	rzheznʸits-tvee
camera shop	**obchod s fotoaparáty**	opkhot sfotoaparahti
chemist's	**lékárna**	lehkahrna
dairy	**mlékárna**	mlehkahrna
delicatessen	**lahůdky**	la-hōōtki
dentist	**zubař**	zoobarzh
department store	**obchodní dům**	opkhodnʸee dōōm
drugstore	**drogerie**	drogehriye
dry cleaner's	**čistírna**	chistʸeerna
electrical goods shop	**elektrické spotřebiče**	elektritskeh spotrzhebiche
fishmonger's	**rybárna**	ribahrna
florist's	**květinářství**	kvyetʸinahrzhstvee
furrier's	**kožešnictví**	kozheshnʸits-tvee
greengrocer's	**zelinářství**	zelinahrzhstvee
grocer's	**potraviny**	potravini
hairdresser's (ladies/ men)	**holičstvi/ kadeřnictví**	holichstvee/kaderzhnʸits-tvee
hardware store	**železářství**	zhelezahrzhstvee

health food shop	**potraviny pro zdravou výživu**	potravini pro zdravoh veezhivoo
hospital	**nemocnice**	nemotsn^{y}it-se
ironmonger's	**železářství**	zhelezahrzhstvee
jeweller's	**klenotnictví**	klenotn^{y}its-tvee
launderette	**samoobslužná prádelna**	samo-opsloozhnah prahdelna
laundry	**prádelna**	prahdelna
library	**knihovna**	kn^{y}ihovna
market	**trh**	t^{u}rkh
newsagent's	**trafika**	trafika
newsstand	**novinový stánek**	novinovee stahnek
optician	**optik**	optik
pastry shop	**cukrárna**	tsookrahrna
photographer	**fotograf**	fotograf
police station	**policejní stanice**	politseyn^{y}ee stan^{y}itse
post office	**pošta**	poshta
second-hand shop	**obchod s použitým zbožím**	opkhot s po-oozhiteem zbozheem
shoemaker's (repairs)	**opravna obuvi**	opravna oboovi
shoe shop	**obuv**	oboof
shopping centre	**nákupní středisko**	nahkoopn^{y}ee strzhed^{y}isko
souvenir shop	**suvenýry**	sooveneeri
sporting goods shop	**sportovní potřeby**	sportovn^{y}ee potrzhebi
stationer's	**papírnictví**	papeern^{y}its-tvee
supermarket	**samoobsluha**	samo-opsloo-ha
sweet shop	**cukrárna**	tsookrahrna
tailor's	**krejčovství**	kreychofstvee
telegraph office	**telegrafní přepážka**	telegrafn^{y}ee przhepahshka
tobacconist's	**tabák**	tabahk
toy shop	**hračky**	hrachki
travel agency	**cestovní kancelář**	tsestovn^{y}ee kantselahrzh
vegetable store	**zelenina**	zelen^{y}ina
veterinarian	**zvěrolékař**	zvyerolehkarzh
watchmaker's	**hodinářství**	hod^{y}inahrzhstvee
wine merchant	**prodej vína**	prodey veena

VCHOD	ENTRANCE
VÝCHOD	EXIT
NOUZOVÝ VÝCHOD	EMERGENCY EXIT

General expressions *Všeobecné výrazy*

Where? *Kde?*

Where's there a good ...?	**Kde je dobrý...?**	gde ye dobree
Where can I find a ...?	**Kde najdu ...?**	gde na-ydoo
Where's the main shopping area?	**Kde je hlavní obchodní centrum?**	gde ye hlavn^{y}ee opkhodn^{y}ee tsentroom
Is it far from here?	**Je to odsud daleko?**	ye to otsood daleko
How do I get there?	**Jak se tam dostanu?**	yak se tam dostanoo

PRODEJ	SALE

Service *Obsluha*

Can you help me?	**Můžete mi pomoci?**	mōōzhete mi pomotsi
I'm just looking.	**Já se jenom dívám.**	yah se yenom d^{y}eevahm
Do you sell ...?	**Prodáváte...?**	prodahvahte
I'd like to buy ...	**Chci si koupit...**	kh-tsi si kohpit
I'd like ...	**Chtěl(a) bych ...**	kht^{y}el(a) bikh
Can you show me some ...?	**Mohl[a] byste mi ukázat nějaké...**	mo-hl[a] bis-te mi ookahzat n^{y}eyakeh
Do you have any ...?	**Máte nějaké...?**	mahte n^{y}eyakeh
Where's the ... department?	**Kde je ...oddělení?**	gde ye ... odd^{y}elen^{y}ee
Where is the lift (elevator)/escalator?	**Kde je výtah/ eskalátor?**	gde ye veeta-h/eskalahtor

That one *Tam ten*

Can you show me ...?	**Můžete mi ukázat ...?**	mōōzhete mi ookahzat
this/that	**tohle/tamto**	to-hle/tamto
the one in the window/in the display case	**ten co je ve výloze/ve vitrině**	ten tso ye veveeloze/ vevitreen^{y}e

Defining the article *Popis předmětu*

I'd like a ... one.	**Chtěl(a) bych ...**	kht^{y}el(a) bikh
big	**velký**	velkee
cheap	**laciný**	latsinee
dark	**tmavý**	tmavee
good	**dobrý**	dobree
heavy	**těžký**	t^{y}eshkee
large	**velký**	velkee
light (weight)	**lehký**	lekhkee
light (colour)	**světlý**	svyetlee
oval	**oválný**	ovahlnee
rectangular	**obdélníkový**	obdehln^{y}eekovee
round	**kulatý**	koolatee
small	**malý**	malee
square	**čtvercový**	ch^{u}tvertsovee
sturdy	**pevný**	pevnee
I don't want anything too expensive.	**Nechci nic drahého.**	nekh-tsi n^{y}its dra-heh-ho

Preference *Dávat přednost*

Can you show me some others?	**Můžete mi ukázat něco jiného?**	mo͞ozhete mi ookahzat n^{y}etso yineh-ho
Don't you have anything ...?	**Nemáte něco ...?**	nemahte n^{y}etso
cheaper/better	**lacinějšího/lepšího**	latsin^{y}eyshee-ho/ lepshee-ho
larger/smaller	**většího/menšího**	vyetshee-ho/menshee-ho

How much? *Kolik*

How much is this?	**Kolik to stojí?**	kolik to stoyee
How much are they?	**Kolik stojí tyhle?**	kolik stoyee tihle
I don't understand.	**Já vám nerozumím.**	yah vahm nerozoomeem
Please write it down.	**Mohl[a] byste to napsat?**	mo-hl[a] bis-te to napsat
I don't want to spend more than ... koruna.	**Nechci utratit víc než ... korun.**	nekh-tsi ootratit veets nesh ... koroon

COLOURS, see page 112

Decision *Rozhodnutí*

It's not quite what I want.	**To není to, co já chci.**	to nen^{y}ee to tso yah kh-tsi
No, I don't like it.	**Ne děkuji, mně se to nelíbí.**	ne d^{y}ekooyi mn^{y}e se to neleebee
I'll take it.	**Já si to vezmu.**	yah si to vezmoo

Ordering *Objednávka*

Can you order it for me?	**Můžu si to objednat?**	m$\overline{oo}$zhoo si to obyednat
How long will it take?	**Jak dlouho to bude trvat?**	yak dloh-ho to boode t^{u}rvat

Delivery *Doručení*

I'll take it with me.	**Já si to hned vezmu.**	yah si to hnet vezmoo
Deliver it to the ... Hotel.	**Dodejte to do Hotelu ...**	dodeyte to do hoteloo
Please send it to this address.	**Pošlete to, prosím, na tuto adresu.**	poshlete to proseem na tooto adresoo
Will I have any difficulty with the customs?	**Budu mít problémy na celnici?**	boodoo meet problehmi na tseln^{y}itsi

Paying *Placení*

How much is it?	**Kolik to stojí?**	kolik to stoyee
Can I pay by traveller's cheque?	**Můžu platit cestovním šekem?**	m$\overline{oo}$zhoo plat^{y}it tsestovn^{y}eem shekem
Do you accept dollars/pounds?	**Berete dolary/libry?**	berete dolari/libri
Do you accept credit cards?	**Je možné platit úvěrovou kartou?**	ye mozhneh plat^{y}it $\overline{oo}$vyerovoh kartoh
Do I have to pay the VAT (sales tax)?	**Musím platit daň z nákupu?**	mooseem plat^{y}it dan^{y} znahkoopoo
I think there's a mistake in the bill.	**V tom účtu je asi chyba.**	ftom $\overline{oo}$chtoo ye asi khiba

Anything else? *A ještě něco?*

No, thanks, that's all.	**Ne, děkuji, to je všechno.**	ne d^{y}ekooyi to ye fshekhno
Yes, I'd like ...	**Ano, ještě bych chtěl(a)...**	ano yesht^{y}e bikh kht^{y}el(a)
Can you show me ...?	**Můžete mi ukázat...?**	mo͞ozhete mi ookahzat
May I have a bag, please?	**Můžete mi dát sáček?**	mo͞ozhete mi daht sahchek
Could you wrap it up for me, please?	**Můžete mi to, prosím, zabalit?**	mo͞ozhete mi to proseem zabalit
May I have a receipt?	**Mohl[a] byste mi dát účtenku**	mo-hl[a] bis-te mi daht oochtenkoo

Dissatisfied? *Nespokojen?*

Can you exchange this, please?	**Mohl[a] byste tohle vyměnit?**	mo-hl[a] bis-te to-hle vimn^{y}en^{y}it
I want to return this.	**Chci tohle vrátit.**	kh-tsi to-hle vraht^{y}it
I'd like a refund. Here's the receipt.	**Chtěl(a) bych vrátit peníze. Tady je moje účtenka.**	kht^{y}el(a) bikh vraht^{y}it pen^{y}eeze. tadi ye moye oochtenka

Můžu vám pomoci?	Can I help you?
Co byste si přál?	What would you like?
Jakou ... byste si přál?	What ... would you like?
barvu/tvar/kvalitu	colour/shape/quality
Je mi líto, ale to my nemáme.	I'm sorry, we don't have any.
To je vyprodáno.	We're out of stock.
Máme to pro vás objednat?	Shall we order it for you?
Chcete si to vzít nebo to máme poslat?	Will you take it with you or shall we send it?
Ještě něco?	Anything else?
To bude ... korun, prosím.	That's ... crowns, please.
Pokladna je tam.	The cash desk is over there.

Bookshop—Stationer's *Knihkupectví—Papírnictví*

Books and stationery are usually sold in separate shops. You'll find newspapers and magazines at newsstands identified with the letters PNS (for *Poštovní Novinová Služba*, post news service) and at post offices. Western dailies and news magazines are available at major hotels and some kiosks in the capital. For foreign periodicals, look out for the sign *Zahraniční časopisy* (za-hrahichn^{y}ee chasopisee).

Where's the nearest ...?	**Kde je nejbližší ...?**	gde ye neyblishee
bookshop	**knihkupectví**	kn^{y}ikhkoopets-tvee
stationer's	**papírnictví**	papeern^{y}its-tvee
newsstand	**novinový stánek**	novinovee stahnek
Where can I buy an English-language newspaper?	**Kde si můžu koupit anglické noviny?**	gde si moozhoo kohpit anglitskeh novini
Where's the guide-book section?	**Kde je oddělení turistických průvodců?**	gde ye odd^{y}elenee tooristitskeekh proovot-tsoo
Where do you keep the English books?	**Kde máte anglické knihy?**	gde mahte anglitskeh kn^{y}ihi
Have you any of ...'s books in English?	**Máte některé knihy od... v angličtině?**	mahte n^{y}ektereh kn^{y}ihi ot ... fanglicht^{y}in^{y}e
Do you have second-hand books?	**Máte nějaké antikvární knihy?**	mahte n^{y}eyakeh antikvahrn^{y}ee kn^{y}ihi
I want to buy a/an/some ...	**Já si chci koupit...**	yah kh-tsi kohpit
address book	**adresář**	adresahrzh
adhesive tape	**lepicí pásku**	lepitsee pahskoo
ball-point pen	**propisovací tužku**	propisovatsee tooshkoo
book	**knihu**	kn^{y}ihoo
calendar	**kalendář**	kalendahrzh
carbon paper	**kopírovací papír**	kopeerovatsee papeer
crayons	**pastelky**	pastelki
dictionary	**slovník**	slovn^{y}eek
Czech-English	**česko-anglický**	chesko-anglitskee
pocket	**kapesní**	kapesn^{y}ee
drawing paper	**kreslicí papír**	kreslitsee papeer
drawing pins	**připínáčky**	przhipeenahchki
envelopes	**obálky**	obahlki
eraser	**korekční barvu**	korekchn^{y}ee barvoo

exercise book	**sešit**	seshit
felt-tip pen	**značkovač**	znachkovach
fountain pen	**plnicí pero**	p^{u}ln^{y}itsee pero
glue	**lepidlo**	lepidlo
grammar book	**gramatiku**	gramatikoo
guidebook	**průvodce**	proovot-tse
ink	**inkoust**	ingohst
black/red/blue	**černý/červený/ modrý**	chernee/chervenee/ modree
(adhesive) labels	**(lepicí) štítek**	(lepitsee) sht^{y}eetek
magazine	**časopis**	chasopis
map	**mapu**	mapoo
street map	**plán města**	plahn mn^{y}esta
road map of ...	**silniční mapa**	siln^{y}ichn^{y}ee mapa
newspaper	**noviny**	novini
American/English	**americké/ anglické**	ameritskeh/anglitskeh
notebook	**blok**	blok
note paper	**poznámkový papír**	poznahmkovee papeer
paintbox	**vodové barvy**	vodoveh barvi
paper	**papír**	papeer
paperback	**knížku v měkké vazbě**	kn^{y}eeshkoo v mn^{y}ekeh vazbye
paperclips	**spínátka**	speenahtka
paper napkins	**papírové ubrousky**	papeeroveh oobrohski
paste	**lepenku**	lepenkoo
pen	**pero**	pero
pencil	**tužku**	tooshkoo
pencil sharpener	**ořezávátko**	orzhezahvahtko
playing cards	**hrací karty**	hratsee karti
pocket calculator	**kalkulačku**	kalkoolachkoo
postcard	**pohled**	po-hled
propelling pencil	**propisovací tužku**	propisovatsee tooshkoo
refill (for a pen)	**náplň (do pera)**	nahpln^{y} (do pera)
rubber	**gumu**	goomoo
ruler	**pravítko**	praveetko
staples	**svorky**	svorki
string	**provázek**	provahzek
thumbtacks	**připínáčky**	przhipeenahchki
travel guide	**turistického průvodce**	tooristitskeh-ho proovot-tse
typewriter ribbon	**pásku do psacího stroje**	pahskoo do psatsee-ho stroye
typing paper	**papír do psacího stroje**	papeer do psatsee-ho stroye
wrapping paper	**balicí papír**	balitsee papeer
writing pad	**dopisní papír**	dopisn^{y}ee papeer

Camping and sports equipment *Stanovací a sportovní potřeby*

I'd like a/an/ some ...	**Chtěl(a) bych ...**	kht^{y}el(a) bikh
I'd like to hire a(n)/ some ...	**Já bych si chtěl(a) pronajmout ...**	yah bikh si kht^{y}el(a) prona-ymoht
air bed (mattress)	**nafukovací matraci**	nafookovatsee matratsi
backpack	**batoh**	batokh
butane gas	**propan-butan**	propan-bootan
campbed	**polní lůžko**	poln^{y}ee looshko
(folding) chair	**(skládací) židli**	(sklahdatsee) zhidli
charcoal	**dřevěné uhlí**	drzhevyeneh oo-hlee
compass	**kompas**	kompas
cool box	**cestovní lednička**	tsestovnee ledn^{y}ichka
deck chair	**lehátko**	le-hahtko
fire lighters	**podpalovače**	podpalovache
fishing tackle	**rybářské potřeby**	ribahrzhskeh potrzhebi
flashlight	**baterku**	baterkoo
groundsheet	**nepromokavou celtu**	nepromokavoh tseltoo
hammock	**houpací sít**	hohpatsee seet^{y}
ice pack	**ledový obal**	ledovee obal
insect spray (killer)	**postřik proti hmyzu**	postrzhik prot^{y}i hmizoo
kerosene	**petrolej**	petroley
lamp	**lampu**	lampoo
lantern	**lucernu**	lootsernoo
mallet	**palici**	palitsi
matches	**zápalky**	zahpalki
(foam rubber) mattress	**(gumovou) matraci**	(goomovoh) matratsi
mosquito net	**sít' proti komárům**	seet^{y} prot^{y}i komahroom
paraffin	**parafín**	parafeen
picnic basket	**košík na piknik**	kosheek na piknik
pump	**pumpu**	poompoo
rope	**lano**	lano
skiing equipment	**lyžařské vybavení**	lizharzhskeh vibaven^{y}ee
skin-diving equipment	**vybavení pro sportovní potápěni**	vibaven^{y}ee pro sportovn^{y}ee potahpyen^{y}ee
sleeping bag	**spacák**	spatsahk
(folding) table	**(skládací) stůl**	(sklahdatsee) stool
tent	**stan**	stan
tent pegs	**stanové kolíky**	stanoveh koleeki
tent pole	**stanové tyče**	stanoveh tiche
torch	**baterku**	baterkoo
water flask	**láhev na vodu**	lahef navodoo
windsurfer	**windsurfer**	vindserfer

CAMPING, see page 32

Chemist's (drugstore) *Lékárna*

Certain pharmacies (*lékárna*) are open after normal business hours. To find the shops on night duty, look for the addresses posted on the door of any pharmacy.

If you need a prescription from a doctor, the visit is free but you pay for the medicine. If you require certain medicines, it's wise to bring an adequate supply from home, for equivalents may not be available.

For toilet articles you need to go to a *drogerie* or *parfumerie*.

This section is divided into two parts:

1. Pharmaceutical—medicine, first-aid, etc.
2. Toiletry—toilet articles, cosmetics

General *Všeobecné dotazy*

Where's the nearest (all-night) chemist's?	**Kde je nejbližší (noční) lékárna?**	gde ye neyblishee (nochn^{y}ee) lehkahrna
What time does the chemist's open/ close?	**V kolik hodin otevírají/zavírají v lékárně?**	fkolik hod^{y}in oteveera-yee/ zaveera-yee vlehkahrn^{y}e

1—Pharmaceutical *Léky*

I'd like something for...	**Potřebuji něco proti...**	potrzhebooyi n^{y}etso prot^{y}i
a cold/a cough	**rýma/kašel**	reema/kashel
hay fever	**senná rýma**	sennah reema
insect bites	**kousnutí**	kohsnoot^{y}ee
sunburn	**spálení sluncem**	spahlen^{y}ee sloontsem
travel/altitude sickness	**nemoc z cestování/ výšková nemoc**	nemots stsestovahn^{y}ee/ veeshkovah nemots
an upset stomach	**žaludeční nevolnosti**	zhaloodechn^{y}ee nevolnost^{y}i
Can you prepare this prescription for me?	**Můžete mi připravit tento předpis?**	moozhete mi przhipravit tento przhetpis
Can I get it without a prescription?	**Můžu to dostat bez předpisu?**	moozhoo to dostat besprzhedpisoo
Shall I wait?	**Mám si počkat?**	mahm si pochkat

DOCTOR, see page 137

Can I have a/an/ some...?	**Chtěl(a) bych ...**	kht^{y}el(a) bikh
adhesive plaster	**leukoplast**	leookoplast
analgesic	**utišující prostředek**	oot^{y}ishooyeetsee prostrzhedek
antiseptic cream	**antiseptický krém**	antiseptitskee krehm
aspirin	**acylpirin**	atsilpireen
bandage	**obvaz**	obvas
elastic bandage	**pružný obvaz**	proozhnee obvas
Band-Aids	**leukoplast**	leookoplast
condoms	**preservativ**	prezervateef
contraceptives	**antikoncepční prostředky**	antikontsepchn^{y}ee prostrzhetki
corn plasters	**náplast na kuří oko**	nahplast nakurzhee oko
cotton wool (absorbent cotton)	**vatu**	vatoo
cough drops	**něco proti kašli**	n^{y}etso prot^{y}i kashli
disinfectant	**desinfekci**	dezinfektsi
ear drops	**kapky do uší**	kapki do ooshee
eye drops	**kapky do očí**	kapki do ochee
first-aid kit	**první pomoc**	p^{u}rvn^{y}ee pomots
gauze	**gázu**	gahzoo
insect repellent/spray	**postřik proti hmyzu**	postrzhik prot^{y}i hmizoo
iodine	**jód**	jōt
laxative	**projímadlo**	proyeemadlo
mouthwash	**ústní výplach**	o͞ostn^{y}ee veeplakh
nose drops	**kapky do nosu**	kapki do nosoo
sanitary towels (napkins)	**vložky**	vloshki
sleeping pills	**prášek na spaní**	prahshek naspan^{y}ee
suppositories	**čípky**	cheepki
... tablets	**... prášky**	... prahshki
tampons	**tampóny**	tampōni
thermometer	**teploměr**	teplomn^{y}er
throat lozenges	**pastilky pro bolavý krk**	pastilki pro bolavee k^{u}rk
tranquillizers	**utišující prostředky**	oot^{y}ishooyeetsee prostrzhetki
vitamin pills	**vitaminové pilulky**	vitameenoveh piloolki

JED	POISON
JEN PRO VNĚJŠÍ POUŽITÍ	FOR EXTERNAL USE ONLY

2—Toiletry *Toaletní potřeby*

I'd like a/an/some ...	**Chtěl(a) bych ...**	kht^{y}el(a) bikh
after-shave lotion	**vodu po holení**	vodoo po holen^{y}ee
astringent	**svíravý prostředek**	sveeratsee prostrzhedek
bath salts	**koupelovou sůl**	kohpelovoh s$\overline{oo}$l
blusher (rouge)	**růž**	r$\overline{oo}$sh
bubble bath	**pěnu do koupele**	pyenoo dokohpele
cream	**krém**	krehm
cleansing cream	**čistící krém**	chist^{y}itsee krehm
foundation cream	**podkladový krém**	potkladovee krehm
moisturizing cream	**výživný krém**	veezhivnee krehm
night cream	**noční krém**	nochn^{y}ee krehm
cuticle remover	**nůžky na kůžičku**	n$\overline{oo}$shki nak$\overline{oo}$zhichkoo
deodorant	**dezodorant**	dezodorant
emery board	**pilníček na nehty**	piln^{y}eechek nanekhti
eyebrow pencil	**tužku na obočí**	tooshkoo naobochee
eyeliner	**štěteček na malování obočí**	sht^{y}etechek namalovahn^{y}ee obochee
eye shadow	**oční stíny**	ochn^{y}ee st^{y}eeni
face powder	**pudr**	pood^{u}r
foot cream	**krém na chodidla**	krehm nakhod^{y}idla
hand cream	**krém na ruce**	krehm narootse
lipsalve	**bezbarvou rtěnku**	bezbarvoh rt^{y}enkoo
lipstick	**rtěnku**	rt^{y}enkoo
make-up remover pads	**vatové tlapky na odstranění líčidla**	vatoveh t^{u}lapki na-otstran^{y}en^{y}ee leechidla
nail brush	**kartáček na nehty**	kartahchek nanekhti
nail clippers	**kleště na nehty**	klesht^{y}e nanekhti
nail file	**pilník na nehty**	piln^{y}eek nanekhti
nail polish	**lak na nehty**	lak nanekhti
nail polish remover	**odlakovač**	odlakovach
nail scissors	**nůžky na nehty**	n$\overline{oo}$shki nanekhti
perfume	**parfém**	parfehm
powder	**pudr**	pood^{u}r
powder puff	**labutěnku**	laboot^{y}enkoo
razor	**břitvu**	brzhitvoo
razor blades	**žiletky**	zhiletki
safety pins	**spínací špendlíky**	speenatsee shpendleeki
shaving brush	**stětku na holení**	sht^{y}etkoo naholen^{y}ee
shaving cream	**mýdlo na holení**	meedlo naholen^{y}ee
soap	**mýdlo**	meedlo
sponge	**houbu**	hohboo
sun-tan cream	**krém na opalování**	krehm naopalovahn^{y}ee
sun-tan oil	**olej na opalování**	oley naopalovahn^{y}ee
talcum powder	**zásyp**	zahsip

tissues	**ubrousky**	oobrohski
toilet paper	**toaletní papír**	toaletn^{y}ee papeer
toilet water	**kolínskou vodu**	koleenskoh vodoo
toothbrush	**kartáček na zuby**	kartahchek nazoobi
toothpaste	**zubní pastu**	zoobn^{y}ee pastoo
towel	**ručník**	roochn^{y}eek
tweezers	**pinsetu**	pinzetoo

For your hair *Pro vaše vlasy*

bobby pins	**sponky**	sponki
colour shampoo	**tónovací šampón**	tohnovatsee shampón
comb	**hřeben**	hrzheben
curlers	**natáčky**	natahchki
dry shampoo	**suchý šampón**	sookhee shampōn
dye	**barvu**	barvoo
hairbrush	**kartáč na vlasy**	kartahch navlasi
hair gel	**pomáda na vlasy**	pomahda navlasi
hairgrips	**sponky**	sponki
hair lotion	**vlasová voda**	vlasovah voda
hairpins	**pinetky**	pinetki
hair slide	**zavírací sponku do vlasů**	zaveeratsee sponkoo dovlas$\overline{oo}$
hair spray	**lak na vlasy**	lak navlasi
setting lotion	**tužidlo na vlasy**	toozhidlo navlasi
shampoo	**šampón**	shampōn
for dry/greasy (oily) hair	**na suché/na mastné vlasy**	nasookheh/namastneh vlasi
tint	**tón**	tōn
wig	**paruka**	parooka

For the baby *Pro miminko*

baby food	**výživa pro kojence**	veezhiva prokoyentse
dummy (pacifier)	**dudlík**	doodleek
feeding bottle	**láhev pro kojence**	lahef prokoyentse
nappies (diapers)	**plenky**	plenki

Clothing *Oděvy*

If you want to buy something specific, prepare yourself in advance. Look at the list of clothing on page 115. Get some idea of the colour, material and size you want. They're all listed on the next few pages.

General *Všeobecné dotazy*

I'd like ...	**Chtěl(a) bych ...**	kht^{y}el(a) bikh
I'd like ... for a 10-year-old boy/ girl.	**Chtěl(a) bych ... pro desetiletého chlapce/pro deseti letou dívku.**	kht^{y}el(a) bikh ... prodeset^{y}ileteh-ho khlaptse/prodeset^{y}letoh d^{y}eefkoo
I'd like something like this.	**Chtěl(a) bych něco podobného.**	kht^{y}el(a) bikh n^{y}etso podobneh-ho
I like the one in the window.	**Chtěl(a) bych ten co je ve výloze.**	kht^{y}el(a) bikh ten tso ye ve veeloze
How much is that per metre?	**Kolik stojí metr?**	kolik stoyee metr

1 centimetre (cm)	= 0.39 in.	1 inch	= 2.54 cm
1 metre (m)	= 39.37 in.	1 foot	= 30.5 cm
10 metres	= 32.81 ft.	1 yard	= 0.91 m

Colour *Barva*

I'd like something in ...	**Chtěl(a) bych něco v ...**	kht^{y}el(a) bikh n^{y}etso v
I'd like a darker/ lighter shade.	**Chtěl(a) bych o něco tmavší/ světlejší odstín.**	kht^{y}el(a) bikh n^{y}etso tmafshee/svyetleyshee otst^{y}een
I'd like something to match this.	**Chtěl(a) bych něco co by se hodilo k tomuto.**	kht^{y}el(a) bikh n^{y}etso tso bi se hod^{y}ilo k tomooto
I don't like the colour.	**Mně se nelíbí ta barva.**	mn^{y}e se neleebee ta barva

beige	**béžový**	behzhovee
black	**černý**	chernee
blue	**modrý**	modree
brown	**hnědý**	hn^{y}edee
fawn	**světle hnědý**	svyetle hn^{y}edee
golden	**zlatavý**	zlatavee
green	**zelený**	zelenee
grey	**šedý**	shedee
mauve	**slézový**	slehzovee
orange	**oranžový**	oranzhovee
pink	**růžový**	roozhovee
purple	**fialový**	fiyalovee
red	**červený**	chervenee
scarlet	**rudý**	roodee
silver	**stříbrný**	st^{u}rzheeb^{u}rnee
turquoise	**tyrkysový**	tirkisovee
white	**bílý**	beelee
yellow	**žlutý**	zhlootee
light . . .	**světlý**	svyetlee
dark . . .	**tmavý**	tmavee

bez vzoru
(bezvzoroo)

kostkovaný
(kostkovan^{y}ee)

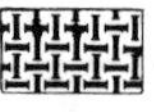

vzorovaný
(vzorovan^{y}ee)

puntíkovaný
(poonteekovan^{y}ee)

Fabric *Látky*

Do you have anything in . . .?	**Máte něco v. . .?**	mahte n^{y}etso v
Is that . . .?	**Je to . . .?**	ye to
handmade	**ruční práce**	roochn^{y}ee prahtse
imported	**z dovozu**	zdovozoo
made here	**tuzemský**	toozemskee
I'd like something thinner.	**Chtěl(a) bych něco tenšího.**	kht^{y}el(a) bikh n^{y}etso tenshee-ho
Do you have anything of better quality?	**Máte něco kvalitnějšího?**	mahte n^{y}etso kvalitn^{y}eyshee-ho

What's it made of?	**Z čeho je to vyrobeno?**	sche-ho ye to virobeno

cambric	**batist**	batist
camel-hair	**velbloudí srst**	velblohd^{y}ee s^{u}rst
chiffon	**šifon**	shifon
corduroy	**manšestr**	manzhestr
cotton	**bavlna**	bav^{u}lna
crepe	**krep**	krep
denim	**džínsovina**	dzheensovina
felt	**plsť**	p^{u}lst^{y}
flannel	**flanel**	flanel
gabardine	**gabardén**	gabardehn
lace	**krajka**	kra-yka
leather	**kůže**	kōōzhe
linen	**plátno**	plahtno
poplin	**popelín**	popeleen
satin	**satén**	satehn
silk	**hedvábí**	hedvahbee
suede	**semiš**	semish
towelling	**froté**	froteh
velvet	**samet**	samet
velveteen	**bavlněný samet**	bav^{u}ln^{y}enee samet
wool	**vlna**	v^{u}lna
worsted	**česaná příze**	chesanah przheeze

Is it ...?	**Je to...?**	ye to
pure cotton/wool	**čistá bavlna/vlna**	chistah bav^{u}lna/v^{u}lna
synthetic	**syntetický materiál**	sintetitskee materiyahl
colourfast	**stálobarevné**	stahlobarevneh
crease (wrinkle) resistant	**nemačkavé**	nemachkaveh
Is it hand washable/ machine washable?	**na praní v ruce/v pračce?**	na pran^{y}ee vrootse/ fprachtse
Will it shrink?	**Sráží se to?**	srazee se to

Size *Velikost*

I take size 38.	**Nosím velikost 38.**	noseem velikost trzhitset osoom
Could you measure me?	**Můžete mě změřit?**	mōōzhete mn^{y}e zmn^{y}erzhit
I don't know the Czech sizes.	**Neznám české velikosti.**	neznahm cheskeh velikost^{y}i

Sizes can vary somewhat from one manufacturer to another, so be sure to try on shoes and clothing before you buy.

Women *Ženy*

Dresses/Suits						
American	8	10	12	14	16	18
British	10	12	14	16	18	20
Continental	36	38	40	42	44	46

Stockings						
American / British	8½	9	9½	10	10½	
Continental	0	1	2	3	4	5

Shoes				
American	6	7	8	9
British	4½	5½	6½	7½
Continental	37	38	40	41

Men *Muži*

Suits/overcoats						
American / British	36	38	40	42	44	46
Continental	46	48	50	52	54	56

Shirts				
American / British	15	16	17	18
Continental	38	40	42	44

Shoes									
American / British	5	6	7	8	8½	9	9½	10	11
Continental	38	39	40	41	42	43	44	44	45

A good fit? *Sedí to dobře?*

Can I try it on?	**Můžu si to zkusit?**	mōōzhoo si to skoosit
Where's the fitting room?	**Kde je zkoušební kabina?**	gde ye skooshebnʸee kabina
Is there a mirror?	**Je tady zrcadlo?**	ye tadi zᵘrtsadlo
It fits very well.	**To dobře padne.**	to dobrzhe padne
It doesn't fit.	**To nesedí.**	to nesedee
It's too ...	**To je moc...**	to ye mots
short/long	**krátké/dlouhé**	krahtkeh/dloh-heh
tight/loose	**těsné/volné**	tʸesneh/volneh

NUMBERS, see page 147

How long will it take to alter?	**Jak dlouho bude trvat ta předělávka?**	yak dloh-ho boode t[u]rvat ta przhed[y]elahfka

Clothes and accessories *Oděvy a doplňky*

I would like a/an/ some...	**Chtěl(a) bych...**	kht[y]el(a) bikh
anorak	**větrovku**	vyetrofkoo
bathing cap	**koupací čepici**	kohpatsee chepitsi
bathing suit	**plavky**	plafki
bathrobe	**koupací plášť**	kohpatsee plahsht[y]
blouse	**halenku**	halenkoo
bow tie	**motýlka**	moteelka
bra	**podprsenku**	potp[u]rsenkoo
braces	**šle**	shle
cap	**čepici**	chepitsi
cardigan	**svetr na zapínání**	svet[u]r nazapeenahn[y]ee
coat	**kabát**	kabaht
dress	**šaty**	shati
with long sleeves	**s dlouhým rukávem**	sdloh-heem rookahvem
with short sleeves	**s krátkým rukávem**	skrahtkeem rookahvem
sleeveless	**bez rukávů**	bezrookahvoo
dressing gown	**župan**	zhoopan
evening dress (woman's)	**večerní šaty**	vechern[y]ee shati
girdle	**podvazkový pás**	podvaskovee pahs
gloves	**rukavice**	rookavitse
handbag	**kabelku**	kabelkoo
handkerchief	**kapesník**	kapesn[y]eek
hat	**klobouk**	klobohk
jacket	**sako**	sako
jeans	**džínsy**	dzheensi
jersey	**svetr**	svet[u]r
jumper (Br.)	**svetr**	svet[u]r
kneesocks	**podkolenky**	potkolenki
nightdress	**noční košili**	nochn[y]ee koshili
overalls	**montérky**	montehrki
pair of...	**pár...**	pahr
panties	**kalhotky**	kalhotki
pants (Am.)	**kalhoty**	kalhoti
panty girdle	**podvazkový pás**	podvaskovee pahs
panty hose	**punčocháče**	poonchokhahche
parka	**sportovní bundu s kapucí**	sportovn[y]ee boondoo skapootsee

pullover	**pulover**	poolovr
polo (turtle)-neck	**s rolákem**	srolahkem
round-neck	**s kulatým výstřihem**	skulateem veest^{u}rzhihem
V-neck	**s véčkem**	svehchkem
with long/short sleeves	**s dlouhým/ krátkým rukávem**	sdloh-heem/krahtkeem rookahvem
without sleeves	**bez rukávů**	bez rookahvoo
pyjamas	**pyžamo**	pizhamo
raincoat	**nepromokavý kabát**	nepromokavee kabaht
scarf	**šálu**	shahloo
shirt	**košili**	koshili
shorts	**šortky**	shortki
skirt	**sukni**	sookn^{y}i
slip	**kombiné**	kombineh
socks	**ponožky**	ponoshki
stockings	**punčochy**	poonchokhi
suit (man's)	**oblek**	oblek
suit (woman's)	**kostým**	kosteem
suspenders (Am.)	**šle**	shle
sweater	**svetr**	svet^{u}r
sweatshirt	**teplákovou bundu**	teplahkovoh boondoo
swimming trunks	**plavky**	plafki
swimsuit	**plavky**	plafki
T-shirt	**tričko**	trichko
tie	**kravatu**	kravatoo
tights	**punčocháče**	poonchokhahche
tracksuit	**teplákovou soupravu**	teplahkovoh sohpravoo
trousers	**kalhoty**	kalhoti
umbrella	**deštník**	deshtn^{y}eek
underpants	**spodky**	spotki
undershirt	**nátělník**	naht^{y}eln^{y}eek
vest (Am.)	**vestu**	vestoo
vest (Br.)	**tílko**	t^{y}eelko
waistcoat	**vestu**	vestoo

belt	**pásek**	pahsek
buckle	**přesku**	przheskoo
button	**knoflík**	knofleek
collar	**límec**	leemets
pocket	**kapsu**	kapsoo
press stud (snap fastener)	**patentku**	patentkoo
zip (zipper)	**zip**	zip

Shoes *Boty*

I'd like a pair of ...	**Chtěl(a) bych pár ...**	kht[y]el(a) bikh pahr
boots	**holínek**	holeenek
moccasins	**mokasín**	mokaseen
plimsolls (sneakers)	**tenisek**	tenisek
sandals	**sandálů**	sandahloo
shoes	**boty**	boti
flat	**bez podpatku**	bespotpatkoo
with a heel	**na podpatku**	napotpatkoo
with leather soles	**s koženou podrážkou**	skozhenoh podrahshkoh
with rubber soles	**s gumovou podrážkou**	sgoomovoh podrahshkoh
slippers	**pantofle**	pantofle
These are too ...	**Tyhle jsou moc...**	ty-hle ysoh mots
narrow/wide	**úzké/široké**	ooskeh/shirokeh
big/small	**velké/malé**	velkeh/maleh
Do you have a larger/ smaller size?	**Máte větší/ menší číslo?**	mahte vyetshee/menshee cheeslo
Do you have the same in black?	**Máte ty samé v černém?**	mahte ti sameh fchernehm
cloth	**látka**	lahtka
leather	**kůže**	koozhe
rubber	**guma**	gooma
suede	**semiš**	semish
Is it real leather?	**Je to z pravé kůže?**	ye to spraveh koozhe
I need some shoe polish/shoelaces.	**Potřebuji krém na boty/tkaničky.**	potrzhebooyi krehm na boti/tkan[y]ichki

Shoes worn out? Here's the key to getting them fixed again:

Can you repair these shoes?	**Můžete mi opravit tyto boty?**	moozhete mi opravit tito boti
Can you stitch this?	**Můžete tohle sešít?**	moozhete to-hle sesheet
I want new soles and heels.	**Chci nové podrážky a podpatky.**	kh-tsi noveh podrahshki a potpatki
When will they be ready?	**Kdy to bude hotové?**	gdi to boode hotoveh

COLOURS, see page 112

Electrical appliances *Elektrické potřeby*

In most places the power is 220-volt, 50-cycle A.C. American appliances will need transformers and plug adaptors.

What's the voltage?	**Jaké je tady napětí?**	yakeh ye tadi nap^{y}etee
Do you have a battery for this?	**Máte pro tohle baterie?**	mahte pro to-hle bateriye
This is broken. Can you repair it?	**Tohle nefunguje. Můžete to opravit?**	to-hle nefoongooye. m$\overline{oo}$zhete to opravit
Can you show me how it works?	**Můžete mi ukázat, jak to funguje?**	m$\overline{oo}$zhete mi ookahzat yak to mahm foongooye
I'd like (to hire) a video cassette.	**Chtěl(a) bych (si půjčit) video kazetu.**	kht^{y}el(a) bikh (si p$\overline{oo}$-ychit) videokazetoo
I'd like a/an/some ...	**Chtěl(a) bych ...**	kht^{y}el(a) bikh
adaptor	**rozdvojku**	rozdvoykoo
amplifier	**zesilovač**	zesilovach
bulb	**žárovku**	zhahrofkoo
CD player	**přehrávač kompaktních disků**	przhe-hrahvach kompaktn^{y}eech disk$\overline{oo}$
clock-radio	**rádio s budíkem**	rahdiyo zbood^{y}eekem
electric toothbrush	**elektrický kartáček na zuby**	elektritskee karahchek nazoobi
extension lead (cord)	**prodlužovací kabel**	prodloozhovatsee kabel
hair dryer	**fén**	fehn
headphones	**sluchátka**	slookhahtka
(travelling) iron	**(cestovní) žehličku**	(tsestovn^{y}ee) zhe-hlichkoo
lamp	**lampu**	lampoo
plug	**zástrčku**	zahst^{u}rchkoo
portable ...	**přenosné...**	przhenosneh
radio	**rádio**	rahdiyo
car radio	**autorádio**	aootorahdiyo
(cassette) recorder	**(kazetový) magnetofon**	(kazetovee) magnetofōn
record player	**gramofón**	gramofōn
shaver	**elektrický holicí strojek**	elektritskee holitsee stroyek
speakers	**reproduktor**	reprodooktor
(colour) television	**(barevná) televize**	(barevnah) televize
transformer	**transformátor**	transformahtor
video-recorder	**video přehrávač**	video przhe-h^{u}rahvach

Grocer's *Obchod s potravinami*

I'd like some bread, please.	**Dejte mi chleba, prosím.**	deyte mi khleba proseem
What sort of cheese do you have?	**Jaké máte druhy sýrů?**	yakeh mahte droo-hi seeroo
A piece of ...	**Kousek ...**	kohsek
that one	**toho**	to-ho
the one on the shelf	**ten na poličce**	ten napolichtse
I'll have one of those, please.	**Já si vezmu jeden z těchto, prosím.**	yah si vezmoo yeden st^{y}ekhto proseem
May I help myself?	**Můžu si sám vzít?**	moozhoo si sahm vzeet
I'd like ...	**Chtěl(a) bych ...**	kht^{y}el(a) bikh
a kilo of apples	**kilo jablek**	kilo yablek
half a kilo of tomatoes	**půl kila rajských jablek**	pool kila ra-yskeekh yablek
100 grams of butter	**sto gramů másla**	sto gramoo mahsla
a litre of milk	**litr mléka**	litr mlehka
half a dozen eggs	**šest vajíček**	shest va-yeechek
4 slices of ham	**čtyři plátky šunky**	chtirzhi plahtki shoonki
a packet of tea	**krabičku čaje**	krabichkoo cha-ye
a jar of jam	**skleničku džemu**	sklen^{y}ichkoo dzhemoo
a tin (can) of peaches	**broskvový kompot**	broskvovee kompot
a tube of mustard	**hořčici**	horzhtitsi
a box of chocolates	**bonbonieru**	bonbonieroo

1 kilogram or kilo (kg.) = 1000 grams (g.)

100 g. = 3.5 oz. ½ kg. = 1.1 lb.

200 g. = 7.0 oz. 1 kg. = 2.2 lb.

1 oz. = 28.35 g.

1 lb. = 453.60 g.

1 litre (l.) = 0.88 imp. quarts = 1.06 U.S. quarts

1 imp. quart = 1.14 l. 1 U.S. quart = 0.95 l.

1 imp. gallon = 4.55 l. 1 U.S. gallon = 3.8 l.

FOOD, see also page 63

Household articles *Potřeby pro domácnost*

aluminium foil	**alobal**	alobal
bottle opener	**otvírač na láhve**	otveerach na lahve
can opener	**otvírač na konzervy**	otveerach nakonzervi
candles	**svíčky**	sveechki
clothes pegs (pins)	**kolíčky na prádlo**	koleechki naprahdlo
dish detergent	**saponát**	saponaht
food box	**krabička na jídlo**	krabichkoo nayeedlo
frying pan	**pánev na smažení**	pahnef nasmazhen^{y}ee
matches	**sirky**	sirki
paper napkins	**papírové ubrousky**	papeeroveh oobrohski
paper towel	**papírové ručníky**	papeeroveh roochn^{y}eeki
plastic bags	**igelitové pytlíky**	igelitoveh pitleeki
saucepan	**pánev**	pahnef
tea towel	**utěrku**	oot^{y}erkoo
vacuum flask	**termosku**	termoskoo
washing powder	**prášek na praní**	prahshek napran^{y}ee
washing-up liquid	**prostředek na mytí nádobí**	prostrzhedek namit^{y}ee nahdobee

Tools *Nářadí*

hammer	**kladivo**	klad^{y}ivo
nails	**hřebíky**	hrzhebeeki
penknife	**kapesní nůž**	kapesn^{y}ee n$\overline{oo}$sh
pliers	**kleště**	klesht^{y}e
scissors	**nůžky**	n$\overline{oo}$shki
screws	**šrouby**	shrohbi
screwdriver	**šroubovák**	shrohbovahk
spanner	**klíč na matice**	kleech na mat^{y}itse

Crockery *Nádobí*

cups/mugs	**hrníčky/hrnky**	h^{u}rn^{y}eechki/h^{u}rnki
plates	**talíře**	taleerzhe
saucers	**podšálky**	pot-shahlki
tumblers	**skleničky**	sklen^{y}ichki

Cutlery (flatware) *Příbory*

forks	**vidličky**	vidlichki
knives	**nože**	nozhe
spoons	**lžíce**	lzheetsi
teaspoons	**lžičky**	lzheechki
(made of) plastic/ stainless steel	**(vyrobeno) z umělé hmoty/nerezu**	(virobeno) zoomyeleh hmoti/znerezoo

Jeweller's—Watchmaker's *Klenoty—Hodiny*

Here are some phrases to help you choose that perfect gift:

Could I see that, please?	**Mohl(a) bych se na tohle podívat?**	mo-hl(a) bikh se na to-hle pod^{y}eevat
Do you have anything in gold?	**Máte nějaké zlaté výrobky?**	mahte n^{y}ey-akee zlateh veeropki
How many carats is this?	**Kolikakarátové je to zlato?**	kolikakarahtoveh ye to zlato
Is this real silver?	**Je to pravé stříbro?**	ye to praveh strzheebro
Can you repair this watch?	**Můžete mi spravit tyhle hodinky?**	mōōzhete mi spravit ti-hle hod^{y}inki
I'd like a/an/some ...	**Chtěl(a) bych ...**	kht^{y}el(a) bikh
alarm clock	**budík**	bood^{y}eek
bangle	**přívěsek**	przheev^{y}esek
battery	**baterii**	bateriyi
bracelet	**náramek**	nahramek
chain bracelet	**řetízkový náramek**	rzhet^{y}eeskovee nahramek
charm bracelet	**náramek s přívěsky**	nahramek s przheevyeski
brooch	**brož**	brosh
chain	**řetízek**	rzhet^{y}eezek
charm	**talisman**	talisman
cigarette case	**cigaretové pouzdro**	tsigaretoveh pohzdro
cigarette lighter	**zapalovač**	zapalovach
clip	**sponu**	sponoo
clock	**hodiny**	hod^{y}ini
cross	**křížek**	k^{u}rzheezhek
cuckoo clock	**hodiny s kukačkou**	hod^{y}ini skookachkoh
cuff links	**manžetové knoflíky**	manzhetoveh knofleeki
cutlery	**příbory**	przheebori
earrings	**náušnice**	nahooshn^{y}etse
gem	**drahokam**	dra-hokam
jewel box	**šperkovnici**	shperkovn^{y}itsi
music box	**krabičku s hudebním strojkem**	krabichkoo shoodebn^{y}eem stroykem
necklace	**náhrdelník**	nah-h^{u}rdeln^{y}eek
pendant	**přívěšek**	przheevyeshek
pin	**špendlík**	shpendleek
pocket watch	**kapesní hodinky**	kapesn^{y}ee hod^{y}inki
powder compact	**pudřenku**	poodrzhenkoo
propelling pencil	**propisovací tužku**	propisovatsee tooshkoo

ring	**prsten**	p^{u}rsten
engagement ring	**zásnubní**	zahsnoobn^{y}ee
signet ring	**pečetní**	pechet^{y}n^{y}ee
wedding ring	**snubní**	snoobn^{y}ee
rosary	**růženec**	r$\overline{oo}$zhenets
silverware	**stříbrné zboží**	st^{u}rzheeb^{u}rneh zbozhee
tie clip	**přesku do kravaty**	przheskoo dokravati
tie pin	**jehlice do kravaty**	ye-hlitse dokravati
watch	**hodinky**	hod^{y}inki
automatic	**automatické**	aootomatitskeh
digital	**digitální**	digitahln^{y}ee
quartz	**quartz**	kvart-ts
with a second hand	**se vteřinovou ručičkou**	sfterzhinovoh roochichkoh
waterproof	**vodotěsné**	vodot^{y}esneh
watchstrap	**řemínek na hodinky**	rzhemeenek na hod^{y}inki
wristwatch	**náramkové hodinky**	nahramkoveh hod^{y}inki

amber	**jantar**	yantar
amethyst	**ametyst**	ametist
chromium	**chróm**	chrōm
copper	**měď**	mn^{y}et^{y}
coral	**korál**	korahl
crystal	**křišťál**	krzhisht^{y}ahl
cut glass	**broušené sklo**	brohsheneh sklo
diamond	**diamant**	diyamant
emerald	**smaragd**	smaragt
enamel	**email**	ema-yl
gold	**zlato**	zlato
gold plate	**pozlacení**	pozlatsen^{y}ee
ivory	**slonovina**	slonovina
jade	**nefrit**	nefrit
onyx	**onyx**	oniks
pearl	**perla**	perla
pewter	**starý cín**	staree tseen
platinum	**platina**	platina
ruby	**rubín**	roobeen
sapphire	**safír**	safeer
silver	**stříbro**	strzheebro
silver plate	**postříbření**	postrzheebrzhen^{y}ee
stainless steel	**nerez**	nerez
topaz	**topaz**	topas
turquoise	**tyrkys**	tirkis

Optician *Optik*

I've broken my glasses.	**Rozbil(a) jsem své brýle.**	rozbil(a) ysem sveh breel-e
Can you repair them for me?	**Můžete mi je spravit?**	m$\overline{oo}$zhete mi ye spravit
When will they be ready?	**Kdy budou hotové?**	gdi boodoh hotoveh
Can you change the lenses?	**Můžete mi vyměnit čočky?**	m$\overline{oo}$zhete mi vimn^{y}en^{y}it chochki
I'd like tinted lenses.	**Chtěl(a) bych tónované čočky.**	kht^{y}el(a) bikh tōnovaneh chochki
The frame is broken.	**Obroučka je zlomená.**	obrohchka ye zlomenah
I'd like a spectacle case.	**Chtěl(a) bych pouzdro na brýle.**	kht^{y}el(a) bikh pohzdro na breele
I'd like to have my eyesight checked.	**Chci si nechat zkontrolovat oči.**	kh-tsi si nekhat skontrolovat ochi
I'm short-sighted/ long-sighted.	**Jsem krátkozraký (-ká)/dalekozraký (-ká).**	ysem krahtkozrakee(-kah)/ dalekozrakee(-kah)
I'd like some contact lenses.	**Chtěl(a) bych kontaktní čočky.**	kht^{y}el(a) bikh kontaktn^{y}ee chochki
I've lost one of my contact lenses.	**Ztratil(a) jsem jednu kontaktní čočku.**	strat^{y}il(a) ysem yednoo kontaktn^{y}ee chochkoo
Could you give me another one?	**Můžete mi dát ještě jednu?**	m$\overline{oo}$zhete mi daht yesht^{y}e yednoo
I have hard/soft lenses.	**Nosím tvrdé/ měkké čočky.**	noseem tv^{u}rdeh/mn^{y}ekeh chochki
Do you have any contact-lens fluid?	**Máte roztok pro kontaktní čočky?**	mahte rostok pro kontaktn^{y}ee chochki
I'd like to buy a pair of sunglasses.	**Chci si koupit sluneční brýle.**	kh-tsi si kohpit sloonechn^{y}ee breele
May I look in a mirror?	**Můžu se podívat do zrcadla?**	m$\overline{oo}$zhoo se pod^{y}eevat doz^{u}rtsadla
I'd like to buy a pair of binoculars.	**Já bych si chtěl(a) koupit dalekohled.**	yah bikh si kht^{y}el(a) kohpit daleko-hlet

Photography *Fotografování*

I'd like a(n) ... camera.	**Chtěl(a) bych ... fotoaparát.**	kht^{y}el(a) bikh ... fotoaparaht
automatic	**automatický**	aootomatitskee
inexpensive	**laciný**	latsinee
simple	**jednoduchý**	yednodookhee
Can you show me some ..., please?	**Můžete mi ukázat nějaké ...?**	mo͞ozhete mi ookahzat n^{y}eyakeh
cine (movie) cameras	**filmové kamery**	filmoveh kameri
video cameras	**videokamery**	videokameri
I'd like to have some passport photos taken.	**Potřebuji fotografie na pas.**	potrzhebooye fotografiye napas

Film *Film*

I'd like a film for this camera.	**Chtěl(a) bych film pro tento fotoaparát.**	kht^{y}el(a) bikh film pro tento fotoaparaht
black and white	**černo-bílý**	chernobeelee
colour	**barevný**	barevnee
colour negative	**barevné negativy**	barevneh negativi
colour slide	**diapozitivy**	diyapoziteevy
cartridge	**kazetu**	kazetoo
disc film	**diskový film**	diskovee film
roll film	**svitkový film**	svitkovee film
video cassette	**video kazetu**	videokazetoo
24/36 exposures	**dvacet čtyři/třicet šest snímků**	dvatset chtirzhi/trzhitset shest sn^{y}eemko͞o
this size	**tuto velikost**	tooto velikost
this ASA/DIN number	**tohle ASA/DIN číslo**	to-hle ASA/DIN cheeslo
artificial light type	**pro umělé světlo**	pro-umn^{y}ekch svyetlo
daylight type	**pro denní světlo**	proden^{y}ee svyetlo
fast (high-speed)	**rychlý**	rikhlee
fine grain	**jemnozrnný**	yemnoz^{u}rnee

Processing *Vyvolání*

How much do you charge for processing?	**Kolik stojí vyvolání?**	kolik stoyee vivolahn^{y}ee

I'd like ... prints of each negative.	**Chtěl(a) bych ... kopie všech negativů.**	kht^{y}el(a) bikh...kopiye fshekh negativoo
with a matt finish	**matné**	matneh
with a glossy finish	**lesklé**	leskleh
Will you enlarge this, please?	**Můžete tohle, prosím, zvětšit?**	moozhete to-hle proseem zvyetshit
When will the photos be ready?	**Kdy budou ty fotografie hotové?**	gdi boodoh ti fotografiye hotoveh

Accessories and repairs *Příslušenství a opravy*

I'd like a/an/some ...	**Chtěl(a) bych ...**	kht^{y}el(a) bikh
battery	**baterie**	batiriye
cable release	**dálkovou spoušť**	dahlkovoh spohsht^{y}
camera case	**pouzdro na fotoaparát**	pohzdro nafotoaparaht
(electronic) flash	**(elektronický) blesk**	(elektronitskee) blesk
filter	**filter**	filtr
for black and white	**pro černobílý**	prochernobeelee
for colour	**pro barvu**	probarvoo
lens	**objektiv**	obyekteef
telephoto lens	**teleobjektiv**	teleobyektif
wide-angle lens	**širokoúhlý objektiv**	shirokooo-hlee obyekteef
lens cap	**víčko objektivu**	veechko obyekteevoo
Can you repair this camera?	**Můžete opravit tento fotoaparát?**	moozhete opravit tento fotoaparaht
The film is jammed.	**Film je zablokovaný.**	film ye zablokovanee
There's something wrong with the ...	**Nefunguje ...**	nefoongooye
exposure counter	**počítač snímků**	pocheetach sn^{y}eemkoo
film winder	**přetáčení filmu**	przhetahchen^{y}ee filmoo
flash attachment	**připevnění blesku**	przhipevn^{y}en^{y}ee bleskoo
lens	**objektiv**	obyekteef
light meter	**expozimetr**	ekspozimet^{u}r
rangefinder	**dálkoměr**	dahlkomn^{y}er
shutter	**spoušť**	spohsht^{y}

NUMBERS, see page 147

Tobacconist's *Tabák*

Cigarettes and tobacco are sold in tobacconist shops (*tabák*), at newspaper kiosks and often in many bars and pubs. Restrictions on smoking in public places are becoming more widespread, including on public transport (except the smoking section on trains), cinemas and theatres and in restaurants between 11 a.m. and 2 p.m.

A packet of cigarettes, please.	**Prosím krabičku cigaret.**	proseem krabichkoo tsigaret
Do you have any American/English cigarettes?	**Máte nějaké americké/anglické cigarety?**	mahte n^{y}eyakeh ameritskeh/anglitskeh tsigareti
I'd like a carton.	**kartón**	kartōn
Give me a/some ..., please.	**Dejte mi, prosím, nějaké ...**	deyte mi proseem n^{y}eyakeh
candy	**bonbóny**	bonbōni
chewing gum	**žvýkačku**	zhveekachkoo
chewing tobacco	**žvýkací tabák**	zhveekatsee tabahk
chocolate	**čokoládu**	chokolahdoo
cigarette case	**pouzdro na cigarety**	pohzdro na tsigareti
cigarette holder	**cigaretovou špičku**	tsigaretovoh shpichkoo
cigarettes	**cigarety**	tsigareti
filter-tipped/ without filter	**s filtrem/bez filtru**	sfiltrem/besfiltroo
light/dark tobacco	**světlý/tmavý tabák**	svyetlee/tmavee tabahk
mild/strong	**slabé/silné**	slabeh/silneh
menthol	**mentolové**	mentoloveh
king-size	**prodloužené**	prodlohzheneh
cigars	**doutníky**	dohtn^{y}eeki
lighter	**zapalovač**	zapalovach
lighter fluid/ gas	**náplň do zapalovače**	nahpln^{y} do zapalovache
matches	**zápalky**	zahpalki
pipe	**dýmka**	deemka
pipe cleaners	**čistič na dýmku**	chistich nadeemkoo
pipe tobacco	**dýmkový tabák**	deemkovee tabahk
pipe tool	**dýmkový nastroj**	deemkovee nastroy
postcard	**pohled**	po-hlet
snuff	**šňupavý tabák**	shn^{y}noopavee tabahk
stamps	**známky**	znahmki
sweets	**bonbóny**	bonbōni
wick	**knot**	knot

Miscellaneous *Rozmanitosti*

Souvenirs *Suvenýry*

For most gift buyers, the Czech republic means crystal and glassware. The best-known brand names are Moser and Bohemia, but like all crystal, they may be subject to customs duty. Leather goods, lace, dolls, embroidery, antiques, Bohemian garnets (*České granáty*) and costume jewellery also make popular purchases to take home.

Porcelain is another promising area; and don't overlook a bottle of *Becherovka*, the aperitif from Karlovy Vary, and *slivovice* (plum brandy).

antique	**starožitnost**	starozhitnost^{y}
art book	**kniha o umění**	kni-ha o oomn^{y}en^{y}ee
ceramics	**keramika**	keramika
chocolate	**čokoláda**	chokolahda
crystal	**křišťál**	krzhisht^{y}ahl
doll	**panna**	pana
embroidery	**výšivka**	veeshivka
glassware	**sklo**	sklo
handicrafts	**ruční práce**	roochnee prahche
jewellery	**klenoty**	klenoti
lace	**krajka**	krayka
leather	**kůže**	k$\overline{oo}$zhe
marionette	**loutka**	lohtka
porcelain	**porcelán**	portselahn
second-hand books	**antikvární knihy**	knihi
sportswear	**sportovní zboží**	sportovnee zbozhee
stoneware	**kamenina**	kamenina

Records—Cassettes *Gramofonové desky—Kazety*

Discs and tapes, particularly abundant in Prague, make interesting souvenirs: there will be a wide choice of locally produced classical, opera, folklore and pop music.

I'd like a ...	**Chtěl(a) bych ...**	kht^{y}el(a) bikh
cassette	**kazetu**	kazetoo
video cassette	**videokazetu**	videokazetoo
compact disc	**kompaktní disk**	kompaktn^{y}ee disk

L.P.(33 rpm)	**dlouhohrající desku**	dloh-ho-hra-yeetsee deskoo
E.P.(45 rpm)	**malou desku**	maloh deskoo
single	**singl**	sing^{u}l

Do you have any records by...?	**Máte nějaké desky od...?**	mahte n^{y}eyakeh deski ot
Can I listen to this record?	**Můžu si poslechnout tuto desku?**	mo͞ozhoo si poslekhnoht tooto deskoo
chamber music	**komorní hudba**	komorn^{y}ee hoodba
classical music	**klasická hudba**	klasitskah hoodba
folk music	**lidová hudba**	lidovah hoodba
folk song	**lidová písnička**	lidovah peesn^{y}ichka
instrumental music	**instrumentální hudba**	instroomentahln^{y}ee hoodba
jazz	**džez**	dzhes
light music	**lehká hudba**	lekhkah hoodba
orchestral music	**orchestrální skladby**	orkhestrahln^{y}ee skladbi
pop music	**populární hudba**	popoolahrn^{y}ee hoodba

Toys *Hračky*

I'd like a toy/game...	**Chtěl(a) bych hračku/hru...**	kht^{y}el(a) bikh hrachkoo/ hroo
for a boy	**pro chlapce**	pro khlaptse
for a 5-year-old girl	**pro pětiletou holčičku**	pro pyet^{y}iletoh holchichkoo
(beach) ball	**míč (na pláž)**	meech (na plahsh)
bucket and spade (pail and shovel)	**kyblík a lopatku**	kibleek a lopatkoo
building blocks (bricks)	**stavební kostky**	stavebn^{y}ee kostki
card game	**karetní hru**	karetn^{y}ee hroo
chess set	**šachy**	shakhi
colouring book	**omalovánky**	omalovahnki
doll	**panenku**	panenkoo
electronic game	**elektronickou hru**	elektronitskoh hroo
roller skates	**kolečkové brusle**	kolechkoveh broosle
snorkel	**šnorkl**	snork^{u}l
toy cars	**autíčka**	aoot^{y}eechka
teddy bear	**medvídka**	medveetka

Your money: banks—currency

The basic unit of currency in the Czech and Slovak republics is the *koruna* (crown), abbreviated to Kčs. The koruna is divided into 100 hellers (hal.).

Coins: 5, 10, 20, 50, 10 hal., 1, 2, 5, 10 Kčs.
Notes: 10, 20, 50, 100, 500, 1,000 Kčs.

There is no restriction on the amount of foreign currency you're allowed to take into or out of the country and you may find American dollars, German Marks and British pounds useful for purchasing certain items or services. However, no Czech currency over 100 Kčs may be imported or exported.

Black market money changers are common in major tourist areas (often proposing *Tauschen*—the German word for exchange); but unofficial money changing is illegal.

Major tourist centres will accept the main international credit cards in shops, hotels, travel agencies and airlines: Access, American Express, Diners Club, Master Card and JCB. Just look for the sign on the door. Traveller's cheques and Eurocheques are also accepted, though you may be asked to show your passport when cashing these.

Official currency exchange offices (*směnárna*) can be found at the frontier, airport and in town at banks, travel agencies and hotels. When changing currency, you'll have to show your passport with currency exchange documents. Some staff usually speak English or German.

Where's the nearest bank?	**Kde je nejbližší banka?**	gde ye neyblishee banka
Where's the nearest currency exchange office?	**Kde je nejbližší směnárna?**	gde ye neyblishee smn^{y}enahrna

At the bank *V bance*

Banks are usually open from 8.00 a.m. to 5.00 p.m. Monday to Friday and on Saturday mornings. They will generally offer a better rate of exchange than currency exchange offices.

I want to change some dollars/pounds.	**Chci si vyměnit nějaké dolary/libry.**	kh-tsi si vimn^{y}en^{y}it n^{y}eyakeh dolari/libri
I want to cash a traveller's cheque.	**Chci si vyměnit cestovní šek.**	kh-tsi si vimn^{y}en^{y}et tsestovn^{y}ee shek
What's the exchange rate?	**Jaký je dnes kurs?**	yakee ye dnes koors
How much commission do you charge?	**Kolik se platí poplatek?**	kolik se plat^{y}ee poplatek
Can you cash a personal cheque?	**Můžete mi vyplatit osobní šek?**	mo͞ozhete mi viplat^{y}it osobn^{y}ee shek
Can you telex my bank in London?	**Můžete poslat telex mé bance v Londýně?**	mo͞ozhete poslat teleks meh bantse vlondeen^{y}e
I have a/an/some ...	**Mám ...**	mahm
credit card	**úvěrovou kartu**	o͞ovyerovoh kartoo
Eurocheques	**Eurošek**	eooroshek
letter of credit	**doporučující dopis**	doporoochooyeetsee dopis
I'm expecting some money from New York. Has it arrived?	**Čekám peníze z New Yorku. Už přišly?**	chekahm pen^{y}eeze zn^{y}oo yorkoo. oosh przhishli
Please give me ... notes (bills) and some small change.	**Dejte mi prosím ... bankovkách a nějaké drobné.**	deyte mi proseem ... bankofkah-kh a n^{y}eyakeh drobneh
Give me ... large notes and the rest in small notes.	**Dejte mi ... me velkých bankovkách a ten zbytek v malých bankovkách.**	deyte mi ... me velkeekh bankofkah-kh a zbitek vmaleekh bankofkah-kh

Deposits—Withdrawals *Uložení—Vyzvednutí*

I want to ...	**Chci ...**	kh-tsi
open an account	**otevřít konto**	otevrzheet konto
withdraw ... koruna	**vyzvednout ... korun**	vizvednoht ... koroon
Where should I sign?	**Kde se mám podepsat?**	gde se mahm podepsat

NUMBERS, see page 147

I'd like to pay this into my account.	**Chci uložit peníze na mé konto.**	kh-tsi oolozhit pen^{y}eeze nameh konto

Business terms *Obchodní výrazy*

My name is ...	**Jmenuji se ...**	ymenooyi se
Here's my card.	**Tady je moje navštívenka.**	tadi ye moye nafsht^{y}eevenka
My company is ...	**Moje společnost je ...**	mo-ye spol^{y}echnost ye
I have an appointment with ...	**Mám domluvenou schůzku s ...**	mahm domloovenoh skhooskoo s
Can you give me an estimate of the cost?	**Můžete mi dát odhadní cenu?**	moozhete mi daht odhadn^{y}ee tsenoo
What's the rate of inflation?	**Kolik procent je inflace?**	kolik protsent ye inflatse
Can you provide me with an interpreter/ a secretary?	**Můžete mi sjednat tlumočníka/ sekretářku?**	moozhete mi syednat tloomochn^{y}eeka/ sekretahrzhkoo
Where can I make photocopies?	**Kde si můžu udělat fotokopie?**	gde si moozhoo ood^{y}elat fotokopiye

amount	**množství**	mnosh-stvee
balance	**bilance**	bilantse
capital	**kapitál**	kapitahl
cheque	**šek**	shek
contract	**smlouva**	smlohva
discount	**sleva**	sleva
expenses	**výlohy**	veelo-hi
interest	**úroky**	ooroki
investment	**investice**	investitse
invoice	**faktura**	faktoora
loss	**ztráta**	strahta
mortgage	**hypotéka**	hipotehka
payment	**splátka**	splahtka
percentage	**procenta**	protsenta
profit	**zisk**	zisk
purchase	**koupě**	kohpye
sale	**prodej**	prodey
share	**akcie**	aktsiye
transfer	**převod**	przhevot
value	**hodnota**	hodnota

At the post office

Czech post offices (*pošta*) handle mail, telegrams, telex and telephone services such as long distance calls between cities (*meziměstský hovor*). Postage stamps are also available where postcards are sold.
Post boxes are attached to buildings and have a distinctive livery: either orange with blue sides or all yellow.

The historic main post office in Prague at Jindřišská 14 is open 24 hours a day.

Where's the nearest post office?	**Kde je tady nejbližší pošta?**	gde ye tadi neyblishee poshta
What time does the post office open/close?	**V kolik hodin otevírají/zavírají na poště?**	fkolik hod^{y}in oteveerayee/zaveerayee na posht^{y}e
A stamp for this letter/postcard, please.	**Známku pro tento dopis/pohled, prosím.**	znahmkoo protento dopis/po-hlet proseem
A ... koruna stamp, please.	**... korunovou známku, prosím.**	... koroonovoh znahmkoo proseem
What's the postage for a letter to London?	**Kolik stojí dopis do Londýna?**	kolik stoyee dopis dolondeena
What's the postage for a postcard to Los Angeles?	**Kolik stojí pohled do Los Angeles?**	kolik stoyee po-hled dolos enzhelis
Where's the letter box (mailbox)?	**Kde je poštovní schránka?**	gde ye poshtovn^{y}ee skhrahnka
I want to send this parcel.	**Chci poslat tento balíček.**	kh-tsi poslat tento baleechek

ODESÍLATEL	SENDER

I'd like to send this (by) . . .	**Chci tohle poslat . . .**	kh-tsi to-hle poslat
airmail	**leteckou poštou**	letetskoh poshtoh
express (special delivery)	**expres**	ekspres
registered mail	**doporučeně**	doporoochen^{y}e
At which counter can I cash an international money order?	**Ukteré přepážky mi mohou vyplatit mezinárodní peněžní poukázku?**	ooktereh przhepahzhki mohoh viplat^{y}it mezinahrodn^{y}ee pen^{y}ezhn^{y}ee po-ookahskoo
Where's the poste restante (general delivery)?	**Kde je Poste Restante?**	gde ye poste restante
Is there any post (mail) for me? My name is . . .	**Je tu pro mne nějaká pošta? Jmenuji se . . .**	ye too promne n^{y}eyakah poshta? ymenooyi se

ZNÁMKY	STAMPS
BALÍKY	PARCELS
PENĚŽNY POUKÁZKY	MONEY ORDERS

Telegrams—Telex—Fax *Telegramy—Telexy—Telefaxy*

Telegrams may be sent from any post office and most hotels, while a telex and fax service is offered by main post offices and principal hotels.

I'd like to send a telegram/telex.	**Já chci poslat telegram/telex.**	kh-tsi poslat telegram/telex
May I have a form, please?	**Máte na to formulář?**	mahte na-to formoolahrzh
How much is it per word?	**Kolik stojí jedno slovo?**	kolik stoyee yedno slovo
How long will a cable to Boston take?	**Jak dlouho půjde telegram do Bostonu?**	yak dloh-ho pōōyde telegram dobostnoo
How much will this telex (fax) cost?	**Kolik bude ten telex (telefax) stát?**	kolik boode ten teleks (telefaks) staht

Telephoning *Používání telefonu*

Coin-operated telephones (*telefonní automat na mince*) are found on the street, in metro stations and other public places. Two principal types of telephone are in operation. The simpler model, coloured yellow, can be used for local calls only. The basic coin valid in all machines is the 1 Kčs piece, but if the cash-box is full, your contribution will be rejected and the line cut.

For international calls avoiding problems with coins, try any post office, main railway station or your hotel. For small towns and villages, all long distance calls go through the exchange (*ústředna*).

Where's the telephone?	**Kde je tady telefon?**	gde ye tadi telefon
I'd like a telephone token.	**Chtěl(a) bych telefonní známku.**	kht^{y}el(a) bikh telefon^{y}ee znahmkoo
Where's the nearest telephone booth?	**Kde je tady nejbližší telefonní budka?**	gde ye tadi neyblishee telefon^{y}ee bootka
May I use your phone?	**Můžu si od vás zatelefonovat?**	mo͞ozhoo si odvahs zatelefonovat
Do you have a telephone directory for Prague?	**Máte telefonní seznam pro Prahu?**	mahte telefon^{y}ee seznam pro pra-hoo
I'd like to call ... in England.	**Chtěl(a) bych zavolat ... v Anglii.**	kh-t^{y}el(a) bikh zavolat ... f anglii
What's the dialling (area) code for ...?	**Jaký je volací kód do ...?**	yakee ye volatsee kōd do
How do I get the international operator?	**Jaké číslo mají mezinárodními hovory?**	yakeh cheeslo ma-yee mazinahrodn^{y}ee hovori

Operator *Telefonista*

I'd like Pilsen 23 45 67.	**Chci zavolat Plžeň dvacet tři čtyřicet pět šedesát sedm.**	kh-tsi zavolat p^{u}lzen^{y} dvatset trzhi chtirzhitset pyet shedesaht sedm
Can you help me get this number?	**Můžete mě spojit s tímto číslem?**	mo͞ozhete mn^{y}e spoyit st^{y}eemto cheeslem

NUMBERS, see page 147

I'd like to place a personal (person-to-person) call.	**Chci objednat osobní hovor.**	kh-tsi obyednat osobn^{y}ee hovor
I'd like to reverse the charges (call collect).	**Chci mít hovor na účet volaného.**	kh-tsi meet hovor naoochet volaneh-ho

Speaking *Prosím!*

Hello. This is ...	**Haló. Tady je ...**	halō. tadi ye
I'd like to speak to ...	**Mohl(a) bych mluvit s ...**	mo-h^{u}l (mo-hla) bikh mloovit s
Give me extension ... please.	**Prosím dejte mi linku ...**	proseem deyte mi linkoo
Speak louder/more slowly, please.	**Mohl[a] byste mluvit hlasitěji/ pomaleji?**	mo-h^{u}l [mo-hla] bis-te mloovit hlasit^{y}eyi/pomaleyi

Not there *Není tady*

Would you try again later, please?	**Můžete to prosím zkusit později?**	moozhete to proseem skoosit pozd^{y}eyi

Telephone alphabet

A	**Adam**	adam	O	**Oto**	oto
B	**Božena**	bozhena	P	**Petr**	petr
C	**Cyril**	tsiril	Q	**Quido**	koovido
D	**David**	davit	R	**Rudolf**	roodolf
'D	**'Dumbier**	d^{y}oombyer	Ř	**Řehoř**	řzhe-hoř
E	**Emil**	emil	S	**Svatopluk**	svatoplook
F	**František**	frant^{y}ishek	Š	**Šimon**	shimon
G	**Gustav**	goostaf	T	**Tomáš**	tomahsh
H	**Helena**	helena	T'	**T'eplá**	t^{y}eplah
I	**Ivan**	ivan	U	**Urban**	oorban
J	**Josef**	yozef	V	**Václav**	vah-tslaf
K	**Karel**	karel	W	**dvojité vé**	dvoyiteh veh
L	**Ludvík**	loodveek	X	**Xaver**	ksaver
L'	**L'ubochňa**	lyoobokhn^{y}a	Y	**ypsilon**	ipsilon
M	**Marie**	mariye	Z	**Zuzana**	zoozana
N	**Norbert**	norbert	Ž	**Žofie**	zhofiye

Operator, you gave me the wrong number.	**Dal jste mi špatné číslo.**	dal yste mi shpatneh cheeslo
Operator, we were cut off.	**Nás někdo přerušil.**	nahs n^{y}egdo przherooshil
When will he/she be back?	**Kdy se vrátí?**	gdi se vraht^{y}ee
Will you tell him /her I called?	**Mohl[a] byste mu/ jí říct, že jsem telefonoval?**	mo-h^{u}l [mo-hla] bis-te moo/ yee rzheets-t zhe ysem telefonoval
Would you ask him/ her to call me?	**Mohl/mohla by mi zavolat?**	mo-h^{u}l/mo-hla bi mi zavolat
Would you give him/ her a message, please?	**Můžete mu/jí vyřídit zprávu?**	m$\overline{oo}$zhete moo/yee virzheed^{y}it zprahvoo

Charges *Poplatky*

What was the cost of that call?	**Kolik stál ten hovor?**	kolik stahl ten hovor
I want to pay for the call.	**Chci platit za ten hovor.**	kh-tsi plat^{y}it zaten hovor

Je tady pro vás telefon.	There's a telephone call for you.
Které číslo voláte?	What number are you calling?
Je to obsazené.	The line's engaged.
Nikdo neodpovídá.	There's no answer.
Máte špatné číslo.	You've got the wrong number.
Ten telefon nefunguje.	The phone is out of order.
Malý moment.	Just a moment.
Prosím čekejte.	Hold on, please.
On/Ona tady momentálne není.	He's/She's out at the moment.

Doctor

The Czech National Health Service is well equipped to handle any unexpected problems. Emergency medical treatment is free of charge, but you will have to pay for medicines. Many Czech doctors and dentists also have private practices.

General *Všeobecné informace*

Can you get me a doctor?	**Můžete mi sehnat lékaře?**	mo͞ozhete mi se-hnat lehkarzhe
Is there a doctor here?	**Je tady lékař?**	ye tadi lehkarzh
I need a doctor, quickly.	**Potřebuji rychle lékaře.**	potrzhebooyi rikhle lehkarzhe
Where can I find a doctor who speaks English?	**Jak najdu lékaře který mluví anglicky?**	yak na-ydoo lehkarzhe kteree mloovee anglitski
Where's the surgery (doctor's office)?	**Kde je lékařská ordinace?**	gde ye lehkarzhskah ordinatse
What are the surgery (office) hours?	**Jaké jsou ordinační hodiny?**	yakeh ysoh ordinachn^{y}ee hod^{y}ini
Could the doctor come to see me here?	**Mohl by lékař přijít ke mě?**	mo-hl bi lehkarzh przhiyeet kemn^{y}e
What time can the doctor come?	**V kolik hodin přijde lékař?**	fkolik hod^{y}in przhiyde lehkarzh
Can you recommend a/an ...?	**Můžete mi doporučit ...?**	mo͞ozhete mi doporoochit
general practitioner	**rodinného lékaře**	rod^{y}ineh-ho lehkarzhe
children's doctor	**dětského lékaře**	d^{y}et-skeh-ho lehkarzhe
eye specialist	**očního specialistu**	ochn^{y}ee-ho spetsialistoo
gynaecologist	**gynekologa**	ginekologa
Can I have an appointment ...?	**Můžu se objednat na ...?**	mo͞ozhoo se obyednat na
tomorrow	**zítra**	zeetra
as soon as possible	**co nejdřív**	tso neydrzheef

CHEMIST'S, see page 107

Parts of the body *Části těla*

appendix	**slepé střevo**	slepeh strzhevo
arm	**paže**	pazhe
back	**záda**	zahda
bladder	**močový měchýř**	mochovee mn^{y}ekheerzh
bone	**kost**	kost
bowel	**střeva**	strzheva
breast	**prs**	p^{u}rs
chest	**hrudník**	hrudn^{y}eek
ear	**ucho**	ookho
eye(s)	**oko**	oko
face	**obličej**	oblichey
finger	**prst**	p^{u}rst
foot	**chodidlo**	khod^{y}idlo
genitals	**přirození**	przhirozen^{y}ee
gland	**žláza**	zhlahza
hand	**ruka**	rooka
head	**hlava**	hlava
heart	**srdce**	s^{u}rtse
jaw	**čelist**	chelist
joint	**kloub**	klohp
kidney	**ledviny**	ledvini
knee	**koleno**	koleno
leg	**noha**	no-ha
ligament	**šlacha**	shlakha
lip	**ret**	ret
liver	**játra**	yahtra
lung	**plíce**	pleetse
mouth	**ústa**	$\overline{oo}$sta
muscle	**sval**	sval
neck	**krk**	k^{u}rk
nerve	**nerv**	nerf
nervous system	**nervový systém**	nervovee sistehm
nose	**nos**	nos
rib	**žebro**	zhebro
shoulder	**rameno**	rameno
skin	**kůže**	k$\overline{oo}$zhe
spine	**páteř**	pahterzh
stomach	**žaludek**	zhaloodek
tendon	**šlacha**	shlakha
thigh	**stehno**	ste-hno
throat	**hrdlo**	h^{u}rdlo
thumb	**palec**	palets
toe	**prst u nohy**	p^{u}rst oo no-hi
tongue	**jazyk**	yazik
tonsils	**mandle**	mandle
vein	**žíla**	zheela

Accident—Injury *Nehoda—Zranění*

There's been an accident.	**Tady se stala nehoda.**	tadi se stala ne-hoda
My child has had a fall.	**Moje dítě upadlo.**	moye d^{y}eet^{y}e oopadlo
He (she) has hurt his (her) head.	**Uhodil(a) se do hlavy.**	oo-hod^{y}il(a) se dohlavi
He's/She's unconscious.	**Je v bezvědomí.**	ye v bezvyedomee
He's/She's bleeding (heavily).	**Krvácí (těžce).**	krvahtsee (t^{y}eshtse)
He's/She's (seriously) injured.	**Je (vážně) zraněný/ zraněná.**	ye (vahzhn^{y}e) zran^{y}enee/ zran^{y}enah
His/Her arm is broken.	**Má zlomenou ruku.**	mah zlomenoh rookoo
His/Her ankle is swollen.	**Má nateklý kotník.**	mah nateklee kotn^{y}eek
I've been stung.	**Mne něco štíplo.**	mn^{y}e n^{y}etso sht^{y}eeplo
I've got something in my eye.	**Mám něco v oku.**	mahm n^{y}etso f okoo
I've got a/an ...	**Mám ...**	mahm
blister	**puchýř**	pookheerzh
boil	**vřed**	vrzhet
bruise	**modřinu**	modrzhinoo
burn	**spáleninu**	spahlen^{y}inoo
cut	**říznutí**	rzheeznoot^{y}ee
graze	**odřeninu**	odrzhen^{y}inoo
insect bite	**štípnutí**	sht^{y}eepnoot^{y}ee
lump	**bouli**	bohli
rash	**vyrážku**	virahshkoo
sting	**žihadlo**	zhihadlo
swelling	**otok**	otok
wound	**ránu**	rahnoo
Could you have a look at it?	**Můžete se na to podívat?**	m$\overline{oo}$zhete se nato pod^{y}eevat
I can't move my ...	**Nemůžu hýbat mojí ...**	nem$\overline{oo}$zhoo heebat moh
It hurts.	**To bolí.**	to bolee

Kde to bolí?	Where does it hurt?
Jaký je to druh bolesti?	What kind of pain is it?
tupý/ostrý/pulsující	dull/sharp/throbbing
trvalá/přijde a odejde	constant/on and off
Je to ...	It's ...
zlomené/vyvrtnuté	broken/sprained
vykloubené/ natržené	dislocated/torn
Nejlepší to bude rentgenovat.	I'd like you to have an X-ray.
Musíme to dát do sádry.	We'll have to put it in plaster.
Je to zanícené.	It's infected.
Měl[a] jste protitetanovou injekci?	Have you been vaccinated against tetanus?
Dám vám prášek proti bolesti.	I'll give you a painkiller.

Illness *Nemoc*

I'm not feeling well.	**Necítím se dobře.**	netseet^{y}eem se dobrzhe
I'm ill.	**Jsem nemocný.**	ysem nemotsnee
I feel dizzy.	**Mám závrat'.**	mahm zahvrat^y
I feel nauseous.	**Mně je špatně od žaludku.**	mn^{y}e ye shpatn^{y}e odzhalootkoo
I feel shivery.	**Třesu se.**	trzhesoo-se
I have a temperature (fever).	**Mám teplotu.**	mahm teplotoo
My temperature is 38 degrees.	**Mám třicet osm stupňů.**	mahm trzhitset osoom stoopn$^y\overline{oo}$
I've been vomiting.	**Zvracel(a) jsem.**	zvratsel(a) ysem
I'm constipated/ I've got diarrhoea.	**Mám zácpu/ průjem.**	mahm zahtspoo/pr$\overline{oo}$yem
My ... hurt(s).	**Bolí mě ...**	bolee mn^{y}e

I've got (a/an) ...	**Mám ...**	mahm
asthma	**astma**	astma
backache	**bolavá záda**	bolavah zahda
cold	**rýmu**	reemoo
cough	**kašel**	kashel
cramps	**křeče**	krzheche
earache	**bolest v uchu**	bolest f ookhoo
hay fever	**senou rýmu**	senoh reemoo
headache	**bolesti hlavy**	bolest^{y}i hlavi
indigestion	**potíže s trávením**	pot^{y}eezhe strahven^{y}eem
nosebleed	**krvácení z nosu**	krvahtsen^{y}ee snosoo
palpitations	**palpitace**	palpitat-se
rheumatism	**revmatismus**	revmatizmoos
sore throat	**bolesti v krku**	bolest^{y}i fk^{u}rkoo
stiff neck	**ztrnulý krk**	st^{u}rnoolee k^{u}rk
stomach ache	**bolesti žaludku**	bolest^{y}i zhalootkoo
sunstroke	**sluneční úpal**	sloonechn^{y}ee o͞opal
I have difficulties breathing.	**Mám potíže s dýcháním.**	mahm pot^{y}eezhe zdeekhahn^{y}eem
I have chest pains.	**Mám bolesti v hrudníku.**	mahm bolest^{y}i vhroodn^{y}eekoo
I had a heart attack ... years ago.	**Měl(a) jsem infarkt před ... lety.**	mn^{y}el(a) ysem infarkt przhet ... leti
My blood pressure is too high/too low.	**Mám vysoký/nízký krevní tlak.**	mahm visokee/n^{y}eeskee krevn^{y}ee tlak
I'm allergic to ...	**Jsem alergický na ...**	ysem alergitskee na
I'm diabetic.	**Jsem diabetik.**	ysem diabetik

Women's section *U gynekologa*

I have period pains.	**Mám bolestivé měsíčky.**	mahm bolest^{y}iveh mn^{y}eseechki
I have a vaginal infection.	**Mám vaginální infekci.**	mahm vaginahln^{y}ee infektsi
I'm on the pill.	**Používám antikoncepční pilulku.**	po-oozheevahm antikontsepchn^{y}ee piloolki
I haven't had a period for 2 months.	**Už dva měsíce nemám měsíčky.**	oozh dva mn^{y}eseetse nemahm mn^{y}eseechki
I'm (3 months) pregnant.	**Jsem (tři měsíce) v jiném stavu.**	ysem (trzhi mn^{y}eseetse) v yinehm stavoo

Jak dlouho se takto cítíte?	How long have you been feeling like this?
Stalo se to poprvé?	Is this the first time you've had this?
Změřím vám teplotu/krevní tlak.	I'll take your temperature/ blood pressure.
Vyhrňte si, prosím, rukáv.	Roll up your sleeve, please.
Prosím, vysvlečte se (do pasu).	Please undress (down to the waist).
Lehněte si, prosím, tady.	Please lie down over here.
Otevřete ústa.	Open your mouth.
Dýchejte z hluboka.	Breathe deeply.
Zakašlete, prosím.	Cough, please.
Kde to bolí?	Where does it hurt?
Máte ...	You've got (a/an) ...
zánět slepého střeva	appendicitis
zánět močového měchýře	cystitis
gastritidu	gastritis
chřipku	flu
zánět ...	inflammation of ...
otravu z jídla	food poisoning
žloutenku	jaundice
pohlavní nemoc	venereal disease
zápal plic	pneumonia
spalničky	measles
To je (není) nakažlivé.	It's (not) contagious.
To je alergie.	It's an allergy.
Dám vám injekci.	I'll give you an injection.
Potřebuji ukázku krve/ stolice/ moči.	I want a specimen of your blood/stools/urine.
Musíte zůstat v posteli ... dnů.	You must stay in bed for ... days.
Doporučím vás ke specialistovi.	I want you to see a specialist.
Pošlu vás do nemocnice na celkovou prohlídku.	I want you to go to the hospital for a general check-up.

Prescription—Treatment *Lékařský předpis—Ošetření*

This is my usual medicine.	**Tohle je můj normální lék.**	to-hle ye mooy normahln^{y}ee lehk
Can you give me a prescription for this?	**Můžete mi dát předpis na tohle?**	moozhete mi daht przhetpis nato-hle
Can you prescribe a/an/some ...?	**Můžete mi předepsat ...?**	moozhete mi przhedepsat ...
antidepressant	**prášky proti depresi**	prahshki prot^{y}i depresi
sleeping pills	**prášky na spaní**	prahshkee naspanee
tranquillizer	**utišující prostředek**	oot^{y}ishooyeetsee prostrzhedek
I'm allergic to certain antibiotics/penicillin.	**Jsem alergický na určitá antibiotika/penicilín.**	ysem alergitskee na oorchitah antibiyotika/penitsileen
I don't want anything too strong.	**Nechci nic silného.**	nekh-tsi n^{y}its silneh-ho
How many times a day should I take it?	**Kolikrát denně to mám brát?**	kolikraht den^{y}e to mahm braht
Must I swallow them whole?	**Musím to spolknout celé?**	mooseem to spolknoht tseleh

Čím se momentálně léčíte?	What treatment are you having?
Jaké berete léky?	What medicine are you taking?
Jsou to injekce nebo prášky?	By injection or orally?
Berte ... lžičky tohoto léku ...	Take ... teaspoons of this medicine ...
Berte jeden prášek se skleničkou vody ...	Take one pill with a glass of water ...
každé ... hodiny	every ... hours
... krát denně	... times a day
před každým/po každém jídle	before/after each meal
ráno/večer	in the morning/at night
když Vás to bude bolet	if there is any pain
... dnů	for ... days

CHEMIST'S, see page 107

Fee *Poplatky*

How much do I owe you?	**Kolik jsem vám dlužen?**	kolik ysem vahm dloozhen
May I have a receipt for my health insurance?	**Můžete mi dát potv^{u}rzení pro mou zdravotní pojišťovnu?**	m$\overline{oo}$zhete mi daht potv^{u}rzen^{y}ee promoh zdravotn^{y}ee poyisht^{y}ovnoo
Can I have a medical certificate?	**Můžete mi dát zdravotní potvrzení?**	m$\overline{oo}$zhete mi daht zdravotn^{y}ee potv^{u}rzen^{y}ee
Would you fill in this health insurance form, please?	**Mohl[a] byste vyplnit tento formulář pro zdravotní pojištění?**	mo-h^{u}l [mo-hla] bis-te vip^{u}ln^{y}it tento formoolahrzh prozdravotn^{y}ee poyisht^{y}en^{y}ee

Hospital *Nemocnice*

Please notify my family.	**Dejte prosím vědět mé rodině.**	de-yte proseem vyed^{y}et meh rod^{y}in^{y}e
What are the visiting hours?	**Kdy jsou návštěvní hodiny?**	gdi ysoh nah-fsht^{y}evn^{y}ee hod^{y}ini
When can I get up?	**Kdy můžu vstát z postele?**	gdi m$\overline{oo}$zhoo fstaht s postele
When will the doctor come?	**Kdy přijde lékař?**	gdi przhiyde lehkarzh
I'm in pain.	**Mám bolesti.**	mahm bolest^{y}i
I can't eat/sleep.	**Nemůžu jíst/spát.**	nem$\overline{oo}$zhoo yeest/spaht
Where is the bell?	**Kde je zvonek?**	gde ye zvonek

nurse	**sestra**	sestra
patient	**pacient**	patsiyent
anaesthetic	**anestetikum**	anestetikoom
blood transfusion	**krevní transfuse**	krevn^{y}ee transf$\overline{oo}$ze
injection	**injekce**	in^{y}ektse
operation	**operace**	operatse
bed	**postel**	postel
bedpan	**lůžková mísa**	l$\overline{oo}$shkovah meesa
thermometer	**teploměr**	teplomn^{y}er

Dentist *Zubař*

Can you recommend a good dentist?	**Můžete mi doporučit dobrého zubaře?**	m$\overline{oo}$zhete mi doporoochit dobreh-ho zoobarzhe
Can I make an (urgent) appointment to see Dr . . .?	**Můžete mě (rychle) objednat k doktoru (doktorce) . . . ?**	m$\overline{oo}$zhete mn^{y}e (rikhle) obyednat k doktoroo (doktortse)
Couldn't you make it earlier?	**Není to možné dřív?**	nen^{y}ee to mozhneh drzheef
I have a broken tooth.	**Zlomil se mi zub.**	zlomil se mi zoop
I have toothache.	**Bolí mě zub.**	bolee mn^{y}e zoop
I have an abscess.	**Mám hnisavý zánět.**	mahm hn^{y}isavee zahn^{y}et
This tooth hurts.	**Tento zub bolí.**	tento zoob bolee
at the top at the bottom at the front at the back	**nahoře** **dole** **vepředu** **vzadu**	na-horzhe dole veprzhedoo vzadoo
Can you fix it temporarily?	**Můžete mi dát vložku?**	m$\overline{oo}$zhete mi daht vloshkoo
I don't want it pulled out.	**Nechci si ho nechat vytrhnout.**	nekh-tsi si ho nekhat vit^{u}rhnoht
Could you give me an anaesthetic?	**Můžete mi dát anestetikum?**	m$\overline{oo}$zhete mi dhat anestetikoom
I've lost a filling.	**Vypadla mi plomba.**	vipadla mi plomba
My gums . . .	**Mé dásně . . .**	meh dahsn^{y}e
are very sore are bleeding	**jsou moc bolestivé** **krvácí**	ysoh mots bolest^{y}iveh krvahtsee
I've broken my dentures.	**Zlomil se mi umělý chrup.**	zlomil se mi oomn^{y}elee khroop
Can you repair my dentures?	**Můžete mi spravit umělý chrup?**	m$\overline{oo}$zhete mi spravit umn^{y}elee khroop
When will they be ready?	**Kdy to bude hotové?**	gdi to boode hotoveh

Reference section

Where do you come from? *Odkud pocházíte?*

Africa	**Afrika**	afrika
Asia	**Asie**	aziye
Australia	**Austrálie**	aoostrahliye
Europe	**Evropa**	evropa
North America	**Severní Amerika**	severn^{y}ee amerika
South America	**Jižní Amerika**	yizhn^{y}ee amerika

Austria	**Rakousko**	rakohsko
Belgium	**Belgie**	belgiye
Bohemia	**Čechy**	che-khee
Canada	**Kanada**	kanada
China	**Čína**	cheena
Commonwealth of Independent States	**Svazu Nezavislých Republik**	svaz nezahvisleekh repooblik
Czech Republic	**Česká Republica**	cheskah repooblika
Denmark	**Dánsko**	dahnsko
England	**Anglie**	angliye
Finland	**Finsko**	finsko
France	**Francie**	frantsiye
Germany	**Německo**	n^{y}emetsko
Great Britain	**Velká Británie**	velkah britahniye
Greece	**Řecko**	rzhetsko
India	**Indie**	indiye
Ireland	**Irsko**	irsko
Israel	**Israelo**	izraelo
Italy	**Itálie**	itahliye
Japan	**Japonsko**	yaponsko
Moravia	**Morava**	morava
Netherlands	**Holandsko**	holansko
New Zealand	**Nový Zéland**	novee zehland
Norway	**Norsko**	norsko
Portugal	**Portugalsko**	portoogalsko
Russia	**Rusko**	roosko
Scotland	**Skotsko**	skot-sko
Slovakia	**Slovensko**	slovensko
South Africa	**Jižní Afrika**	yizhn^{y}ee afrika
Spain	**Španělsko**	shpan^{y}elsko
Sweden	**Švédsko**	shvehtsko
Switzerland	**Švýcarsko**	shveetsarsko
Turkey	**Turecko**	turetsko
Ukraine	**Ukrajina**	ookra-yina
United States	**Spojené Státy**	spoyeneekh stahti
Wales	**Wales**	velz

Numbers *Čísla*

0	**nula**	noola
1	**jedna**	yedna
2	**dvě**	dvye
3	**tři**	trzhi
4	**čtyři**	chtirzhi
5	**pět**	pyet
6	**šest**	shest
7	**sedm**	sedoom
8	**osm**	osoom
9	**devět**	devyet
10	**deset**	deset
11	**jedenáct**	yedenahts-t
12	**dvanáct**	dvanahts-t
13	**třináct**	trzhinahts-t
14	**čtrnáct**	cht^{u}rnahts-t
15	**patnáct**	patnahts-t
16	**šestnáct**	shestnahts-t
17	**sedmnáct**	sedoomnahts-t
18	**osmnáct**	osoomnahts-t
19	**devatenáct**	devatenahts-t
20	**dvacet**	dvatset
21	**dvacet jedna**	dvatset yedna
22	**dvacet dva**	dvatset dva
23	**dvacet tři**	dvatset trzhi
24	**dvacet čtyři**	dvatset chtirzhi
25	**dvacet pět**	dvatset pyet
26	**dvacet šest**	dvatset shest
27	**dvacet sedm**	dvatset sedoom
28	**dvacet osm**	dvatset osoom
29	**dvacet devět**	dvatset devyet
30	**třicet**	trzhitset
31	**třicet jedna**	trzhitset yedna
32	**třicet dva**	trzhitset dva
33	**třicet tři**	trzhitset trzhi
40	**čtyřicet**	chtirzhitset
41	**čtyřicet jedna**	chtirzhitset yedna
42	**čtyřicet dva**	chtirzhitset dva
43	**čtyřicet tři**	chtirzhitset trzhi
50	**padesát**	padesaht
51	**padesát jedna**	padesaht yedna
52	**padesát dva**	padesaht dva
53	**padesát tři**	padesaht trzhi
60	**šedesát**	shedesaht
61	**šedesát jedna**	shedesaht yedna
62	**šedesát dva**	shedesaht dva

63	**šedesát tři**	shedesaht trzhi
70	**sedmdesát**	sedoomdesaht
71	**sedmdesát jedna**	sedoomdesaht yedna
72	**sedmdesát dva**	sedoomdesaht dva
73	**sedmdesát tři**	sedoomdesaht trzhi
80	**osmdesát**	osoomdesaht
81	**osmdesát jedna**	osoomdesaht yedna
82	**osmdesát dva**	osoomdesaht dva
83	**osmdesát tři**	osoomdesaht trzhi
90	**devadesát**	devadesaht
91	**devadesát jedna**	devadesaht yedna
92	**devadesát dva**	devadesaht dva
93	**devadesát tři**	devadesaht trzhi
100	**sto**	sto
101	**sto jedna**	sto yedna
102	**sto dva**	sto dvye
110	**sto deset**	sto deset
120	**sto dvacet**	sto dvatset
130	**sto třicet**	sto trzhitset
140	**sto čtyřicet**	sto chtirzhitset
150	**sto padesát**	sto padesaht
160	**sto šedesát**	sto shedesaht
170	**sto sedmdesát**	sto sedoomdesaht
180	**sto osmdesát**	sto osoomdesaht
190	**sto devadesát**	sto devadesaht
200	**dvě stě**	dvye st^{y}e
300	**tři sta**	trzhi sta
400	**čtyři sta**	chtirzhi sta
500	**pět set**	pyet set
600	**šest set**	shest set
700	**sedm set**	sedoom set
800	**osm set**	osoom set
900	**devět set**	devyet set
1000	**tisíc**	t^{y}iseets
1100	**jedenáct set**	yedenahts set
1200	**dvanáct set**	dvanahts set
2000	**dva tisíce**	dva t^{y}iseetse
5000	**pět tisíc**	pyet t^{y}iseets
10,000	**deset tisíc**	deset t^{y}iseets
50,000	**padesát tisíc**	padesaht t^{y}iseets
100,000	**sto tisíc**	sto t^{y}iseets
1,000,000	**milión**	miliyōn
1,000,000,000	**bilión**	biliyōn

first	**první**	p^{u}rvn^{y}ee
second	**druhý**	droo-hee
third	**třetí**	trzhet^{y}ee
fourth	**čtvrtý**	ch^{u}tv^{u}rtee
fifth	**pátý**	pahtee
sixth	**šestý**	shestee
seventh	**sedmý**	sedmee
eighth	**osmý**	osmee
ninth	**devátý**	devahtee
tenth	**desátý**	desahtee
once/twice	**jednou/dvakrát**	yednoh/dvakraht
three times	**třikrát**	trzhikraht
a half	**půl**	p$\overline{oo}$l
half a ...	**půl ...**	p$\overline{oo}$l
half of ...	**půlka ...**	p$\overline{oo}$lka
half (adj.)	**poloviční**	polovichn^{y}ee
a quarter/one third	**čtvrtina/ třetina**	ch^{u}tv^{u}rt^{y}ina/trzhet^{y}ina
a pair of	**pár**	pahr
a dozen	**tucet**	tootset
one per cent	**jedno procento**	yedno protsento
3.4%	**tři celé čtyři desetiny procenta**	trzhi tseleh chtirzhi deset^{y}ini protsenta

Date and time *Datum a čas*

1981	**devatenát set osmdesát jedna**	devatenahts set osoomdesaht yedna
1993	**devatenát set devadesát tři**	devatenahts set devadesaht trzhi
2003	**dva tisíce tři**	dva t^{y}iseetse trzhi

Year and age *Rok a věk*

year	**rok**	rok
leap year	**přestupný rok**	przhestoopnee rok
decade	**desetiletí**	deset^{y}itet^{y}ee
century	**století**	stolet^{y}ee
this year	**tento rok**	tento rok
last year	**vloni**	vlon^{y}i
next year	**příští rok**	przheesht^{y}ee rok
each year	**každý rok**	kazhdee rok
2 years ago	**před lety**	przhed dvyema leti
in one year	**v jednom roce**	v yednom rotse
in the nineties	**v devadesátých letech**	v devadesahteekh letekh
the 16th century	**šestnácté století**	shestnahts-teh stolet^{y}ee
in the 20th century	**ve dvacátém století**	vedvatsahtehm stolet^{y}ee

How old are you?	**Kolik je vám let?**	kolik ye vahm let
I'm 30 years old.	**Je mi třicet let.**	ye mi trzhitset let
He (she) was born in 1960.	**Narodil(a) se v roce devatenáct set šedesát.**	narod^{y}il(a) se vrotse devatenahts-t set shedesaht
What is his/her age?	**Jak je starý/stará?**	yak ye staree/starah
Children under 16 are not admitted.	**Dětem do šestnácti let vstup zakázán.**	d^{y}etem do shestnah-ts-t^{y}i let fstoop zakahzahn

Seasons *Roční období*

spring/summer	**jaro/léto**	yaro/lehto
autumn/winter	**podzim/zima**	podzim/zima
in spring	**na jaře**	na yarzhe
during the summer	**během léta**	bye-hem lehta
in autumn	**na podzim**	napodzim
during the winter	**během zimy**	bye-hem zimi
high season	**sezóna**	sezōna
low season	**mimo sezónu**	mimo sezōnoo

Months *Měsíce*

January	**Leden**	leden
February	**Únor**	$\overline{oo}$nor
March	**Březen**	brzhezen
April	**Duben**	dooben
May	**Květen**	kvyeten
June	**Červen**	cherven
July	**Červenec**	chervenets
August	**Srpen**	s^{u}rpen
September	**Září**	zahrzhee
October	**Říjen**	rzheeyen
November	**Listopad**	listopat
December	**Prosinec**	prosinets
in September	**v září**	vzahrzhee
since October	**od října**	od rzheeyna
the beginning of January	**začátek ledna**	zachahtek ledna
the middle of February	**uprostřed února**	uprostrichet $\overline{oo}$nora
the end of March	**konec března**	konets brzhezna

Days and Date *Dny a Datum*

What day is it today?	**Co je dnes za den?**	tso ye dnes zaden
Sunday	**neděle**	ned^{y}ele
Monday	**pondělí**	pond^{y}elee
Tuesday	**úterý**	$\overline{oo}$teree
Wednesday	**středa**	strzheda
Thursday	**čtvrtek**	ch^{u}tv^{u}rtek
Friday	**pátek**	pahtek
Saturday	**sobota**	sobota
It's . . .	**Je . . .**	ye
July 1	**prvního července**	p^{u}rvn^{y}ee-ho cherventse
March 10	**desátého března**	desahteh-ho brzhezna
in the morning	**ráno**	rahno
during the day	**během dne**	bye-hem dne
in the afternoon	**odpoledne**	otpoledne
in the evening	**večer**	vecher
at night	**v noci**	*vnotsi
the day before yesterday	**předevčírem**	przhedefcheerem
yesterday	**včera**	vchera
today	**dnes**	dnes
tomorrow	**zítra**	zeetra
the day after tomorrow	**pozítří**	pozeetrzhee
the day before	**den před tím**	den przhet t^{y}eem
the next day	**příští den**	przheesht^{y}ee den
two days ago	**před dvěma dny**	przhed dvyema dni
in three days' time	**za tři dny**	zatrzhi dni
last week	**minulý týden**	minoolee teeden
next week	**příští týden**	przheesht^{y}ee teeden
for a fortnight (for two weeks)	**na čtrnáct dnů (na dva týdny)**	nach^{u}t^{u}rnahts-t dn$\overline{oo}$ (nadva teedni)
birthday	**narozeniny**	narozen^{y}ini
day off	**volný den**	volnee den
holiday	**prázdniny**	prahzdn^{y}ini
holidays/vacation	**prázdniny/ dovolená**	prahzdn^{y}ini/dovolenah
week	**týden**	teeden
weekend	**víkend**	veekent
working day	**pracovní den**	pratsovn^{y}ee den

Public holidays *Státní svátek*

Banks, offices and shops are closed on the following days:

January 1	**Nový rok**	New Year's Day
May 1	**Svátek práce**	May Day
May 9	**Vítězství nad fašismem**	Victory over Fascism
July 5	**Slóvanští věrozvěsti sv. Cyril a Metoděj**	Slavic Missionaries St. Cyril and St. Methodius
October 28	**První Československá republika**	First Czechoslovak Republic
December 24	**Štědrý den**	Christmas Eve
December 25-26	**Svátek vánoční**	Christmas/Boxing Day
Moveable date:	**Velikonoční pondělí**	Easter Monday

Greetings and wishes *Pozdravy a přání*

Merry Christmas!	**Veselé vánoce!**	veseleh vahnotse
Happy New Year!	**Štastný nový rok!**	sht^{y}astnee novee rok
Happy Easter!	**Veselé velikonoce!**	veseleh velikonotse
Happy birthday!	**Všechno nejlepší k narozeninám!**	fshekhno neylepshee k narozen^{y}inahm
Best wishes!	**Všechno nejlepší!**	fshekhno neylepshee
Congratulations!	**Gratuluji!**	gratoolooyi
Good luck/ All the best!	**Hodně štěstí!**	hodn^{y}e sht^{y}est^{y}ee
Have a good trip!	**Příjemnou cestu!**	przheeyemnoh tsestoo
Have a good holiday!	**Mějte hezkou dovolenou!**	mn^{y}eyte heskoh dovolenoh
Best regards from ...	**Srdečné pozdravy od ...**	srdechneh pozdravi ot
My regards to ...	**Pozdravujte prosím ...**	pozdravooyte proseem

What time is it? *Kolik je hodin?*

Excuse me. Can you tell me the time?	**Promiňte, prosím. Můžete mi říct kolik je hodin?**	promin^{y}te proseem. moozhete mi rzheets-t kolik ye hod^{y}in
It's ...	**Teď je ...**	tet^{y} ye
five past one	**jedna a pět minut**	yedna a pyet minoot
ten past two	**dvě a deset minut**	dvye a deset minoot
a quarter past three	**čtvrt na čtyři**	ch^{u}tvrt na chtirzhi
twenty past four	**za deset minut půl páté**	za deset minoot pool pahteh
twenty-five past five	**za pět minut půl šesté**	za pyet minoot pool shesteh
half past six	**půl sedmé**	pool sedmeh
twenty-five to seven	**za deset minut tři čtvrtě na sedm**	zadeset minoot trzhi ch^{u}tv^{u}rt^{y}e na sedoom
twenty to eight	**za dvacet minut osm**	zadvatset minoot osoom
a quarter to nine	**tři čtvrtě na devět**	trzhi ch^{u}tv^{u}rt^{y}e na devyet
ten to ten	**za deset minut deset**	zadeset minoot deset
five to eleven	**za pět minut jedenáct**	zapyet minoot yedenahts-t
twelve o'clock (noon/ midnight)	**dvanáct hodin (poledne/půlnoc)**	dvanahts-t hod^{y}in (poledne/ poolnots)
in the morning	**ráno**	rahno
in the afternoon	**odpoledne**	otpoledne
in the evening	**večer**	vecher
The train leaves at ...	**Vlak odjíždí ve ...**	vlak odyeezhd^{y}ee ve
13.04 (1.04 p.m.)	**třináct hodin čtyři minuty**	trzhinahts-t hod^{y}in chtirzhi minooti
0.40 (0.40 a.m.)	**čtyřicet minut po půlnoci**	chtirzhitset minoot popoolnotsi
in five minutes	**za pět minut**	zapyet minoot
in a quarter of an hour	**za čtvrt hodiny**	zach^{u}tv^{u}rt hod^{y}ini
half an hour ago	**před půl hodinou**	przhet pool hod^{y}inoh
about two hours	**asi za dvě hodiny**	asi zadvye hod^{y}ini
more than 10 minutes	**víc než deset minut**	veets nezhdeset minoot
less than 30 seconds	**míň než třicet vteřin**	meen^{y} nesh-trzhitset fterzhin
The clock is fast/slow.	**Ty hodiny jdou rychle/pomalu.**	ti hod^{y}ini ydoh rikhle/ pomaloo

Common abbreviations *Běžné zkratky*

atd.	**a tak dále**	etc.
č/čís	**čislo**	number, No.
Čedok	**Čedok**	Czechoslovak Tourist Agency
čs	**československé**	Czechoslovak
ČSA	**Československé aerolinie**	Czechoslovak Airlines
ČSAD	**Československá státní automobilová doprava**	Czechoslovak Bus and Road Haulage Company
ČSAO	**Československé automobilové opravny**	Czechoslovak Motor Repair Works
ČSD	**Československé státní dráhy**	Czechoslovak State Railways
ČT	**Československá televize**	Czechoslovak Television
dop.	**dopoledne**	a.m.
h	**haléř**	heller (Czech currency)
h/hod.	**hodina**	hour
hl.	**hlavní**	main, chief
j.	**jih, jižní**	south, southern
Kčs	**koruna československá**	Czechoslovak crown (currency)
KU/UK	**Karlova universita**	Charles University (Prague)
nám.	**náměstí**	square, place
n.m.	**nad mořem**	above sea-level
odd.	**oddělení**	department, section
odp.	**odpoledne**	p.m.
p.	**pan**	Mr.
pí	**paní**	Mrs., Ms.
r.	**roku**	(in . . .) year
RaJ	**Restaurace a jídelny**	Restaurants and cafés
s.	**sever, severní**	north, northern
SBČ	**Státni banka československá**	Czechoslovak State Bank
SK	**sportovní klub**	sports club
sl.	**slečna**	Miss
str.	**strana**	page
sv.	**svatý/tá**	Saint
tj	**to jest**	that is
tř	**třída**	Road, Avenue
ul.	**ulice**	street
v.	**východ, východní**	east, eastern
VB	**Veřejná vezpečnost**	police
vt.	**vteřina, vtěrin**	seconds
z.	**západ(ní)**	west(ern)

Signs and notices *Nápisy a oznámení*

Čerstvě natřeno	Wet paint
Dámy	Ladies
Dolů	Down
Horký	Hot
Informace	Information
Kouření zakázáno	No smoking
K pronajmutí	For hire
K pronajmutí	To let
Nahoru	Up
Na prodej	For sale
Nebezpečí (smrti)	Danger (of death)
Neblokujte vchod	Do not block entrance
Nedotýkejte se	Do not touch
Nepovolaným vstup zakázán	Trespassers will be prosecuted
Nerušit	Do not disturb
Nouzový východ	Emergency exit
Obsazeno	No vacancies
Obsazeno	Occupied
Otevřeno	Open
Páni/Muži	Gentlemen
Pokladna	Cash desk
Porucha	Out of order
Pozor	Caution
Pozor zlý pes!	Beware of the dog
Prosím počkejte	Please wait
Reservováno	Reserved
Soukromá cesta	Private road
Studený	Cold
Táhnout	Pull
Tlačit	Push
Veřejné záchodky	Toilets
Volné	Vacant
Vstupte bez klepání	Enter without knocking
Vstup/Vchod	Entrance
Vstup zakázán	No admittance
Vstup zdarma	Free admittance
Vyprodáno	Sold out
Výprodej	Sale
Výstup/Východ	Exit
Výtah	Lift
. . . zakázáno	. . . forbidden
Zákaz odhazování odpadků	No littering
Zazvoňte	Please ring

Emergency *Pohotovost*

Call the police	**Zavolejte policii**	zavoleyte politsiyi
Consulate	**Konzulární oddělení**	konzoolahrn^{y}ee odd^{y}elen^{y}ee
DANGER	**NEBEZPEČÍ**	nebespechee
Embassy	**Vyslanectví**	vislanets-tvee
FIRE	**POŽÁR**	pozhahr
Gas	**plyn**	plin
Get a doctor	**Zavolejte lékaře**	zavoleyte lehkarzhe
Go away	**Odejděte**	odeyd^{y}ete
HELP	**POMOC**	pomots
Get help quickly	**Běžte rychle pro pomoc**	byeshte rikhle pro pomots
I'm ill	**Jsem nemocný (nemocena)**	ysem nemotsn^{y}ee (nemotsena)
I'm lost	**Zabloudil(a) jsem**	zabloh-dil(a) ysem
Leave me alone	**Nechte mne na pokoji**	nekhte mne na pokoyi
LOOK OUT	**DÁVEJTE POZOR**	dahveyte pozor
Poison	**Jed**	yet
POLICE	**POLICIE**	politsiye
Stop that man/ woman	**Chyťte toho člověka/ tu paní**	kheet-te to-ho chlovyeka/ too panee
STOP THIEF	**CHYŤTE ZLODĚJE**	khit^{y}te zlod^{y}eye

Emergency telephone numbers *Pohotovostní čísla*

158	**Police**	**150**	**Fire**	**155**	**Ambulance**

Lost property—Theft *Ztráty a nálezy—Loupež*

Where's the ...?	**Kde je ...?**	gde ye
lost property (lost and found) office	**ztráty a nálezy**	ztrahti a nahlezi
police station	**policejní stanice**	politseyn^{y}ee stan^{y}itse
I want to report a theft.	**Chci oznámit krádež.**	kh-tsi oznahmit krahdezh
My ... has been stolen.	**Někdo mi ukradl ...**	n^{y}egdo mi ookradl
I've lost my ...	**Ztratil(a) jsem ...**	strat^{y}il(a) ysem
handbag	**kabelku**	kabelkoo
passport	**pas**	pas
wallet	**peněženku**	pen^{y}ezhenkoo

CAR ACCIDENTS, see page 79

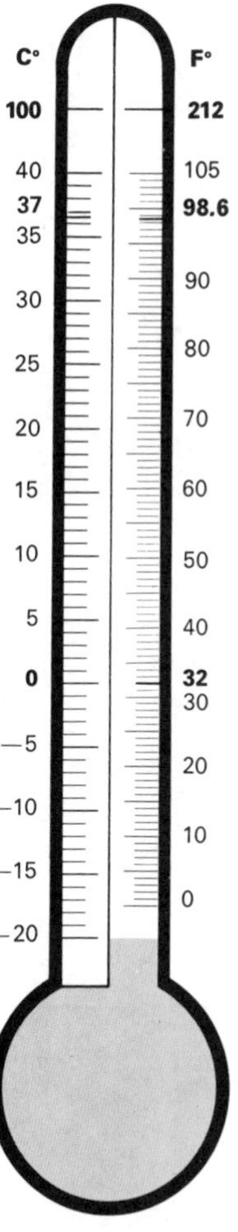

Conversion tables

Centimetres and inches

To change centimetres into inches, multiply by .39.

To change inches into centimetres, multiply by 2.54.

	in.	feet	yards
1 mm	0.039	0.003	0.001
1 cm	0.39	0.03	0.01
1 dm	3.94	0.32	0.10
1 m	39.40	3.28	1.09

	mm	cm	m
1 in.	25.4	2.54	0.025
1 ft.	304.8	30.48	0.304
1 yd.	914.4	91.44	0.914

(32 metres = 35 yards)

Temperature

To convert Centigrade into degrees Fahrenheit, multiply Centigrade by 1.8 and add 32.

To convert degrees Fahrenheit into Centigrade, subtract 32 from Fahrenheit and divide by 1.8.

inches 1 2 3 4

cm. 1 2 3 4 5 6 7 8 9 10 11 12

Kilometres into miles

1 kilometre (km.) = 0.62 miles

km.	10	20	30	40	50	60	70	80	90	100	110	120	130
miles	6	12	19	25	31	37	44	50	56	62	68	75	81

Miles into kilometres

1 mile = 1.609 kilometres (km.)

miles	10	20	30	40	50	60	70	80	90	100
km.	16	32	48	64	80	97	113	129	145	161

Fluid measures

1 litre (l.) = 0.88 imp. quart or 1.06 U.S. quart

1 imp. quart = 1.14 l. 1 U.S. quart = 0.95 l.

1 imp. gallon = 4.55 l. 1 U.S. gallon = 3.8 l.

litres	5	10	15	20	25	30	35	40	45	50
imp. gal.	1.1	2.2	3.3	4.4	5.5	6.6	7.7	8.8	9.9	11.0
U.S. gal.	1.3	2.6	3.9	5.2	6.5	7.8	9.1	10.4	11.7	13.0

Weights and measures

1 kilogram or kilo (kg.) = 1000 grams (g.)

100 g. = 3.5 oz. ½ kg. = 1.1 lb.

200 g. = 7.0 oz. 1 kg. = 2.2 lb.

1 oz. = 28.35 g.

1 lb. = 453.60 g.

CLOTHING SIZES, see page 114/YARDS AND INCHES, see page 112

Basic grammar

Nouns

In Czech there are no indefinite or definite articles corresponding to "a', "an" and "the", but three genders are distinguished: masculine, feminine and neuter. You can usually determine the gender of a noun by its ending. The typical endings for genders are as follows:

masculine: the great majority of nouns ending in a consonant:

vlak	train	**muž**	man	**čaj**	tea

feminine: most nouns ending in **-a** and **-e**; a smaller number ending in a consonant:

hlava	head	**ulice**	street	**velikost**	size

neuter: nouns ending in **-o** and also in **-e** and **-í**:

město	town	**pole**	field	**náměstí**	square

Plural: Although there are exceptions, most masculine and feminine nouns end in **-y** or **-e**; while neuter nouns generally end in **-a** and **-í**:

klíce (m.pl)	keys	**ponožky** (f.pl)	socks	**města** (n.pl)	towns

Declension

The endings of nouns vary according to their use in a sentence. There are six difference cases in Czech, both for singular and plural.

The **nominative** (N)* refers to the subject of the sentence—the person or thing performing the action:

***Žena* pracuje.**	*The woman* is working.
***Vlak* přijel.**	*The train* has arrived.

The **accusative** (A) most often denotes the direct object of an action:

psát *knihu*	to write *a book*
potkat *ženu*	to meet *a woman*

* The capital letters designate the case.

The **genitive** (G) designates a person to whom, or an object to which, somebody or something belongs or refers (it is often translated by *of* or *'s* in English):

sklenice *vody*	a glass *of water*
pokoj *ženy*	*the woman's* room

The **dative** (D) designates the person or object to whom or which something is given or done:

Dám to *ženě*.	I will give it *to the woman.*
Zaplatil *číšnici*.	He paid *the waitress.*

The **instrumental** (I) answers the questions "by whom?", "how?", "by what means?", etc.:

Dopis byl poslán *poštou*.	The letter was sent *by mail.*
Píše *perem*.	He/she writes *with a pen.*

The **locative** (L) is always used with a preposition; the most common are **na**, **v** (on, in) and **o** (about):

Kniha je *na polici*.	The book is *on the shelf.*
Klíč je *v pokoji*.	The key is *in the room.*
Píše *o práci*.	He/she is writing *about work.*

The **vocative** (V) is used to address a person:

Ivane! [addressing] Ivan **Miloši!** Miloš **Anno!** Anna

Adjectives

Adjectives agree in number and gender with the noun they modify. There are two types of adjective declension: adjectives with nominative singular endings of (1) **-ý** (masculine), **-á** (feminine), **-é** (neuter); or (2) with endings for all genders of **-í**. In the following table the more common first group is shown, together with noun declensions.

	Masculine (old suit)	Feminine (nice woman)	Neuter (small car)
sing. N	**starý oblek**	**milá žena**	**malé auto**
A	**starý oblek**	**milou ženu**	**malé auto**
G	**starého obleku**	**milé ženy**	**malého auta**
D	**starému obleku**	**milé ženě**	**malému autu**
I	**starým oblekem**	**milou ženou**	**malým autem**
L	**starém obleku**	**milé ženě**	**malém autě**

plur. N	**staré obleky**	**milé ženy**	**malá auta**
A	**staré obleky**	**milé ženy**	**malá auta**
G	**starých obleků**	**milých žen**	**malých aut**
D	**starým oblekům**	**milým ženám**	**malým autům**
I	**starými obleky**	**milými ženami**	**malými auty**
L	**starých oblecích**	**milých ženách**	**malých autech**

Personal pronouns

	I	you	he	she	it	we	you	they
N	**já**	**ty**	**on**	**ona**	**ono**	**my**	**vy**	**oni/ony**
A	**mě**	**tě/tebe**	**jeho/ho**	**ji**	**he/ho**	**nás**	**vás**	**je**
G	**mě**	**tě/tebe**	**jeho**	**jí**	**jeho**	**nás**	**vás**	**jich**
D	**mně/mi**	**tobě/ti**	**jemu/mu**	**jí**	**jemu/mu**	**nám**	**vám**	**jím**
I	**mnou**	**tebou**	**jím**	**jí**	**jím**	**námi**	**vámi**	**jimi**
L	**mně**	**tobě**	**něm**	**ní**	**něm**	**nás**	**vás**	**nich**

Note: There are two forms of "you" in Czech: **ty** (plural: **vy**) is used when talking to relatives, friends and children, and between young people; in all other situations **vy** is used.

If the personal pronoun is used with a preposition in any other case than in the locative, **j-** becomes **n-**, e.g. **bez ní** (G) without her

Possessives

These agree with the noun in number and gender and are declined like adjectives.

	singular			plural		
	masc.	fem.	neut.	masc.	fem.	neut.
my	**můj**	**má**	**mé**	**mé**	**mé**	**má**
your	**tvůj**	**tvá**	**tvé**	**tvé**	**tvé**	**tvá**
his/its	**jeho**	**jeho**	**jeho**	**jeho**	**jeho**	**jeho**
her	**její**	**její**	**její**	**její**	**její**	**její**
our	**náš**	**naše**	**naše**	**naše**	**naše**	**naše**
you	**váš**	**vaše**	**vaše**	**vaše**	**vaše**	**vaše**
their	**jejich**	**jejich**	**jejich**	**jejich**	**jejich**	**jejich**

Verbs

The infinitive ("to do" form) of most verbs ends in **-t**. Here are four typical verbs in the present tense:

	dělat (to do)	**vidět** (to see)	**kupovat** (to buy)	**nést** (to carry)
já	**dělám**	**vidím**	**kupuju**	**nesu**
ty	**děláš**	**vidíš**	**kupuješ**	**neseš**
on/ona/ono	**dělá**	**vidí**	**kupuje**	**nese**
my	**děláme**	**vidíme**	**kupujeme**	**neseme**
vy	**děláte**	**vidíte**	**kupujete**	**nesete**
oni/ony	**dělají**	**vidí**	**kupují**	**nesou**

. . . and some useful irregular verbs:

	jít (to go)	**chtít** (to want)	**mít** (to have)	**moci** (to be able)
já	**jdu**	**chci**	**mám**	**můžu**
ty	**jdeš**	**chceš**	**máš**	**můžeš**
on/ona/ono	**jde**	**chce**	**má**	**může**
my	**jdeme**	**chceme**	**máme**	**můžeme**
vy	**jdete**	**chcete**	**máte**	**můžete**
oni/ony	**jdou**	**chtějí**	**mají**	**můžou**

There are three tenses in Czech: past, present and future. Here are three tenses of the verb **být** (to be):

	present	past	future
já	**jsem**	**byl/byla/bylo jsem**	**budu**
ty	**jsi**	**byl/byla/bylo jsi**	**budeš**
on/ona/ono	**je**	**byl/byla/bylo**	**bude**
my	**jsme**	**byli/byly jsme**	**budeme**
vy	**jste**	**byli/byly jste**	**budete**
oni/ony/ona	**jsou**	**byli/byly/byla**	**budou**

Note: the pronoun subject (I - **já**, he - **on**, etc.) may normally be omitted, because the verb endings indicate the subject

Some more remarks about verbs

In the past tense, the verb agrees in gender and number with the subject of the sentence, i.e. there is a masculine, a feminine and a plural form in both singular and plural form. For regular verbs, you just take off the infinitive ending **-t** and add **-l** for masculine, **-la** for feminine and **-lo** for neuter. The present forms of the verb **být** (to be) are added for I, you and we.

čekat (to wait)	**čekal(a) jsem**	I waited
	čekal	he waited
	čekala	she waited
	čekalo	it waited

Almost every verb in Czech occurs in two different forms called **aspects**:
— the imperfective is used for continuous, repeated or uncompleted action. For the present tense, this form of the verb is always used.
— the perfective aspect is used for a single or completed action.

Every verb, then, has two infinitives, one for each aspect. The perfective infinitive is usually formed by adding a prefix to the imperfective infinitive or by changing its ending, e.g.:

to write:	imperfective form — **psát**
	perfective form — **napsat**
to sell:	imperfective form — **prodávat**
	perfective form — **prodat**

Both aspects form their past tense in the same way, e.g.:

psal	he was writing	**napsal**	he wrote/has written

N.B. For reasons of space, we only give one of the two aspects in our dictionary. You will find out how it's used by looking up the phrase on the cross-referenced page.

The **future tense** is expressed in two ways, depending on whether the verb is perfective or perfective:
imperfective verbs: the future form of the verb **být** (to be) plus the infinitive of the imperfective verb

budeš psát	you will be writing

and for **perfective verbs**, the present tense endings are used:

napíšeš	you will write

Negation: To make a verb negative add the prefix **ne-**:

nerozumím	I don't understand	**nenapíšu**	I will not write

Dictionary
and alphabetical index

English–Czech

f feminine *m* masculine *nt* neuter *pl* plural

For adjectives only the masculine ending (-ý and -é) is given; see GRAMMAR section for feminine and neuter endings.

abbey opatství *nt* 81
abbreviation zkratka *f* 154
able, to be moci 163
about *(approximately)* asi 153
above nad 15, 63
abscess hnisavý zánět *m* 145
absorbent cotton vata *f* 108
accept, to přijmout 62; brát 102
accessories doplňky *pl* 115; příslušenství *nt* 125
accident nehoda *f* 78, 139
accommodation ubytování *nt* 22
account konto *nt* 130, 131
ache bolest *f* 141
adaptor rozdvojka *f* 118
address adresa *f* 21, 31, 76, 102
address book adresář *m* 104
adhesive label lepicí štítek *m* 105
adhesive tape lepicí páska *f* 104
admission vstupné *nt* 82
admittance vstup *m* 155
admitted vstup povolen 150
adult dospělý *m* 82
Africa Afrika *f* 146
after po 15, 77
afternoon, in the odpoledne *nt* 151, 153
after-shave lotion voda po holení *f* 109
again znovu 96
age věk *m* 149; starý 150
ago před 149, 151
air bed nafukovací matrace *f* 106
air conditioning klimatizace *f* 23, 28
airmail letecká pošta *f* 133
air mattress nafukovací matrace *f* 106
airplane letadlo *nt* 65
airport letiště *nt* 16, 21, 65
aisle seat sedadlo u uličky *nt* 65
alarm clock budík *m* 121
alcohol alkohol *m* 37, 59
alcoholic alkoholický 59
all všechno 103
allergic alergický 141, 143
almond mandle *f* 53
alphabet abeceda *f* 9
also také 15
alter, to *(garment)* změnit 116
altitude sickness nemoc výšková nemoc *f* 107
always vždycky 15
amazing neuvěřitelný 84
amber jantar *m* 122
ambulance ambulance *f* 79
American americký 93, 105, 126
American plan se všemi jídly 24
amethyst ametyst *m* 122
amount množství *nt* 62, 131
amplifier zesilovač *m* 118
anaesthetic anestetikum *nt* 144, 145
analgesic utišující prostředek *m* 108
and a 15
animal zvíře *nt* 85
aniseed anýz *m* 51
ankle kotník *m* 139
anorak větrovka *f* 115
another ještě 58, 123
answer odpověď *f* 136
antibiotic antibiotikum *nt* 143
antidepressant prášek proti depresi *m* 143
antiques starožitnosti *pl* 83
antique shop starožitnictví *nt* 98
antiseptic cream antiseptický krém *m* 108
any žádné 14
anyone někdo 11, 16
anything něco 17, 24, 25, 101, 112
anywhere někde 89

apartment byt *m* 23
aperitif aperitiv *m* 58
appendicitis zánět slepého střeva *f* 142
appetizer předkrm *m* 41
apple jablko *nt* 53, 64, 119
apple juice jablečná šťáva 60
appliance potřeba *f* 118
appointment schůzka *f* 131
appointment, to make an objednat se 145
apricot meruňka *f* 54
April duben *m* 150
archaeology archeologie *f* 83
architect architect *m* 83
area code volací kód *m* 134
arm paže *f* 138; ruka *f* 139
around kolem 31
arrangement *(set price)* podmínky 20
arrival příjezd, přílet *m* 16, 65
arrive, to přijet 65, 68, 70, 130
art umění *nt* 83
art gallery galerie *f* 81, 98
artichoke artyčok *m* 49
article předmět *m* 101
artificial umělý 124
artificial light umělé světlo *nt* 124
artist umělec *m* 81, 83
ashtray popelník *m* 36
Asia Asie *f* 146
ask for, to chtít 25, 61; zavolat 136
asparagus chřest *m* 49
aspirin acylpyrin *m* 108
asthma astma *nt* 141
astringent svíravý prostředek *m* 109
at v 15
at least nejméně 24
at once okamžitě 31
aubergine lilek *m* 49
August srpen *m* 150
aunt teta *f* 93
Australia Austrálie *f* 146
Austria Rakousko *nt* 146
automatic automatický 20, 122, 124
autumn podzim *m* 150
average průměr *m* 91
awful hrozný 84, 94

B

baby miminko *nt* 24, 110
baby food pokrmy pro kojence 110
babysitter hlídání dětí *nt* 27
back záda *pl* 138
back, to be/to get vrátit se 21, 80, 136
backache bolavá záda *f* 141
backpack batoh *m* 106
bacon slanina *f* 40
bacon and eggs slanina s vejci 40
bad špatný 14, 95
bag taška *f* 18; sáček *m* 103
baggage zavazadlo *nt* 18, 26, 71
baggage cart vozík pro zavazadla *m* 18, 71
baggage check odbavení zavazadel *f* 67, 71
baggage locker úschovna zavazadel *f* 18, 67, 71
baked pečený 45, 47
baker's pekařství *nt* 98
balance *(finance)* bilance *f* 131
balcony balkón *m* 23
ball *(inflated)* míč *m* 128
ballet balet *m* 88
ball-point pen propisovací tužka *f* 104
banana banán *m* 53, 64
bandage obvaz *m* 108
Band-Aid leukoplast *f* 108
bangle přívěsek *m* 121
bank *(finance)* banka *f* 98, 129, 130
banknote bankovka *f* 130
bar *(room)* bar *m* 33
barber's holič *m* 30; holičství *nt* 98
basil bazalka *f* 51
basketball košíková *f* 89
bath koupelna *f* 23, 25, 27
bathing cap koupací čepice *f* 116
bathing hut plavecká kabina *f* 91
bathing suit plavky *pl* 116
bathrobe koupací plášť *m* 115
bathroom koupelna *f* 27
bath salts koupelová sůl *f* 110
bath towel velký ručník *m* 27
battery baterie *f* 75, 78, 119, 121, 125
bay leaf bobkový list *m* 51
be, to být 162
beach pláž *f* 90
beach ball míč na pláž *m* 128
bean fazole *f* 49
beard vousy *pl* 31
beautiful krásný 14, 84
beauty salon salón krásy 98
bed postel *f* 24, 28, 142, 144
bed and breakfast nocleh se snídaní *f* 24
bedpan lůžková mísa *f* 144
beef hovězí 44, 45, 46
beer pivo *nt* 56, 63
beet(root) červená řepa *f* 49
before *(place)* před 15; *(time)* před 15

begin, to začínat 80, 87, 88
beginner začátečník *m* 91
beginning začátek *m* 150
behind za 15, 77
beige béžový 113
Belgium Belgie *f* 146
bell *(electric)* zvonek *m* 144
below pod 14
belt pásek *m* 117
berth lůžko *nt* 69, 70, 71
better lepší 14, 25, 101
between mezi 15
beverage nápoj *m* 39
bicycle kolo *nt* 74
big velký 14, 101
bilberry borůvka *f* 54
bill účet *m* 28, 31, 62, 102; *(banknote)* bankovka *f* 130
billion *(Am.)* bilión *m* 148
binoculars dalekohled *m* 123
bird pták 85
birth narození *nt* 25
birthday narozeniny *pl* 151, 152
biscuit *(Br.)* sušenka *f* 63
bitter hořký 61
black černý 113
black and white *(film)* černobílý 124, 125
black coffee černá káva *f* 40, 60
blackcurrant černý rybíz *m* 54
bladder měchýř *m* 138
blade žiletka *f* 110
blanket deka *f* 27
bleach odbarvení *nt* 30
bleed, to krvácet 139, 145
blind *(window shade)* roleta *f* 29
blister puchýř *m* 139
blocked ucpaný 28
blood krev *f* 142
blood pressure krevní tlak *m* 141, 142
blood transfusion transfúze krve *f* 144
blouse halenka *f* 116
blow-dry vyfoukat 30
blue modrý 112
blueberry borůvka *f* 54
blusher růž 110
boar divoké prase *nt* 47
boat člun *m* 74
bobby pin sponka *f* 110
body tělo *nt* 138
Bohemia Čechy *f* 146
boil vřed 139
boiled vařený 40
boiled egg vařené vajíčko 40
bone kost *f* 138
book kniha *f* 12, 104
booking office pokladna *f* 19, 67
booklet *(of tickets)* blok jízdenek *m* 72
bookshop knihkupectví *nt* 98, 104
boot holinka *f* 117
boring nudný 84
born narozený 150
botanical gardens botanická zahrada 81
botany botanika *f* 83
bottle láhev *f* 17, 59
bottle-opener otvírač na lahve *m* 120
bottom dole 145
bowel střeva *pl* 138
bow tie motýlek *m* 116
box krabička *f* 120
boxing rohování *nt* 89
boxing match box *m* 90
boy chlapec *m* 111, 128
boyfriend mládenec *m* 93
bra podprsenka *f* 115
bracelet náramek *m* 121
braces *(suspenders)* šle *pl* 115
braised dušený 45, 47
brake brzda *f* 78
brake fluid brzdová kapalina *f* 75
brandy koňak *m* 60
bread chleb *m* 36, 64, 119
breaded obalený v housce 45
break, to zlomit 139, 145; pokazit 29; rozbít 123
break down, to pokazit se 78
breakdown porucha 78
breakdown van havarijní služba *f* 78
breakfast snídaně *f* 24, 27, 34, 40
breast prs *m* 138
breathe, to dýchat 141, 142
bridge most *m* 85
bring, to přinést 13, 59
bring down, to snést 31
British britský 93
broken zlomený 139, 140; nefungovat 118; rozbít 123
brooch brož *f* 121
broth vývar 42
brother bratr *m* 93
brown hnědý 112
bruise modřina *f* 139
brush kartáč *m* 110
Brussels sprouts růžičková kapusta *f* 50
bubble bath pěna do koupele *f* 109
bucket *(toy)* kyblík *m* 128
buckle přeska *f* 116
build, to postavit 83

building budova *f* 81, 83
building blocks/bricks stavební kostky *pl* 128
bulb *(light)* žárovka *f* 28, 76, 118
bump *(lump)* boule *f* 139
burn spálenina *f* 139
burn out, to *(bulb)* prasknout 28
bus autobus *m* 18, 19, 65, 72, 80
bus stop autobusová zastávka *f* 73; stanice *f* 73
business obchod *m* 16, 131
business class business třída 65
business district obchodní čtvrť *f* 81
business trip služební cesta *f* 93
busy mít moc práce 96
but ale 15
butane gas plynová bomba *f* 32; propan-butan *m* 106
butcher's řeznictví *nt* 98
butter máslo *nt* 36, 40, 64
button knoflík *m* 29, 116
buy, to koupit 82, 100, 104, 123

C

cabana plavecká kabina 91
cabbage zelí *nt* 48
cabin *(ship)* kabina *f* 74
cable telegram *m* 133
cable car lanovka *f* 74
cable release dálková spoušť *f* 125
café kavárna *f* 33
cake dort *m* 37, 55, 64
calculator kalkulačka *f* 105
calendar kalendář *m* 104
call *(phone)* telefonní hovor *m* 135, 136
call, to *(give name)* říct 11; *(phone)* telefonovat 134, 136; *(summon)* zavolat 79, 156
calm klidný 90
cambric batist *m* 113
camel-hair velbloudí srst 113
camera fotoaparát *m* 124, 125
camera case pouzdro na fotoaparát *nt* 125
camera shop obchod s fotoaparáty 98
camp, to stanovat 32
campbed polní lůžko *nt* 106
camping kemping *m*, stanování 32
camping equipment stanovací potřeby *pl* 106
camp site kemping *m* 32
can *(container)* konzerva *f* 119
can *(be able to)* moci 12, 162
Canada Kanada 146
Canadian Kanad'an 93
cancel, to zrušit 65
candle svíčka *f* 120
candy cukroví 63, 126
candy store cukrárna *f* 99
can (tin) opener otvírač na konservy *m* 120
cap čepice *nt* 115
capers kapary 52
capital *(finance)* kapitál *m* 131
car auto *nt* 19, 20, 32, 75, 78
carat karát *m* 121
caravan obytný přívěs *m* 32
caraway kmín *m* 52
carbon paper kopírovací papír *m* 104
carbonated *(fizzy)* šumivý 60
carburettor karburátor *m* 78
card karta *f* 131
card game karetní hra *f* 128
cardigan svetr na zapínání *m* 115
car hire půjčovna aut 20
car mechanic automechanik *m* 78
carp kapr *m* 43
car park parkoviště *nt* 77
car racing automobilové závody *pl* 89
car radio autorádio *nt* 118
car rental půjčovna aut 20
carrot mrkev *f* 50
carry, to nést 21
cart vozík *m* 18
carton *(of cigarettes)* kartón 17, 126
cartridge *(camera)* kazeta *f* 124
case pouzdro *nt* 123, 125
cash, to vyplatit 130, 133
cash desk pokladna *f* 103, 155
cassette kazeta *f* 118, 127
cassette recorder kazetový magnetofon *m* 119
castle zámek *m* 81
catacombs katakomby *pl* 81
catalogue katalog *m* 82
cathedral katedrála *f* 81
Catholic katolický 84
cauliflower květák *m* 50, 51
caution pozor *m* 155
cave jeskyně *f* 81
celery celer *m* 50
cemetery hřbitov *m* 81
centimetre centimetr *m* 111
centre střed *m* 19, 21, 76, 81
century století *nt* 149
ceramics keramika *f* 83
cereal obilniny *pl* 40

certain určitý 143
certificate potvrzení *nt* 144
chain *(jewellery)* řetízek *m* 121
chain bracelet řetízkový náramek 121
chair židle *f* 106; *(deck chair)* lehátko *nt* 106
chamber music komorní hudba *f* 128
change *(money)* drobné *pl* 62, 77
change, to změnit 61, 65, 68, 73, 75, 123; *(money)* 18, 130
chapel kaple *f* 81
charcoal dřevěné uhlí *nt* 106
charge poplatek *m* 20, 32, 77, 89, 136
charge, to platit 24, 130
charm *(trinket)* přívěsek *m* 121
cheap laciný 14, 24, 25, 101
cheque šek *m* 130, 131; *(restaurant)* 62
check, to zkontrolovat 75, 123; *(luggage)* odbavení 71
check in, to *(airport)* odbavení *nt* 65
check out, to odjet 31
check-up *(medical)* lékařská prohlídka *f* 142
cheers! na zdraví! 57
cheese sýr *m* 52, 53, 64
chemist's lékárna *f* 98, 107
cheque šek *m* 130, 131
cherry třešeň *f* 54
chess set šachy *pl* 128
chest hrudník *m* 138, 141
chestnut kaštan *m* 53
chewing gum žvýkačka *f* 126
chewing tobacco žvýkací tabák *m* 126
chicken kuře *nt* 47
chicken breast kuřecí prsa 47
chicory cikorka *f* 50
chiffon šifon *m* 113
child dítě *nt* 24, 61, 82, 93, 139, 150
children's doctor dětský lékař *m* 137
China Čína *f* 146
chips *(French fries)* hranolky *pl* 48
chives pažitka *f* 52
chocolate čokoláda *f* 64, 119, 126; *(hot)* horká 40, 60
chocolate bar čokoláda *f* 64
choice výběr *m* 40
chop *(meat)* kotleta *f* 44
Christmas Vánoce *pl* 152
chromium chróm *m* 122
church kostel *m* 81, 84
cigar doutník *m* 126
cigarette cigareta *f* 17, 95, 126
cigarette case pouzdro na cigarety *nt* 121, 126
cigarette holder cigaretová špička *f* 126
cigarette lighter zapalovač *m* 121, 126
cine camera filmová kamera *f* 124
cinema kino *nt* 86, 96
cinnamon skořice *f* 51
circle *(theatre)* balkón *m* 87
city město *nt* 81
city centre městské centrum 81, 100
classical klasický 128
clean čistý 61
clean, to vyčistit 29, 76
cleansing cream čistící prostředek *m* 110
cliff skála *f* 85
clip spona *f* 121
cloakroom šatna *f* 87
clock hodiny *pl* 121, 153; *(alarm)* budík *m* 121
clock-radio radio s budíkem 118
close, to zavírat 11, 82, 107, 132
closed zavřeno 155
cloth látka *f* 117
clothes šaty 29, 115
clothes peg/pin kolíčka na prádlo *f* 120
clothing oděvy 111
cloud mrak *m* 94
clove hřebíček *m* 52
coach *(bus)* autobus *m* 72
coat kabát *m* 115
coconut kokos *m* 53
cod treska *f* 45
coffee káva *f* 40, 60, 64
coin mince *f* 83, 130
cold studený 14, 25, 39, 61, 94, 155
cold *(illness)* rýma *f* 107, 141
cold cuts studené maso *nt* 64; uzeniny *pl* 39
collar límec *m* 116
collect call hovor na účet volaného *m* 135
colour barva *f* 103, 111, 124, 125
colour chart ukázky barvy 30
colourfast stálobarevný 113
colour rinse přeliv *m* 30
colour shampoo tónovací šampon *m* 110
colour slide diapositiv *m* 124
comb hřeben *m* 110
come, to přijít 16, 35, 92, 95, 137, 144, 146
comedy komedie *f* 86
commission *(fee)* poplatek *m* 130
common *(frequent)* běžný 154

Commonwealth of Independent States (CIS) Svaz Nezávislých Republik *m* 146
compact disc kompaktní disk *m* 127
compartment *(train)* kupé *nt* 66
compass kompas *m* 106
complaint stížnost *f* 61
concert koncert *m* 88
concert hall koncertní hala *f* 81, 88
condom preservativ *m* 108
conductor *(orchestra)* dirigent *m* 88
confectioner's cukrárna *f* 99
conference room konferenční sál *m* 23
confirm, to potvrdit 65
confirmation potvrzení 23
congratulation gratuluji *f* 152
connection *(transport)* spojení *nt* 65, 68
consommé vývar *m* 42
constipation zácpa *f* 140
consulate konsulát *m* 156
contact lens kontaktní čočky 123
contagious nakažlivý 142
contain, to obsahovat 37
contraceptive antikoncepční prostředek 108
contract smlouva *f* 131
control kontrola *f* 16
convent klášter *m* 81
cookie cukroví *nt* 64
cool box cestovní lednička *f* 106
copper měď *f* 122
coral korál 122
corduroy manšestr *m* 113
corkscrew otvírač na láhve *m* 120
corn *(Am.)* obilí *nt* 50; *(foot)* kuří oko *nt* 108
corner roh *m* 21, 35, 77
corn plaster náplast na kuří oko *f* 108
cost cena *f* 131, 136
cost, to stát 11, 80, 133, 136
cotton bavlna *f* 113
cotton wool vata *f* 108
cough kašel *m* 108, 141
cough, to kašlat 142
cough drops něco proti kašli 108
counter přepážka *f* 133
country země *f* 93, 146
countryside venkov *m* 85
court house soud *m* 81
cousin bratranec *m* 93
cover charge poplatek za stůl *m* 62
crab krab *m* 43
cramp křeč *f* 141
crayon pastelka *f* 104
cream *(whipping)* šlehačka *f* 56, 60; *(sour)* smetana *f* 49, 53; *(toiletry)* krém *m* 110
crease resistant nemačkavý 113
credit úvěr *m* 130
credit card úvěrová karta *f* 20, 31, 62, 102, 130
crepe krep 113
crisps brambůrky *pl* 64
crockery nádobí *nt* 120
cross křížek *m* 121
cross-country skiing běh na lyžích 91
crossing *(maritime)* přeplavba *f* 74
crossroads křižovatka *f* 77
cruise cesta lodí 74
crystal křišťál *m* 122, 127
cucumber okurka *f* 50, 51
cuff link manžetové knoflíky 121
cuisine kuchyně *f* 35
cup šálek *m* 36, 60, 120
curler natáčka *f* 110
currants hrozinky *pl* 54
currency měna *f* 129
currency exchange office směnárna 18, 67, 129
current proud *m* 90
curtain záclona *f* 28
curve *(road)* zatáčka *f* 79
customs celnice *f* 16, 102
cut *(wound)* říznutí *nt* 139
cut, to *(with scissors)* stříhat 30
cut off, to *(interrupt)* přerušit 135
cut glass broušené sklo *nt* 122
cuticle remover nůžky na kůžičku *pl* 109
cutlery příbory *pl* 120, 121
cutlet kotleta *f* 44
cycling cyklistika *f* 89
cystitis zánět močového měchýře *f* 142
Czech *(language)* česky 11, 95
Czech Republic česká republika *f* 146

D

dairy mlékárna *f* 98
dance tanec *m* 88, 96
dance, to tančit 88, 96
danger nebezpečí *nt* 155, 156
dangerous nebezpečný 90
dark tmavý 25, 101, 111, 112, 113
date *(day)* datum *nt* 25, 151; *(appointment)* schůzka *f* 95; *(fruit)* datle *pl* 53, 64
daughter dcera *f* 93

day den *m* 20, 24, 32, 80, 94, 151
daylight denní světlo *nt* 124
day off volný den *m* 151
decade desetiletí *nt* 149
decaffeinated bez kofeinu 40, 60
December prosinec 150
decision rozhodnutí 24, 102
deck *(ship)* paluba *f* 74
deck chair lehátko *nt* 91, 106
declare, to *(customs)* proclít 17
deep hluboký 142
degree *(temperature)* stupeň *m* 140
delay zpoždění *nt* 69
delicatessen lahůdky *pl* 98
delicious vynikající 62
deliver, to dodat 102
delivery doručení 102
denim džínsovina *f* 113
Denmark Dánsko *nt* 146
dentist zubař *m* 98, 145
denture umělý chrup *f* 145
deodorant dezodorant *m* 109
department *(museum)* oddělení *nt* 83; *(shop)* 100
department store obchodní dům *m* 98
departure odjezd/odlet *m* 65
deposit *(down payment)* záloha 20; *(bank)* uložení *nt* 130
dessert moučník *m* 38, 54
detour *(traffic)* objížďka *f* 79
diabetic diabetik *m* 37, 141
dialling code volací kód *m* 134
diamond diamant *m* 122, 127
diaper plenka *f* 111
diarrhoea průjem *m* 140
dictionary slovník *m* 104
diesel nafta *f* 75
diet dieta *f* 37
difficult složitý 14
difficulty problém *m* 28, 102; *(illness)* potíže *pl* 141
digital digitální 122
dill kopr *m* 52
dine, to večeřet 94
dining car jídelní vůz *m* 68, 71
dining room jídelna *f* 27
dinner večeře *f* 34, 94
direct přímý 65
direct, to ukázat 13, 86
direction směr *m* 76
director *(theatre)* režisér *m* 86
directory *(phone)* telefonní seznam *m* 134
disabled tělesně postižený 82
disc disk *m* 124, 127
discotheque diskotéka *f* 88, 96
discount sleva *f* 131
disease nemoc *f* 142
dish jídlo *nt* 37, 39
dishwashing detergent saponát 120
disinfectant desinfekce *f* 108
dislocated vykloubený 140
display case vitrina *f* 100
dissatisfied nespokojený 103
district *(of town)* čtvrť *f* 81
disturb, to vyrušit 155
diversion *(traffic)* objížďka *f* 79
dizzy závrať 140
do, to dělat 162
doctor doktor *m* 79, 137, 144, 145
doctor's office ordinace *f* 137
dog pes *m* 155
doll panenka *f* 128
dollar dolar *m* 18, 102, 130
double bed dvojitá postel *f* 23
double room dvoulůžkový pokoj *m* 19, 23
down dolů 15
downhill skiing sjezd na lyžích *nt* 91
downtown centrum města 81
dozen tucet *m* 149
drawing paper kreslicí papír *m* 104
drawing pins připínáčky *pl* 104
dress šaty *pl* 115
dressing gown župan *m* 116
drink nápoj *m* 56, 59, 60, 61, 95
drink, to pít 35, 36, 37
drinking water pitná voda *f* 32
drip, to kapat 28
drive, to jet 21, 76
driving licence řidičský průkaz *m* 20
drop *(liquid)* kapka *f* 108
drugstore drogerie *f* 98, 107
dry suchý 30, 59, 111
dry cleaner's čistírna *f* 29, 98
dry shampoo suchý šampon *m* 111
duck kachna *f* 48
dummy *(baby's)* dudlík *m* 110
during během 15, 150, 151
duty *(customs)* clo *nt* 17
duty-free shop obchod bez cla 19
dye obarvení *nt* 30

E

each každý 149
ear ucho *nt* 138
earache bolest v uchu 141
ear drops kapky do uší *pl* 108

early brzo 14, 31
earring náušnice *pl* 121
east východ *m* 77
Easter velikonoce *pl* 152
easy jednoduchý 14
eat, to jíst 36, 37, 144
eel úhoř *m* 43
egg vajíčko *nt* 40, 41, 64
eggplant lilek *m* 50
eight osm 147
eighth osmý 149
eighteen osmnáct 147
eighty osmdesát 148
elastic bandage pružný obvaz *m* 108
Elastoplast leukoplast *f* 108
electric(al) elektrický 119
electrical appliance elektrické potřeby *pl* 119
electrical goods shop elektrické spotřebiče *pl* 98
electricity elektřina 32
electronic elektronický 128
elevator výtah *m* 27, 100
eleven jedenáct 147
embarkation point nalodit se *m* 74
embassy vyslanectví *nt* 156
embroidery výšivka *f* 127
emerald smaragd *m* 122
emergency pohotovost *f* 156
emergency exit nouzový východ *m* 27, 99
emery board pilníček na nehty 109
empty prázdný 14
enamel emajl 122
end konec *m* 150
engaged *(phone)* obsazeno 136
engagement ring zásnubní prsten *m* 122
engine *(car)* motor *m* 78
England Anglie *f* 134, 146
English *(language)* anglický 11, 16, 80, 82, 84, 104, 105, 126
English *(nationality)* Angličan(ka) 93
enjoyable příjemný 31
enjoy oneself, to bavit se 96
enlarge, to zvětšit 125
enough to stačí 14
entrance vstup *m* 67, 99, 155
entrance fee vstupné *nt* 82
envelope obálka *f* 104
equipment zařízení *nt* 91, 106
eraser korekční barva *f* 105
escalator eskalátor *m* 100
estimate *(cost)* odhadní cena *m* 78, 131
Eurocheque Eurošek *m* 130
Europe Evropa *f* 146
evening večer *m* 95, 96
evening, in the večer *m* 151, 153
evening dress večerní šaty *pl* 88, 116
every každý 143
everything všechno 31, 62
exchange, to vyměnit 103
exchange rate kurs *m* 18, 130
excuse, to prominout 10
exercise book sešit *m* 105
exhaust pipe výfuk *m* 78
exhibition výstava *f* 81
exit východ *m* 67, 99, 155
expect, to čekat 130
expenses výlohy *pl* 131
expensive drahý 14, 19, 24, 101
exposure *(photography)* snímek *m* 124
exposure counter počítač snímků *m* 125
express expres 133
expression výraz *m* 10, 100
expressway dálnice *f* 76
extension *(phone)* linka *nt* 135
extension cord/lead prodlužovací kabel *m* 118
extra víc, navíc 24, 27
eye oko *nt* 138, 139
eyebrow pencil tužka na obočí 109
eye drops kapky do očí *pl* 108
eye shadow očni stíny *pl* 109
eyesight oči *pl* 123
eye specialist oční specialista *m* 137

F

fabric *(cloth)* látka *f* 112
face obličej *m* 138
face powder pudr *m* 110
factory továrna *f* 81
fair pouť *f* 81
fall *(autumn)* podzim *m* 149
fall, to upadnout 139
family rodina *f* 93, 144
fan belt náhonný řemen *m* 76
far daleko 14, 100
fare *(ticket)* lístek *m* 68, 73
farm statek *f* 85
fast rychlý 124
fat *(meat)* tuk *m* 37
father otec *m* 93
faucet *(tap)* kohoutek *m* 28
fax telefax *m* 133

February únor *m* 150
fee *(doctor's)* poplatek *m* 144
feeding bottle láhev pro kojence *f* 110
feel, to *(physical state)* cítit 140, 142
felt plsť *f* 113
felt-tip pen značkovač *m* 105
ferry převoz *m* 74
fever teplota *f* 140
few málo 14; *(a few)* několik 14
field pole *nt* 85
fifteen patnáct 147
fifth pátý 149
fifty padesát 147
fig fík 53
fill in, to vyplnit 26, 144
filling *(tooth)* plomba *f* 145
filling station benzinová pumpa *f* 75
film film *m* 86, 124, 125
film winder přetáčení filmu *nt* 125
filter filtr *m* 125
filter-tipped s filtrem 126
find, to najít 11, 12, 76, 84, 100
fine *(OK)* dobře 10, 25, 92
fine arts umění *nt* 83
finger prst *m* 138
Finland Finsko *nt* 146
fire požár *m* 156
first první 68, 73, 77, 149
first-aid kit první pomoc *f* 108
first class první třída *f* 69
first course *(appetizer)* předkrm *m* 38, 41
first name křestní jméno *nt* 25
fish ryba *f* 43
fishing lovit ryby 90
fishing permit povolení *nt* 90
fishing tackle rybářské potřeby *pl* 106
fishmonger's rybárna *f* 98
fit, to *(clothes)* sedět 115
fitting room zkušební kabina *f* 115
five pět 147
fix, to opravit 75, 145
fizzy *(mineral water)* minerálka *f* 60
flannel flanel 113
flash *(photography)* blesk *m* 125
flash attachment připevnění blesku *nt* 125
flashlight baterka *f* 106
flat *(shoe)* bez podpatku 117
flat *(apartment)* byt *m* 23
flat tyre píchlá duše *f* 75, 78
flea market trh *m* 81
flight let *m* 65
floor patro *nt* 27
florist's květinářství *nt* 98
flour mouka *f* 37
flower květina *f* 85
flu chřipka *f* 142
fluid roztok *m* 123; *(brake)* kapalina *f* 75
foam rubber mattress gumová matrace *f* 106
fog mlha *f* 94
folding chair skládací židle *f* 106
folding table skládací stůl *m* 106
folk music lidová hudba *f* 128
follow, to sledovat 77
food jídlo *nt* 37, 61
food box krabička na jídlo *f* 120
food poisoning otrava z jídla 142
foot chodidlo *nt* 138
football fotbal *m* 89
foot cream krém na chodidlo *m* 109
footpath pěšina *f* 85
for pro 15
forbidden zakázaný 155
forecast předpověď *f* 94
forest les *m* 85
forget, to zapomenout 61
fork vidlička *f* 36, 61, 120
form *(document)* formulář *m* 25, 26, 133, 144
fortnight čtrnáct dnů 151
fortress pevnost *f* 81
forty čtyřicet 147
foundation cream podkladový krém *m* 109
fountain fontána *f* 81
fountain pen plnicí pero *nt* 105
four čtyři 147
fourteen čtrnáct 147
fourth čtvrtý 149
frame *(glasses)* obroučky *pl* 123
France Francie *f* 146
free volný 14, 70, 80, 82, 96, 155
fresh čerstvý 53, 61
Friday pátek *m* 151
fried smažený 40, 53
fried egg smažené vejce *nt* 38
friend přítel *m* 92, 93, 95
fringe ofina *f* 30
from od 15
front vepředu 75
frost mráz *m* 94
fruit ovoce *nt* 53, 55
fruit cocktail ovocný pohár *m* 53
fruit juice ovocná šťáva *f* 40, 60
fruit salad ovocný salát *m* 53
frying pan pánev na smažení *f* 120
full plný 14

full board se všemi jídly *pl* 24
full insurance plné pojištění 20
furniture nábytek *m* 83
furrier's kožešnictví *nt* 98

G

gabardine gabarděn 113
gallery galerie *f* 81, 98
game hra *f* 128; *(food)* zvěřina *f* 39, 46
garage garáž *f* 26, 78
garden zahrada *f* 85
gardens zahrady *pl* 81
garlic česnek 47, 51
gas plyn *m* 32, 156
gasoline benzin *m* 75, 78
gastritis gastritida *f* 142
gauze gáza *f* 108
gem drahokam *m* 121
general základní 27; všeobecný 100, 137
general delivery Poste Restante 133
general practitioner rodinný lékař *m* 137
genitals přirození *nt* 138
gentleman pán *m* 155
genuine pravý 117, 121
geology geologie *f* 83
Germany Německo *nt* 146
get, to *(find)* najít 11, 21; *(fetch)* objednat 31, 134; *(obtain)* sehnat 19, 32, 137
get off, to vystoupit 73
get past, to projít 11, 70
get to, to dostat se 19, 76
get up, to vstát 144
gherkin nakládaná okurka *f* 52, 64
gift dárek *m* 17
gin gin *m* 58
gin and tonic gin s tonikem 60
ginger zázvor *m* 52
girdle podvazkový pas *m* 115
girl dívka *f* 111; holčička 128
girlfriend dívka *f* 93
give, to dát 13, 63, 75, 123, 126, 130, 135
give way, to *(traffic)* dát přednost 79
gland žláza *f* 138
glass sklenice *f* 36, 58, 61, 143
glasses brýle *pl* 123
gloomy chmurný 84
glove rukavice *f* 115
glue lepidlo *nt* 105
go, to jít 11, 21, 72, 77, 96, 162
go away! odejděte! 156
go back, to vrátit se 77
go out, to jít ven 96
gold zlato *nt* 121, 122
golden zlatiný 112
gold plated pozlacený 122
golf course golfové hřiště 90
good dobrý 14, 86, 101
good afternoon dobré odpoledne 10
goodbye na shledanou 10
good evening dobrý večer 10
good morning dobré ráno 10
good night dobrou noc 10
goose husa *f* 46, 47
gooseberry angrešt *m* 53
gram gram *m* 119
grammar gramatika *f* 159
grammar book gramatika *f* 105
grape hrozen *m* 53, 64
grapefruit grapefruit *m* 53
grapefruit juice grapefruitový džus *f* 40, 60
gray šedý 112
graze odřenina *f* 139
greasy mastný 30, 110
great *(excellent)* vynikající 95
Great Britain Velká Británie *f* 146
Greece Řecko *nt* 146
green zelený 112
green bean zelené fazolky *pl* 50, 51
greengrocer's zelinářství *nt* 98
green salad hlávkový salát *m* 51
greeting pozdrav *m* 10, 152
grey šedý 112
grilled grilovaný 45, 47
grocer's potraviny *pl* 98, 119
groundsheet nepromokavá celta *f* 106
group skupina *f* 82
guesthouse pension *m* 22, 23
guide průvodce *m* 80
guidebook průvodce *m* 82, 104, 105
guinea fowl perlička *f* 47
gum *(teeth)* dásně *pl* 145
gynaecologist gynekolog *m* 137, 141

H

hair vlasy *pl* 30, 110
hairbrush kartáč na vlasy *m* 110
haircut ostříhat 30
hairdresser's kadeřnictví *nt* 98; *(men)* holičstvi *nt* 30, 98
hair dryer fén *m* 118
hair gel pomáda na vlasy *nt* 30, 110

hairgrip sponka *f* 110
hair lotion vlasová voda *f* 110
hairpin sponka *f* 110
hair slide zavírací sponka do vlasů *f* 110
hair spray lak na vlasy *m* 30, 110
half půl 149
half an hour půl hodiny 153
half board s večeří a snídaní 24
half price poloviční cena *f* 69
hall *(large room)* hala *f* 81, 88
hall porter vrátný *m* 26
ham šunka *f* 40, 64
ham and eggs šunka s vajíčky 40
hammer kladivo *nt* 120
hammock houpací síť *f* 106
hand ruka *f* 138
handbag kabelka *f* 115, 156
hand cream krém na ruce *m* 110
handicrafts řemesla *pl* 83, 127
handkerchief kapesník *m* 116
handmade ruční práce *f* 112
hand washable na praní v ruce 113
hanger ramínko *nt* 27
happy šťastný 152
harbour *(port)* přístav *m* 74, 81
hard tvrdý 123
hard-boiled *(egg)* vejce na tvrdo 40
hardware store železářství *nt* 98
hare zajíc 47
hat klobouk *m* 115
have, to mít 162
have to, to *(must)* muset 68, 69, 77, 95, 140
haversack batoh *m* 106
hay fever senná rýma *f* 107, 141
hazelnut lískový ořech *m* 53
he on 161
head hlava *f* 138, 139
headache bolest hlavy 141
headphones sluchátka *pl* 118
head waiter pan vrchní *m* 61
health food shop potraviny pro zdravou výživu *pl* 99
health insurance *(company)* zdravotní pojišťovna *f* 144
health insurance formulář prozdravotní pojištěni *nt* 144
heart srdce *nt* 138
heart attack infarkt *m* 141
heat, to vytápět 90
heating topení *nt* 28
heavy těžký 14, 101, 139
helicopter helikoptéra *f* 74
hello ahoj 10; *(on the phone)* haló 135
help pomoc *f* 156
help! pomoc! 156
help, to pomoci 13, 21, 71, 100, 134
her jí 161
herbs bylinky *pl* 51
herb tea bylinkový čaj 60
here tady 13
herring sleď 44
hi ahoj 10
high vysoký 85, 141
high season hlavní sezóna *f* 150
hill kopec *m* 85
hire nájem *m* 20, 74
hire, to pronajmout 19, 20, 74, 90, 91
his jeho 161
history historie *m* 83
hitchhike, to stopovat 74
hold on! *(phone)* čekejte ! 136
hole díra *f* 29
holiday dovolená *f* 151, 152
holidays prázdniny *pl* 16, 151
home domů 96
home address domácí adresa 31
home town trvalé bydliště *nt* 25
honey med *m* 40
hope, to doufat 96
hors d'oeuvre předkrm *m* 41
horseback riding jezdectví *nt* 89
horse racing dostihy *pl* 89
horseradish křen *m* 52
hospital nemocnice *f* 99, 142, 144
hot *(boiling)* horký 14, 25, 40; *(warm)* teplý 28, 94
hotel hotel *m* 19, 21, 22, 26, 80, 96, 102
hotel directory/guide seznam hotelů *m* 19
hotel reservation hotelová rezervace *f* 19
hot water horká voda *f* 23, 28
hot-water bottle ohřívací láhev *f* 27
hour hodina *f* 80, 143, 153
house dům *m* 83, 85
household article potřeby pro domácnost *pl* 120
how jak 11
how far jak daleko 11, 76, 85
how long jak dlouho 11, 24
how many kolik 11
how much kolik 11, 24
hundred sto 148
hungry hladový 13, 35
hunting lov 89
hurry, to be in a spěchat 21
hurt, to bolet 139, 140, 142, 145; uhodit se 139

husband manžel *m* 93
hydrofoil křídlový člun *m* 74

I

I já 161
ice náledí *nt* 94
ice cream zmrzlina *f* 39, 55
ice cubes ledové kostky *pl* 27
iced tea ledový čaj *m* 60
ice pack ledový obal *m* 106
if když 143
ill nemocný 140
illness nemoc 140
important důležitý 13
imported z dovozu 112
impressive impozantní 84
in v 15
include, to zahrnovat 24; započítat 31, 80
included zahrnutý 20; včetně 20, 32
India Indie *f* 146
indigestion potíže s trávením 141
indoor *(swimming pool)* krytý 90
inexpensive laciný 35, 124
infected zanícený 140
infection infekce *f* 141
inflammation zánět *m* 142
inflation inflace *f* 131
inflation rate procento inflace *nt* 131
influenza chřipka *f* 142
information informace *f* 67, 155
injection injekce *f* 142, 143, 144
injure, to zranit 139
injured zraněný 79, 139
injury zranění *nt* 139
ink inkoust *m* 105
inn zájezdní hospoda *f* 33
inquiry dotaz *m* 68
insect bite štípnutí 139
insect repellent postřik proti hmyzu *m* 108
insect spray postřik proti hmyzu *m* 106, 108
inside vevnitř 14
instead of místo 37
insurance pojištění *nt* 20, 144
insurance company pojišťovna *f* 79
interest *(finance)* úrok *m* 131
interested, to be mít zájem 83, 96
interesting zajímavý 84
international mezinárodní 133, 134
interpreter tlumočník *m* 131
introduce, to představit 92
introduction *(social)* představování *nt* 92
investment investice *f* 131
invitation pozvání *nt* 94
invite, to pozvat 94
invoice faktura *f* 131
iodine jód *m* 108
Ireland Irsko *nt* 146
Irish Irčan *m*; Irčanka *f* 93
iron *(for laundry)* žehlička *f* 119
iron, to žehlit 29
ironmonger's železářství *nt* 99
Israel Israel *m* 146
it to 161
Italy Itálie *f* 146
its jeho 161
ivory slonovina *f* 122

J

jacket sako *nt* 115
jade nefrit *m* 122
jam *(preserves)* džem *m* 40
jam, to zablokovat 28, 125
January leden *m* 150
Japan Japonsko *nt* 146
jaundice žloutenka *f* 142
jar sklenička *f* 119
jaw čelist *f* 138
jazz džez *m* 128
jeans džínsy *pl* 115
jersey svetr *m* 115
jewel box šperkovnice *f* 121
jeweller's klenotnictví *nt*, klenoty 99, 121
joint kloub *m* 138
journey cesta *f* 72
juice šťáva *f* 37, 60; džus 40
July červenec *m* 150
jumper svetr *m* 115
June červen *m* 150
just *(only)* jenom 12, 16, 100

K

keep, to nechat 62
kerosene petrolej *m* 106
key klíč *m* 27
kidney ledviny *pl* 138
kilo(gram) kilo *nt* 119
kilometre kilometr *m* 20, 78
kind milý 95

kind *(type)* druh *m* 85, 140
knee koleno 138
kneesocks podkolenky *pl* 115
knife nůž *m* 36, 61, 120
knock, to zaklepat 155
know, to vědět 16, 24, 96, 113

L

label štítek *m* 105
lace krajka *f* 113
lady dáma *f* 155
lake jezero *nt* 81, 85, 90
lamb *(meat)* jehněcí *nt* 44
lamp lampa *f* 29, 106, 118
language jazyk *m* 104
lantern lucerna *f* 106
large velký 20, 101, 130
last poslední 14, 68, 73, 149, 151
last name příjmení *nt* 25
late pozdě 14
later později 135
laugh, to smát se 95
launderette prádelna *f* 99
laundry *(place)* prádelna *f* 29, 99; *(clothes)* prát 29
laundry service prádelní služba *f* 23
laxative projímadlo *nt* 108
lead *(theatre)* hlavní role 86; *(metal)* olovo *m* 75
leap year přestupný rok *m* 149
leather kůže *f* 113, 117
leave, to nechat 31, 68, 95; *(leave behind)* zapomenout 20, 71; *(deposit)* uložit 26
leeks pórek *m* 50
left levý 21, 69, 77
left-luggage office úschovna zavazadel *f* 67, 71
leg noha *f* 138
lemon citrón *m* 36, 40, 53, 60
lemonade limonáda *f* 60, 64
lens *(glasses)* čočky *pl* 123; *(camera)* objektiv *m* 125
lentils čočka *f* 50
less méně 14
lesson hodina *f* 91
let, to *(hire out)* pronajmout 155
letter dopis *m* 132
letter box poštovní schránka *f* 132
lettuce salát *m* 50
library knihovna *f* 81, 99
licence *(driving)* řidičský průkaz *m* 20, 79
lie down, to lehnout si 142
life belt záchranný pás *m* 74
life boat záchranný člun *m* 74
life guard *(beach)* plavčík *m* 90
lift *(elevator)* výtah *m* 27, 100
light světlo *nt* 14, 28, 55, 101, 128; *(colour)* světlý 101, 112; *(weight)* lehký 14, 101; *(for cigarette)* zapalovač 95
lighter zapalovač *m* 126
lighter fluid/gas náplň do zapalovače *f* 126
light meter exposimetr *m* 125
lightning blesk *m* 94
like jako 111
like, to líbit se 13, 20, 23, 61, 96, 112; *(please)* 25, 92, 102
line linka *f* 72
linen *(cloth)* plátno *m* 113
lip ret *m* 138
lipsalve bezbarvá rtěnka *f* 110
lipstick rtěnka *f* 109
liqueur likér *m* 58
listen, to poslouchat 128
litre litr *m* 57, 75, 119
little *(a little)* trochu 14
live, to žít 83
liver játra *pl* 138
lobster humr *f* 43
local místní 36, 69
long dlouhý 114
long-sighted dalekozraký 123
look, to podívat se 100; 123, 139
look for, to hledat 13
look out! pozor! 156
loose *(clothes)* volný 114
lose, to ztratit 123, 156
loss ztráta *f* 131
lost ztracený 13
lost and found office/lost property office ztráty a nálezy 67, 156
lot hodně 14
lotion *(hair)* vlasová voda *f* 110; *(setting)* tužidlo 110
loud *(voice)* hlasitý 135
love, to milovat 95
lovely krásný 94
low nízký 141
lower spodní 69, 71
low season mimo sezónu 150
luck štěstí *nt* 152
luggage zavazadla *pl* 17, 18, 21, 26, 31, 71
luggage locker skříňka na zavazadla *f* 67, 71

luggage trolley vozík na zavazadla *m* 18, 71
lump *(bump)* boule *f* 139
lunch oběd *m* 34, 80, 94
lung plíce *pl* 138

M

machine *(washable)* na praní v pračce 113
magazine časopis *m* 105
magnificent překrásný 84
maid pokojská *f* 26
mail pošta *f* 28, 133
mail, to poslat poštou 28
mailbox poštovní schránka *f* 132
main hlavní 67, 80, 100
make, to udělat 131, 162
make up, to *(bed)* ustlat 28, 71
make-up líčidlo *nt* 109
make-up remover pad vatové tlapky na odstranění líčidla 109
mallet palice *f* 106
man muž *m* 114; člověk *m* 156
manager ředitel *m* 26
manicure manikůra *f* 30
many hodně 14
map mapa *f* 76, 89, 105
March březen *m* 150
marinated marinovaný 43
marjoram majoránka 52
market trh *m* 81, 99
marmalade pomerančový džem 40
married ženatý/vdaná 93
mass *(church)* bohoslužba *f* 84
matt *(finish)* matný 125
match *(matchstick)* zápalka *f* 106, 126; *(sport)* zápas *m* 89
match, to *(colour)* sladit 111
material *(fabric)* látka *f* 112
matinée odpolední představení *nt* 87
mattress matrace *f* 106
May květen *m* 150
may *(can)* moci 12, 163
meadow louka *f* 85
meal jídlo *nt* 24, 34, 61, 143
mean, to znamenat 11
means způsoby *pl* 74
measles spalničky *pl* 142
measure, to měřit 113
meat maso *nt* 37, 44, 45, 61
meatball masové kuličky *pl* 44
mechanic mechanik *m* 78
medical certificate zdravotní potvrzení *nt* 144
medicine lékařství 83; *(drug)* lék *m* 143
medium *(meat)* středně udělané 45
medium-sized středně velký 20
meet, to setkat 96
melon meloun *m* 53
memorial pomník *m* 81
mend, to opravit 75; *(clothes)* spravit 29
menthol *(cigarettes)* mentolový 126
menu *(printed)* jídelní lístek *m* 36, 39; *(food)* jídlo *nt* 37, 38
merry veselý 152
message zpráva *f* 28, 136
metre metr *m* 111
mezzanine *(theatre)* první balkón *m* 87
middle uprostřed 69, 150
midnight půlnoc *f* 153
mild *(light)* slabý 126
mileage poplatek za kilometr *m* 20
milk mléko *nt* 40, 60, 64
milkshake koktejl *m* 60
milliard miliarda *f* 148
million milion *m* 148
mineral water minerálka *f* 60, 64
minister *(religion)* kněz *m* 84
mint máta peprná *f* 52
minute minuta *f* 21, 69, 153
mirror zrcadlo *nt* 114, 123
miscellaneous rozmanitosti *pl* 127
Miss slečna *f* 10
miss, to chybět 18, 29, 61
mistake chyba *f* 31, 62, 102
mixed salad míchaný salát *m* 51
moccasin mokasiny *pl* 117
modified American plan s večeří a snídaní 24
moisturizing cream výživný krém *m* 109
moment moment *m* 12, 136
monastery klášter *m* 81
Monday pondělí *nt* 151
money peníze *pl* 18, 129, 130
money order peněžní poukázka *f* 133
month měsíc *m* 16, 150
monument pomník *m* 81
moon měsíc *m* 94
moped moped *m* 74
Moravia Morava *f* 146
more víc 12, 14
morning, in the ráno *nt* 143, 151, 153
mortgage hypotéka *f* 131
mosque mešita *f* 84
mosquito net síť proti komárům *f* 106
motel motel *m* 22

mother matka *f* 93
motorbike motocykl *m* 74
motorboat motorový člun *m* 91
motorway dálnice *f* 76
mountain hora *f* 85
mountaineering horolezectví *nt* 89
moustache knír *m* 31
mouth ústa *pl* 138, 142
mouthwash ústní výplach *m* 108
move, to hýbat 139
movie camera filmová kamera *f* 124
movies kino *nt* 86, 96
Mr. pan *m* 10
Mrs. paní *f* 10
much moc 11, 14
mug hrnek *m* 120
muscle sval *m* 138
museum muzeum *nt* 81
mushroom houba *f* 41, 45, 50, 51
music hudba *f* 83, 128
musical muzikál 86
must *(have to)* muset 31, 61, 95, 142; *(must not)* nesmět 37
mustard hořčice *f* 52, 64
my můj 161
myself já sám 119

N

nail *(human)* nehet *m* 109
nail brush kartáček na nehty *m* 109
nail clippers kleště na nehty *pl* 109
nail file pilník *m* 109
nail polish lak na nehty *m* 109
nail polish remover odlakovač *m* 109
nail scissors nůžky na nehty *pl* 109
name jméno *nt* 23, 25, 79, 92, 131, 133
napkin ubrousek *m* 36, 105, 120
nappy plena *f* 110
narrow úzký 117
national národní 40
nationality národnost *f* 25, 92
natural přírodní 83
natural history přírodověda *f* 83
nausea špatně od žaludku 140
near blízko 14, 15, 32
nearby blízko 77
nearest nejbližší 75, 78, 98
neat *(drink)* čistý 59
neck krk *m* 30, 138
necklace náhrdelník *m* 121
need, to potřebovat 29, 90, 137
needle jehla *f* 27
negative negativy *pl* 124, 125
nephew synovec *m* 93
nerve nerv *m* 138
nervous system nervový systém *m* 138
Netherlands Holandsko *nt* 146
never nikdy 15
new nový 14
newsagent's Tabák *nt* 99, 126
newspaper noviny *pl* 104, 105
newsstand novinový stánek *m* 19, 67, 99, 104
New Year Nový rok *m* 152
New Zealand Nový Zéland *m* 146
next příští 14, 65, 68, 73, 76, 149, 151
next time příště 95
next to vedle 15, 77
nice *(beautiful)* hezký 94
niece neteř *f* 93
night noc *f* 10, 24, 151
night, at v noci 151
nightclub noční klub *m* 88
night cream noční krém *m* 109
nightdress/-gown noční košile *f* 115
nine devět 147
nineteen devatenáct 147
ninety devadesát 148
ninth devátý 149
no ne 10
noisy hlučný 25
nonalcoholic nealkoholický 60
none žádný 15
nonsmoker nekuřák *m* 70
noodle nudle *f* 49
noon poledne *nt* 31, 153
normal normální 30
north sever *m* 77
North America Severní Amerika *f* 146
Norway Norsko *nt* 146
nose nos *m* 138
nosebleed krvácení z nosu 141
nose drops kapky do nosu *pl* 108
not ne 15, 163
note *(banknote)* bankovka *f* 130
notebook poznámkovy blok *m* 105
note paper poznámkový papír 105
nothing nic 15, 17
notice *(sign)* oznámení nápis *nt* 155
notify, to dát vědět 144
November listopad *m* 150
now ted' 15
number číslo *nt* 26, 65, 135, 136, 147
nurse sestra *f* 144
nutmeg muškátový oříšek *m* 52

O

occupation *(profession)* zaměstnání *nt* 25
occupied obsazený 14, 155
o'clock hodin 153
October říjen *m* 150
office *(booking)* rezervace *f* 19, 67; *(lost property)* ztráty a nálezy *pl* 156; *(post)* pošta *f* 99, 132, 133; *(telegraph)* telegrafní přepážka *f* 99
oil olej *m* 36, 75, 110
oily *(greasy)* mastný 30, 111
old starý 14
old town staré město *m* 81
on na 15
once jednou 149
one jeden 147
one-way ticket jízdenka jedním směrem *f* 65, 69
one-way *(traffic)* jednosměrný 77, 79
on foot pěšky 76
onion cibule *f* 50
only jenom 15, 80, 87, 108
on request na požádání 73
on time na čas 68
onyx onyx 122
open otevřený 14, 82, 155
open, to otevřít 11, 17, 82, 107, 130, 132, 142
opera opera *f* 88
opera house operní divadlo *nt* 81, 88
operation operace *f* 144
operator telefonní ústředna *f* 134
operetta opereta *f* 88
opposite naproti 77
optician optik *m* 99, 123
or nebo 15
orange *(colour)* oranžový 112
orange *(fruit)* pomeranč *m* 54, 64
orange juice pomerančový džus *m* 40, 60
orangeade oranžáda 61
orchestra orchestr *m* 88; *(seats)* přízemí *nt* 87
order *(goods, meal)* objednávka *f* 36, 102
order, to *(goods, meal)* objednat si 61, 102, 103
oregano oregano *nt* 50
ornithology ornitologie *f* 83
other jiný 74, 101
our náš 161
out of order nefunguje 136
out of stock vyprodáno 103
outlet *(electric)* zástrčka *f* 27
outside venku 15, 35
oval oválný 101
overalls montérky *pl* 116
overdone *(meat)* příliš upečené 61
overheat, to *(engine)* přehřát 78
overtake, to předjet 79
owe, to dlužit 144
oyster ústřice *f* 44

P

pacifier *(baby's)* dudlík *m* 110
packet krabička *f* 126
pain bolest *f* 140, 141, 144
painkiller prášek proti bolesti *m* 140
paint barva *f* 155
paint, to malovat 83
paintbox vodové barvy *pl* 105
painter malíř *m* 83
painting malířství *nt* 83
pair pár *m* 117, 118, 149
pajamas pyžamo *nt* 116
palace palác *m* 81
palpitations palpitace *pl* 141
pancake palačinka *f* 56
panties kalhotky *pl* 115
pants *(trousers)* kalhoty *pl* 115
panty girdle podvazkový pás *m* 115
panty hose punčocháče *pl* 115
paper papír *m* 105
paperback kniha v měkké vazbě *f* 105
paperclip spínátko *nt* 105
paper napkin papírový ubrousek *m* 105, 120
paraffin *(fuel)* parafín *m* 106
parcel balík *m* 132, 133
pardon, I beg your promiňte 10
parents rodiče *pl* 93
park park *m* 81
park, to zaparkovat 26, 77
parka sportovní bunda s kapucí *f* 115
parking parkoviště *nt* 77, 79
parking lot parkoviště *nt* 79
parking meter parkovací hodiny *pl* 77
parliament building budova parlamentu *f* 81
parsley zelená petržel *f* 50
part část *f* 138
partridge koroptev *f* 46
party *(social gathering)* společnost *f* 95
pass *(mountain)* průsmyk *m* 85
passport pas *m* 16, 17, 25, 26, 156
passport photo fotografie na pas *f* 124

pass through, to projíždět 16
pasta těstoviny *pl* 49
paste *(glue)* lepidlo *nt* 105
pastry těsto *nt* 55, 56
pastry shop cukrárna *f* 99
patch, to *(clothes)* záplatovat 29
path pěšina *f* 85
patient pacient *m* 144
pattern vzor *m* 112
pay, to platit 17, 31, 62, 102, 136
payment splátka *f* 131; *(paying)* placení *nt* 102
pea hrášek *m* 50
peach broskev *f* 53
peak vrchol *m* 85
peanut burský oříšek *m* 53
pear hruška *f* 53
pearl perla *f* 122
pedestrian *(zone)* pěší zóna *f* 79
peg *(tent)* kolík *m* 106
pen pero *nt* 105
pencil tužka *f* 105
pencil sharpener ořezávátko *nt* 105
pendant přívěsek *m* 121
penicillin penicilín *m* 143
penknife kapesní nůž *m* 120
pensioner důchodce *m* 82
people lidé *pl* 92
pepper pepř *m* 36, 40, 51, 64
per cent procento *nt* 149
percentage procenta *pl* 131
perch okoun *m* 43
per day za den 20, 32, 89
perform, to *(theater)* hrát 86
perfume parfém *m* 109
perhaps možná 15
per hour za hodinu 77, 89
period *(monthly)* měsíčky *pl* 141
period pains bolestivé měsíčky 141
permanent wave trvalá *f* 30
permit povolení *nt* 90
per night za noc 24
per person za osobu 32
personal osobní 17, 130
personal call/person-to-person call osobní hovor *m* 135
per week za týden 20, 24
petrol benzín *m* 75, 78
pewter starý cín *m* 122
pharmacy lékárna *f* 107
pheasant bažant *m* 46, 47
photo fotografie *f* 82, 124, 125
photocopy fotokopie *f* 131
photograph, to fotografovat 82
photographer fotograf *m* 99
photography fotografování *nt* 124
phrase výraz *m* 12
pick up, to *(person)* vyzvednout 80, 96
picnic piknik *m* 63
picnic basket košík na piknik *m* 106
picture *(painting)* obraz *m* 83; *(photo)* fotografie *f* 82
piece kousek *m* 18, 63, 119
pig selátko *nt* 44
pigeon holub *m* 46
pike štika *f* 43
pill pilulka *f* 141, 143
pillow polštář *m* 27
pin špendlík *m* 110, 121; *(safety)* sponka *f* 110
pineapple ananas *m* 53
pink růžový 112
pipe dýmka *f* 126
pipe cleaner čistič na dýmku *m* 126
pipe tobacco dýmkový tabák *m* 126
pipe tool dýmkový nástroj *m* 126
place místo *nt* 25, 76
place, to objednat 135
place of birth místo narození *nt* 25
plain *(colour)* jednobarevný 112
plane letadlo *nt* 65
planetarium planetárium *nt* 81
plaster sádra *f* 140
plastic z umělé hmoty 120
plastic bag igelitový pytlík *m* 120
plate talíř *m* 36, 61, 120
platform *(station)* nástupiště *nt* 67, 68, 69, 70
platinum platina *f* 122
play *(theatre)* hra *f* 86
play, to hrát 86, 88, 89, 93
playground dětské hřiště *nt* 32
playing card hrací karty *pl* 105, 128
please prosím 10
plimsolls tenisky *pl* 117
plug *(electric)* zástrčka *f* 29, 118
plum švestka *f* 54
pneumonia zápal plic *m* 142
poached ztracený 40
pocket kapsa *f* 116
pocket calculator kalkulačka *f* 105
pocket knife kapesní nůž *m* 120
pocket watch kapesní hodinky *pl* 121
point of interest *(sight)* zajímavé místo *m* 80
point, to ukázat 12
poison jed *m* 108, 156
poisoning otrava *f* 142
pole *(tent)* tyč *f* 106; *(ski)* hůl *f* 91
police policie *f* 78, 156

police station policejní stanice *f* 99, 156
pond rybník *m* 85
poplin popelín *m* 113
porcelain porcelán *m* 127
pork vepřové maso *nt* 44
port přístav *m* 74
portable přenosný 118
porter vrátný *m* 18, 26, 71
portion porce *f* 37, 55, 61
Portugal Portugalsko *nt* 146
possible, as soon as co nejdřív 137
post *(mail)* pošta *f* 28, 133
post, to poslat poštou 28
postage poštovné *nt* 132
postage stamp poštovní známka *f* 28, 126, 132, 133
postcard pohled *m* 105, 126; 132
poste restante poste restante 133
post office pošta *f* 99, 132
potato brambor *m* 50
pottery hrnčířství *nt* 83; *(ceramics)* keramika *f* 127
poultry drůbež *f* 46
pound libra *f* 18, 102, 130
powder *(talcum)* zásyp *m* 110
powder compact pudřenka *f* 121
powder puff labutěnka *f* 109
prawn krevetka *f* 43
pregnant v jiném stavu 141
premium *(gasoline)* super *m* 75
prescribe, to předepsat 143
prescription předpis *m* 107, 143
present dárek *m* 17
press, to *(iron)* vyžehlit 29
press stud patentka *f* 116
pressure tlak *m* 75, 141
pretty hezký 84
price cena *f* 24, 69
priest kněz *m* 84
print *(photo)* kopie *f* 125
private soukromý 23; 80, 91, 155
processing *(photo)* vyvolání *nt* 124
profession povolání *nt* 25
profit zisk *m* 131
programme program *m* 87
pronounce, to vyslovovat 12
pronunciation výslovnost *f* 6
propelling pencil propisovací tužka *f* 105, 121
Protestant protestant *m* 84
provide, to poskytnout/sjednat 131
prune sušená švestka *f* 54
public holiday státní svátek *m* 152
pull, to táhnout 155; *(tooth)* trhat 145
pullover svetr *m* 116
pump pumpa *f* 106
pumpkin dýně *f* 50
puncture píchnout*m* 75, 78
purchase koupě *f* 131
pure čistý 113
purple fialový 112
push, to tlačit 155
put, to dát 24
pyjamas pyžamo *nt* 116

Q

quail křepelka *f* 46
quality kvalita *f* 103, 112
quantity množství *f* 14
quarter čtvrt' *f* 81; *(a quarter)* čtvrtina *f* 149
quarter of an hour čtvrt hodiny *f* 153
question otázka *f* 11
quick(ly) rychle 14, 79, 137, 156
quiet tichý 23, 25

R

rabbi rabín *m* 84
rabbit králík *m* 44
race závod *m* 89
race course/track dostihová dráha *f* 90
racket *(sport)* raketa *f* 90
radiator *(car)* chladič *m* 78
radio rádio *nt* 23, 28, 118
radish ředkvička *f* 50
railway železnice *f* 66, 154
railway station nádraží *nt* 19, 21, 67
rain déšt' *m* 94
rain, to pršet 94
raincoat nepromokavý kabát *m* 116
raisin hrozinka *f* 53
rangefinder dálkoměr *m* 125
rare *(meat)* syrový 45, 61
rash vyrážka *f* 139
raspberry malina *f* 53
rate *(price)* sazba *f* 20; *(inflation)* procento inflace *nt* 131; *(of exchange)* kurs *m* 18, 130
razor břitva *f* 109
razor blades žiletky *pl* 109
read, to číst 39
reading lamp noční lampa *f* 27
ready hotový 29, 117, 123, 125, 145
real *(genuine)* pravý 117, 121
rear vzadu 69, 75

receipt účtenka *f* 103
reception recepce *f* 23
receptionist recepční *m/f* 26
recommend, to doporučit 35, 36, 80, 86, 88, 137, 145
record *(disc)* deska *f* 127, 128
recorder magnetofon *m* 118
record player gramofon *m* 118
rectangular obdélníkový 101
red červený 105, 112; *(wine)* 58
redcurrant červený rybíz *m* 54
reduction sleva *f* 24, 82
refill *(pen)* náplň *f* 105
refund *(to get a)* vrátit peníze 103
regards pozdrav *m* 152
register, to *(luggage)* registrovat 71
registered mail doporučeně 133
registration registrace *f* 25
registration form registrační formulář *m* 25, 26
regular *(petrol)* normál 75
religion náboženství *nt* 83
religious service bohoslužba *f* 84
rent, to pronajmout 19, 20, 74, 90, 91, 118, 155
rental půjčovna *m* 20, 74
repair oprava *f* 125
repair, to opravit, spravit 29, 117, 118, 121, 123, 125, 145
repeat, to opakovat 12
report, to *(a theft)* oznámit 156
request *(stop)* na požádání *f* 73
required požadovat 88
requirement potřeba *f* 27
reservation rezervace *f* 19, 23, 65, 69
reservations office rezervace *pl* 19, 67
reserve, to reservovat 19, 23, 35, 69, 87
reserved rezervovaný 155
rest zbytek *m* 130
restaurant restaurace *f* 19, 32, 34, 35, 67
return ticket zpáteční lístek *m* 65, 69
return, to *(come back)* vrátit se 21, 80; *(give back)* vrátit 103
rheumatism revmatismus *m* 141
rib žebro *nt* 46, 138
ribbon páska *f* 105
rice rýže *f* 49
right *(correct)* správný 14; *(direction)* vpravo 21, 69, 77
ring *(jewellery)* prsten *m* 122
ring, to *(doorbell)* zazvonit 155
river řeka *f* 81, 85, 90
river trip cesta říční lodí *f* 74
road silnice *f* 76, 77, 85
road map silniční mapa *f* 105
road sign dopravní značka *f* 79
roasted pečený 47
roast beef pečené hovězí 46
roll houska *f* 40, 64
roller skate kolečková brusle *f* 128
roll film svitkový film *m* 124
roll-neck rolák *m* 116
room pokoj *m* 19, 23, 24, 25, 26, 27; *(space)* místo *nt* 32
room number číslo pokoje *nt* 26
room service pokojová služba *f* 23
rope lano *nt* 106
rosary růženec *m* 122
rosemary rozmarýnka *f* 52
round kulatý 101
round *(golf)* kolo *nt* 90
round-neck kulatý výstřih *m* 116
round-trip ticket zpáteční lístek *m* 65, 69
round up, to zaokrouhlit 62
route trasa *f* 85
rowing boat loďka *f* 91
royal královský 81
rubber *(eraser)* korekční barva *f* 104; *(material)* guma *f* 117
ruby rubín *m* 122
ruin zřícenina *f* 81
ruler *(for measuring)* pravítko *nt* 105
rum rum *m* 58

S

safe *(free from danger)* bezpečný 90
safe trezor *m* 26
safety pin spínací špendlík *m* 109
saffron šafrán *m* 52
sage šalvěj *f* 52
sailing boat plachetnice *f* 91
salad salát *m* 38, 51
sale prodej *m* 100, 131; *(bargains)* výprodej *m* 155
salmon losos *m* 43
salt sůl *f* 36, 40, 52, 64
salty slaný 61
same *(the same)* ten samý 117
sand písek *m* 90
sandal sandál *m* 118
sandwich sendvič *m* 63
sanitary napkin/towel vložka *f* 108
sapphire safír *m* 122
sardine sardinka *f* 43
satin satén *m* 113

Saturday sobota *f* 151
sauce omáčka *f* 51
saucepan pánev *f* 120
saucer podšálek *m* 120
sauerkraut kyselé zelí *nt* 50
sausage klobása *f* 64; *(salami)* salám *m* 41, 44
scarf šála *f* 116
scarlet rudý 113
scenic route vyhlídková trasa *f* 85
school škola *f* 79
scissors nůžky *pl* 109
scooter skútr *m* 74
Scotland Skotsko *nt* 146
scrambled eggs míchaná vejce *pl* 40
screwdriver šroubovák *m* 120
sculptor sochař *m* 83
sculpture sochařství *nt* 83
sea moře *nt* 85
seafood mořské ryby *pl* 39, 43
season sezóna *f* 150
seasoning koření *nt* 36
seat sedadlo *nt* 65, 69, 70, 87
seat belt ochranný pás *m* 75
second druhý 149
second vteřina *f* 153
second class druhá třída *f* 69
second-hand shop obchod s použitým zbožím *m* 99
secretary sekretářka *f* 27, 131
section oddělení *nt* 104
see, to vidět 24, 26, 87, 89, 96, 121
self-service shop samoobsluha *f* 99
sell, to prodat 100
send, to poslat 78, 102, 103, 132, 133
sentence věta *f* 12
separately zvlášť 62
September září *nt* 150
seriously vážně 139
service služba *f* 24, 62, 98, 100; *(church)* bohoslužba *f* 84
serviette ubrousek *m* 36
set *(hair)* natočit 30
set menu standardní menu 36, 40
setting lotion tužidlo *nt* 30, 110
seven sedm 147
seventeen sedmnáct 147
seventh sedmý 149
seventy sedmdesát 148
sew, to přišít 29
shade *(colour)* odstín *m* 111
shampoo šampon *m* 30, 110
shampoo and set umýt a natočit 30
shape tvar *m* 103
share *(finance)* akcie *pl* 131
sharp *(pain)* ostrý 140
shave oholit 30
shaver holicí strojek *m* 27, 118
shaving brush štětka na holení *f* 109
shaving cream mýdlo na holení *nt* 109
she ona 161
shelf polička *f* 119
ship loď *f* 74
shirt košile *f* 116
shivery třást se 140
shoe bota *f* 117
shoelace tkanička *f* 117
shoemaker's opravna obuvi *f* 99
shoe polish krém na boty *m* 117
shoe shop obuv *f* 99
shop obchod *m* 98
shopping nakupování *nt* 97
shopping centre nákupní středisko *nt* 99
shop window výloha *f* 100, 111
short krátký 30, 114
shorts šortky *pl* 116
short-sighted krátkozraký 123
shoulder rameno *nt* 138
shovel lopata *f* 128
show představení 86, 87; 88
show, to ukázat 13, 76, 100, 101, 103, 124
shower sprcha *f* 23, 32
shrimp kreveta 43
shrink, to srazit se 113
shut zavřený 14
shutter *(window)* okenice *f* 29; *(camera)* spoušť *f* 125
sick *(ill)* nemocný 140
sickness *(illness)* nemoc *f* 140
side strana *f* 30
sideboards/-burns licousy/kotlety *pl* 31
sightseeing prohlížení památek *nt* 80
sightseeing tour vyhlídková cesta *f* 80
sign *(notice)* nápis *m* 77, 79, 155
sign, to podepsat 26, 130
signature podpis *m* 25
signet ring pečetní prsten *m* 122
silk hedvábí *nt* 113
silver *(colour)* stříbrný 112
silver stříbro *nt* 121, 122
silver plated postříbřený 122
silverware stříbrné zboží *pl* 122
simple jednoduchý 124
since od 15, 150
sing, to zpívat 88
single *(ticket)* jedním směrem 65, 69; *(unmarried)* svobodný 93

single cabin jednolůžková kabina *f* 74
single room jednolůžkový pokoj *m* 19, 23
sister sestra *f* 93
sit down, to posadit se 95
six šest 147
sixteen šestnáct 147
sixth šestý 149
sixty šedesát 147
size velikost *f* 124; *(clothes)* 114; *(shoes)* číslo *nt* 117
skate brusle *f* 91
skating rink kluziště *nt* 91
ski lyže *f* 91
ski, to lyžovat 91
ski boot lyžařská bota *f* 91
skiing lyžování *nt* 89, 91
skiing equipment lyžařské vybavení *pl* 91
skiing lessons hodiny lyžováni *pl* 91
ski lift lyžarský vlek *m* 91
skin kůže *f* 138
skin-diving potápění *nt* 89, 91
skin-diving equipment potápěčské vybavení *pl* 91, 106
skirt sukně *f* 116
ski run sjezdovka *f* 91
sky obloha *f* 94
sled sáňky *pl* 91
sleep, to spát 144
sleeping bag spacák *m* 106
sleeping car spací vůz *m* 66, 68, 69, 70
sleeping pill prášek na spaní *m* 108, 143
sleeve rukáv *m* 116, 142
sleeveless bez rukávů 116
slice plátek *m* 119
slide *(photo)* diapositiv *m* 124
slip *(underwear)* kombiné *nt* 116
slipper pantofle 117
Slovakia Slovensko *f* 146
slow(ly) pomalý (u) 14, 21, 135
slow down, to zpomalit 79
small malý 14, 20, 25, 101, 118, 130
smoke, to kouřit 95, 155
smoked uzený 45
smoker kuřák *m* 70
snack rychlé občerstvení *nt* 63
snack bar občerstvení *nt* 34, 67
snap fastener patentka *f* 116
sneaker teniska *f* 117
snow sníh *m* 94
snow, to sněžit 94
snuff šňupavý tabák *m* 126
soap mýdlo *nt* 27, 109
soccer fotbal *m* 89
sock ponožka *f* 116
socket *(electric)* zástrčka *f* 27
soft měkký 123
soft-boiled *(egg)* vajíčko na měkko 40
soft drink nealkoholický nápoj *m* 64
sold out vyprodáno 87
sole *(shoe)* podrážka *f* 117
soloist sólista *m* 88
some několik 14
someone někdo 95
something něco 29, 36, 55, 108, 111, 112, 125, 139
somewhere někde 87
son syn 93
song písnička *f* 128
soon brzo 15
sore *(painful)* bolestivý 145
sore throat bolesti v krku 141
sorry promiňte 10, 16, 87, 103, 153
sort *(kind)* druh *m* 119
soup polévka *f* 42
south jih *m* 77
South Africa Jihoafrická republika *f* 146
South America Jižní Amerika *f* 146
souvenir suvenýr *m* 127
souvenir shop suvenýry *pl* 99
spade lopatka *f* 128
Spain Španělsko *nt* 146
spare tyre náhradní pneumatika *f* 75
spark(ing) plug svíčka *f* 76
sparkling *(wine)* šumivé 59
speak, to mluvit 11, 16, 84, 135
speaker *(loudspeaker)* reproducktor *m* 118
special speciální 20; 37
special delivery expres 133
specialist specialista *m* 142
specimen *(medical)* ukázka *f* 142
spectacle case pouzdro na brýle *nt* 123
spell, to hláskovat 12
spend, to utratit 101
spice koření *nt* 52
spinach špenát *m* 50
spine páteř *f* 138
sponge houba *f* 109; *(dessert)* piškot *m* 55
spoon lžíce *f* 36, 61, 120
sport sport *m* 89
sporting goods shop sportovní potřeby *pl* 99
sports jacket sportovní sako *nt* 115
sprained vyvrtnutý 140
spring *(season)* jaro *nt* 150; *(water)*

pramen *m* 85
square čtvercový *m* 101
square *(town)* náměstí *nt* 81
stadium stadion *m* 82
staff *(personnel)* zaměstnanci *pl* 26
stain skvrna *f* 29
stainless steel nerez *m* 120, 122
stalls *(theatre)* přízemí *nt* 87
stamp *(postage)* známka *f* 28, 126, 132, 133
staple svorka *f* 105
star hvězda *f* 94
start, to začít 80, 87, 88; *(car)* nastartovat 78
starter *(meal)* předkrm *m* 41
station *(railway)* nádraží *nt* 19, 21, 67, 70; *(underground, subway)* stanice *f* 73
stationer's papírnictví *nt* 99, 104
statue socha *f* 82
stay pobyt *m* 31, 92
stay, to zůstat 16, 24, 26, 142; *(reside)* ubytovat se 93
steak biftek *m* 44, 45
steal, to ukrást 156
steamed uvařený v páře 43
stew dušené maso 45
stewed dušený 45, 47
stiff neck ztrnulý krk *m* 141
sting žihadlo *nt* 139
sting, to štípnout 139
stitch, to sešít 29, 117
stock exchange bursa *f* 82
stocking punčocha *f* 116
stomach žaludek *m* 138
stomach ache bolesti žaludku *f* 141
stools stolice *f* 142
stop *(bus)* stanice *f* 72, 73
stop! zastavte! 156
stop, to zastavit 21, 68, 70, 72
stop thief! zastavte zloděje! 156
store *(shop)* obchod *m* 98
straight *(drink)* čistý 59
straight ahead rovně 21, 77
strange zvláštní 84
strawberry jahoda *f* 53
street ulice *f* 25, 77
streetcar tramvaj *f* 73
street map plán města *m* 19; 105
string provázek *m* 105
strong silný 126, 143
student student *m* 82, 93
study, to studovat 93
stuffed plněný 46, 47
sturdy pevný 101
subway *(railway)* metro *nt* 72
suede semiš 113, 117
sugar cukr *m* 36, 64
suit *(man's)* oblek *m* 116; *(woman's)* kostým *m* 116
suitcase kufr *m* 18
summer léto *nt* 150
sun slunce *nt* 94
sunburn spálený sluncem 107
Sunday neděle *f* 151
sunglasses sluneční brýle *pl* 123
sunshade *(beach)* slunečník *m* 91
sunstroke úpal *m* 141
sun-tan cream krém na opalování *m* 109
sun-tan oil olej na opalování *m* 109
super *(petrol)* super benzin *m* 75
superb ohromné 84
supermarket samoobsluha *f* 99
suppository čípek *m* 108
surgery *(consulting room)* ordinace *f* 137
surname příjmení *nt* 25
suspenders *(Am.)* podvazky *pl* 116
swallow, to spolknout 143
sweater svetr *m* 116
sweatshirt tepláková bunda *f* 116
Sweden Švédsko *nt* 146
sweet sladký 59, 61
sweet *(confectionery)* bonbón *m* 126
sweet corn kukuřice *f* 50
sweetener sladidlo *nt* 37
sweet shop cukrárna *f* 99
swell, to natéct 139
swelling otok *m* 139
swim, to plavat 90
swimming plavání *nt* 89, 91
swimming pool plavecký bazén *m* 32, 90
swimming trunks plavky *pl* 117
swimsuit plavky *pl* 117
switch *(electric)* vypínač *m* 29
switchboard operator telefonní centrála *f* 26
Switzerland Švýcarsko *nt* 146
swollen nateklý 139
synagogue synagoga *f* 84
synthetic syntetický 114
system systém *m* 138

T
table stůl *m* 35, 106
tablet *(medical)* prášek *m* 108

tailor's krejčovství *nt* 99
take, to vzít 8, 25, 72, 73, 102, 143
take away, to odnést 63, 102
take to, to zavézt 21, 67
taken *(occupied)* obsazený 70
talcum powder zásyp 109
tampon tampón *m* 108
tangerine mandarinka *f* 54
tap *(water)* kohoutek *m* 28
tape recorder magnetofon *m* 116
tarragon estragon *m* 51
tart koláč *m* 55
tax daň *f* 32, 102
taxi taxi 19, 21, 31, 67
taxi rank/stand stanoviště taxi *nt* 21
tea čaj *m* 40, 60, 64
team tým *m* 89
tear, to trhat 140
teaspoon čajová lžička *f* 120, 143
telegram telegram *m* 133
telegraph office telegrafní přepážka *f* 99
telephone telefon *m* 28, 78, 79, 134
telephone, to *(call)* telefonovat 134
telephone booth telefonní budka *f* 134
telephone call telefonní hovor *m* 135, 136
telephone directory telefonní seznam *m* 134
telephone number telefonní číslo *nt* 135, 136, 156
telephoto lens teleobjektiv *m* 125
television televize *f* 23, 28
telex telex *m* 133
telex, to poslat telex 130
tell, to říct 13, 73, 76, 136, 153
temperature teplota *f* 140, 142
temporary dočasný 145
ten deset 147
tendon šlacha *f* 138
tennis tenis *m* 89
tennis court tenisový kurt *m* 90
tennis racket tenisová raketa *f* 90
tent stan *m* 32, 106
tenth desátý 149
tent peg stanový kolík *m* 106
tent pole stanová tyč *f* 106
term *(word)* výraz *m* 131
terrace terasa *f* 35
terrifying úděsný 84
terrycloth froté 113
tetanus tetanus *m* 140
than než 15
thank, to poděkovat 10, 96
thank you děkuji 10
that tamten 11, 100, 162
theatre divadlo *nt* 82, 86
theft krádež *f* 156
their jejich 161
then pak 15
there tam 13, 14
thermometer teploměr *m* 108, 144
these tyto 163
they oni 161
thief zloděj *m* 156
thigh stehno *nt* 138
thin tenký 113
think, to *(believe)* věřit, myslet si 31, 62, 94, 102
third třetí 149
third (jedna) třetina *f* 149
thirsty, to be mít žízeň 13, 35
thirteen třináct 147
thirty třicet 147
this tohle 11, 100, 160
those tamty 160
thousand tisíc 148
thread nit' *f* 27
three tři 147
throat hrdlo *nt* 138, 141
throat lozenge pastilka *f* 108
through skrz 15
through train rychlík *m* 66, 68
thumb palec *m* 138
thumbtack připínáček *m* 105
thunder hrom *m* 94
thunderstorm bouřka *f* 94
Thursday čtvrtek *m* 151
thyme tymián *m* 52
ticket lístek *m* 65, 69, 73, 87, 89; jízdenka *f* 73
ticket office pokladna *f* 67
tie kravata *f* 116
tie clip přeska do kravaty *f* 122
tie pin jehlice do kravaty *f* 122
tight *(close-fitting)* těsný 114
tights punčocháče *pl* 116
time čas *m* 68, 80, 95 ,153; *(occasion)* čas *m* 142, 143
timetable *(trains)* jízdní řád *m* 68
tin *(container)* konzerva *f* 120
tint tón *m* 110
tinted tónovaný 123
tire pneumatika *f* 75, 76
tired unavený 13
tissue *(handkerchief)* papírový kapesník *m* 110, 115
to do15
toast topinka *f* 40
tobacco tabák *m* 126

tobacconist's Tabák 99, 126
today dnes 29, 151
toe prst na noze *m* 138
toilet paper toaletní papír *m* 110
toiletry toaletní potřeby *pl* 109
toilets toalety, záchody *pl* 23, 27, 32, 37, 67
toilet water kolínská voda *f* 110
tomato rajské jablíčko *m* 50
tomato juice rajská šťáva *f* 60
tomb hrobka *f* 82
tomorrow zítra 29, 96, 151
tongue jazyk *m* 138
tonic water tonik *m* 60
tonight dnes večer 29, 86, 87, 96
tonsils mandle *pl* 138
too příliš 15; *(also)* také 15
tools nářadí *pl* 120
too much moc 14
tooth zub *m* 145
toothache bolest zubu *f* 145
toothbrush kartáček na zuby *m* 110, 118
toothpaste zubní pasta 110
top, at the nahoře 30, 145
torch *(flashlight)* baterka *f* 106
torn natržený 140
touch, to dotýkat se 155
tough *(meat)* tvrdý 61
tour cesta 80
tourist office turistické informace *f* 80
tourist tax turistický poplatek *m* 32
towards směrem 15
towel ručník *m* 27, 110, 120
towelling *(terrycloth)* froté *f* 113
tower věž *f* 82
town město *nt* 19, 76, 88
town center střed města *m* 21, 73, 76
town hall radnice *f* 82
tow truck havarijní služba *f* 78
toy hračka *f* 128
toy shop hračkářství *nt* 99
tracksuit tepláková souprava *f* 117
traffic provoz *f* 76
traffic light semafor *m* 77
trailer *(caravan)* obytný přívěs *m* 32
train vlak *m* 66, 68, 69, 70, 153
tram tramvaj *f* 73
tranquillizer utišující prostředek *m* 108, 143
transfer *(finance)* převod *m* 131
transformer transformátor *m* 118
translate, to přeložit 12
transport, means of dopravní prostředky *pl* 74
travel, to cestovat 93
travel agency cestovní kancelář *f* 99
travel guide průvodce *m* 105
traveller's cheque cestovní šek *m* 18, 62, 102, 130
travelling bag cestovní taška *f* 18
travel sickness nemoc z cestování *f* 107
treatment ošetření *nt* 143
tree strom *m* 85
tremendous obrovský 84
trim, to *(a beard)* přistříhnout 31
trip cesta *m* 93, 152; 72
trolley vozík *m* 18, 71
trousers kalhoty *pl* 117
trout pstruh *m* 43
truck nákladní auto *nt* 78
truffle nepečená kulička 56
try on, to zkusit si 114
T-shirt tričko *nt* 117
Tuesday úterý *nt* 151
tumbler sklenice *f* 120
tuna tuňák *m* 43
tunny tuňák *m* 43
Turkey Turecko *nt* 146
turkey krůta *f* 48
turn, to *(change direction)* zahnout 21, 77
turnip tuřín *m* 50
turquoise *(colour)* tyrkysový 112
turquoise tyrkys *m* 122
turtleneck rolák *m* 116
tweezers pinseta *f* 110
twelve dvanáct 147
twenty dvacet 147
twice dvakrát 149
twin beds dvojitá postel *f* 23
two dva 147
typewriter psací stroj *m* 27
typing paper papír do psacího stroje *m* 105
tyre pneumatika *f* 75, 76

U

ugly ošklivý 14, 84
umbrella deštník *m* 116; *(beach)* slunečník *m* 91
uncle strýc *m* 93
unconscious bezvědomí 139
under pod 15
underdone *(meat)* nedodělaný 45, 61
underground *(railway)* metro *nt* 72
underpants spodky *pl* 116

undershirt nátělník *f* 116
understand, to rozumět 12, 16
undress, to vysvléct se 142
United States Spojené Státy *pl* 146
university universita *f* 82
unleaded bezolovnatý 75
until až do 15
up nahoru 15
upper horní 69
upset stomach žaludeční nevolnost *f* 108
upstairs nahoře 15
urgent spěchat 13, 145
urine moč *f* 142
use použití *nt* 17, 108
use, to používat 78, 134
useful užitečný 15
usually normálně 94, 143

V

vacancy volné místo *nt* 23
vacant volný 14, 155
vacation dovolená *f* 151
vaccinate, to očkovat 140
vacuum flask termoska *f* 120
vaginal infection vaginální infekce *f* 141
valley údolí *nt* 85
value hodnota *f* 131
value-added tax daň z přidané hodnoty *f* 24, 102
vanilla vanilka *f* 52
veal telecí *nt* 44
vegetable zelenina *f* 39, 50
vegetable store zelenina *f* 99
vegetarian vegetarián *m* 37
vein žíla *f* 138
velvet samet *m* 113
velveteen bavlněný samet *m* 113
venereal disease pohlavní nemoc *f* 142
venison zvěřina *f* 47
vermouth vermut *m* 59
very velmi 15
vest tílko *nt* 116; *(Am.)* 116
veterinarian veterinář *m* 99
video camera video kamera *f* 124
video cassette video kazeta *f* 118, 124, 127
video recorder video přehrávač *m* 118
view *(panorama)* výhled *m* 23, 25
village vesnice *f* 76, 85
vinegar ocet *m* 36
vineyard vinice *f* 85
visit návštěva *f* 92
visiting hours návštěvní hodiny *pl* 144
visit, to navštívit 95
vitamin pill vitaminová pilulka *f* 108
v-neck véčko *nt* 117
vodka vodka *f* 59
volleyball volejbal *m* 89
voltage napětí proudu *nt* 27, 119
vomit, to zvracet 140

W

waist pas *m* 142
waistcoat vesta *f* 116
wait, to čekat 21, 95, 108, 162
waiter číšník *m* 26, 36
waiting room čekárna *f* 67
waitress číšnice *f* 26; 36
wake, to vzbudit se 27, 71
Wales Wales *m* 146
walk, to jít 74, 85
wall zeď *f* 85
wallet peněženka *f* 156
walnut vlašský ořech *m* 54
want, to chtít 13, 101, 102
warm teplý 94, 155
wash, to prát 29, 114
washable prací 114
washbasin umyvadlo *nt* 28
washing powder prášek na praní *m* 120
washing-up liquid prostředek na mytí nádobí *m* 120
watch hodinky *pl* 121, 122
watchmaker's hodinářství *nt* 99
watchstrap řemínek na hodinky *m* 122
water voda *f* 23, 28, 32, 75, 90
watercress potočnice *f* 52
waterfall vodopád *m* 85
water flask láhev na vodu *f* 106
waterproof vodotěsný 122
water-skis vodní lyže *pl* 91
way směr *m* 76
we my 161
weather počasí *nt* 94
weather forecast předpověď počasí *f* 94
wedding ring snubní prsten *m* 122
Wednesday středa *f* 151
week týden *m* 16, 20, 24, 80, 92; 151
weekday den v týdnu *m* 151
weekend víkend *m* 20, 151
well dobře 10, 140

well-done *(meat)* dobře udělané 45
west západ *m* 77
what co 11
wheel kolo *nt* 78
when kdy 11
where kde 11
where from odkud 92, 146
which který 11
whipped cream šlehačka *f* 56, 60
whisky whisky 17, 59
white bílý 58, 112
who kdo 11
whole celý 143
why proč 11
wick knot *m* 126
wide široký 117
wide-angle lens širokoúhlý objektiv *m* 125
wife manželka *f* 93
wig paruka *f* 111
wild boar divoké prase *nt* 46
wind vítr *m* 94
window okno *nt* 28, 35, 65, 69; *(shop)* výloha *f* 100, 111
windscreen/shield přední sklo *nt* 76
windsurfer windsurfer *m* 91
wine víno *nt* 45, 47, 58, 61, 64
wine list vinný lístek *m* 58
wine merchant's prodej vína *m* 99
winter zima *f* 150
winter sports zimní sporty *pl* 91
wiper *(car)* stěrač *m* 76
wish přání *nt* 152
with s 15
withdraw, to *(from account)* vyzvednout 130
withdrawal vyzvednutí *nt* 130
without bez 15
woman žena *f* 114
wonderful krásný 96
wood les *m* 85
wool vlna *f* 113
word slovo *nt* 12, 15, 133
work, to fungovat 28, 118
working day pracovní den *m* 151
worse horší 14
worsted česaná příze *f* 114
wound rána *f* 139
wrap up, to zabalit 103
wrapping paper balicí papír *m* 105
wrinkle resistant nemačkavý 113
wristwatch náramkové hodinky *pl* 122
write, to psát 12, 101
writing pad dopisní papíry *pl* 105
writing paper dopisní papíry *pl* 27, 105
wrong špatný 14, 77, 135

X

X-ray rentgen *m* 140

Y

year rok *m* 149
yellow žlutý 113
yes ano 10
yesterday včera 151
yet ještě 15, 16, 24
yield, to *(traffic)* dát přednost 79
yoghurt jogurt *m* 40, 64
you ty 161
young mladý 14
your tvůj 161
youth hostel turistická ubytovna *f* 22, 32

Z

zero nula *f* 147
zip(per) zip *m* 116
zoo zoologická zahrada *f* 82
zoology zoologie *f* 83
zucchini zucchini 49

Český rejstřík

POLAND
Leipzig
Dresden
Wrołcaw
Kraków
Ústí
Teplice
Hradec Králové
Karlovy Vary
PRAHA
Cheb
Kutná Hora
Mariánské Lázně
Ostrava
Labe
ČECHY
Olomouc
Plzeň
Tábor
Vltava
Telč
MORAVA
České Budějovice
Třeboň
Brno
Český Krumlov
Lednice
Morava
GERMANY
Poprad
Prešov
Váh
Žilina
Košice
SLOVENSKO
Trenčín
Banská Bystrica
Hron
Piešťany
Trnava
Nitra
BRATISLAVA
Dunaj
VIENNA
Nové Zámky
HUNGARY
UKRAINE
BUDAPEST
AUSTRIA